The Obedience of Faith, the Eschatological People of God, and the Purpose of Romans

SOCIETY
OF BIBLICAL
LITERATURE

DISSERTATION SERIES
Saul M. Olyan, Old Testament Editor
Mark Allan Powell, New Testament Editor

Number 177
THE OBEDIENCE OF FAITH,
THE ESCHATOLOGICAL PEOPLE OF GOD,
AND THE PURPOSE OF ROMANS

by
James C. Miller

James C. Miller

The Obedience of Faith, the Eschatological People of God, and the Purpose of Romans

Society of Biblical Literature
Atlanta, Georgia

The Obedience of Faith, the Eschatological People of God, and the Purpose of Romans

by
James C. Miller
Ph.D., Union Theological Seminary and
Presbyterian School of Christian Education, 1999
John T. Carroll, Dissertation Advisor

Library of Congress Cataloging-in-Publication Data

Miller, James C., 1956–
    The obedience of faith, the eschatological people of God, and the purpose
of Romans / James C. Miller.
      p. cm. — (Dissertation series ; no. 177)
    Originally presented as the author's thesis (Ph. D.)—Union Theological
Seminary and Presbyterian School of Christian Education, 1999.
    Includes bibliographical references (p.) and indexes.
    ISBN 0-88414-027-X (alk. paper)
    1. Bible. N.T. Romans—Criticism, interpretation, etc. I. Title. II. Dissertation
series (Society of Biblical Literature) ; no. 177.

BS2665.2 M54 2000
227'.106—dc21   00-061208

08 07 06 05 04 03 02 01 00   5 4 3 2 1

Printed in the United States of America
on acid-free paper

TABLE OF CONTENTS

ACKNOWLEDGMENTS

The idea that a doctoral dissertation gets finished through the long hours a student spends alone in the library is only partially correct. This project could not have been completed without the assistance of a considerable number of people to whom I am deeply indebted.

The Governing Council of Daystar University and the Board of Directors of Daystar U. S. granted me an extended leave from teaching responsibilities in Nairobi. Professor Stephen Talitwala, Vice-Chancellor of Daystar University, has especially been supportive of this project.

Throughout our years in the United States, a faithful team of financial supporters made time for concentrated study feasible. In addition, liberal financial assistance from Union Theological Seminary—PSCE more than covered educational expenses. The generosity of these people and this institution made the impossible possible.

The people of Third Presbyterian Church in Richmond have been the body of Christ for us as a family in ways too numerous to count. Special mention goes to Bob and Elaine Metcalf, Steve and Susie Hartman, Tommy and Weezie Thompson, and Bill and Ann Nell Jackson.

My dissertation committee consisted of Professors John Carroll (advisor), Jack Dean Kingsbury, and Paul J. Achtemeier. Their timely advice and corrections, not to mention their patience, improved the final product in multiple ways. Any errors remaining are solely my own. I am especially grateful to them for working with me on my tight time schedule.

Finally, my three children, Wesley, Susanna, and Caroline, have put up with an overly busy father for four years of doctoral study. As a result, my wife, Ann, often bore the burden of parenting alone. With profound gratitude, I dedicate this dissertation to her.

ABBREVIATIONS

The abbreviations in this dissertation follow those in *JBL* 117 (1998): 560–79 with the following addition.

DPL   *Dictionary of Paul and His Letters*

Chapter One

THE ROMANS DEBATE: DEFINING THE PROBLEM

Few documents in history have been analyzed as thoroughly as Paul's letter to the Romans. The most extensive, recent bibliography lists 2,109 studies published in this century, through 1995.[1] Ironically, in spite of all this analysis, what Paul intended to accomplish by sending his letter remains a matter of sharp disagreement among scholars. Yet, a decision regarding the letter's purpose inevitably shapes how one understands Paul's argument.

The amount of literature generated by the search for the purpose of the letter has earned the controversy its own name, "The Romans Debate," after the title of a collection of essays on the subject.[2] Within this dissertation, therefore, the phrase "Romans Debate" or simply "Debate" will be used to refer to the search for Paul's purpose(s) in writing Romans. Frequent summaries of the history of this Debate have

---

[1]Watson E. Mills, comp., *Bibliographies for Biblical Research, New Testament Series*, vol. 6, *Romans* (Lewiston, N.Y.: Mellen Biblical Press, 1996). Mills's compilation is not exhaustive.

[2]Karl P. Donfried, ed., *The Romans Debate*, rev. and expanded ed. (Peabody, Mass.: Hendrickson, 1991). Though concerned with more than just the purpose of Romans, the debate focuses primarily on that topic. See F. F. Bruce, "The Romans Debate—Continued?" in *The Romans Debate*, 175; Mark Nanos, *The Mystery of Romans: The Jewish Context of Paul's Letter* (Minneapolis: Fortress Press, 1996), 85, n. 1.

1

appeared, making a rehash of that history unnecessary here.[3]
Careful definition of recurring problems in the Debate, however, is a must. I contend that one problem occupies a place of
importance above the rest. This chapter will identify and
define that key problem, in the process illustrating unsatisfactory attempts at a solution. Following this identification, I
offer a proposed solution to that problem in the form of a thesis. The chapter concludes by outlining the path followed in
arguing that thesis in the rest of the dissertation.

Defining the Issue

The search for Paul's purpose in writing Romans
involves a number of interrelated issues. In question form,
these matters include: What is the specific genre of this letter? Did Paul's original letter to Rome include all sixteen
chapters as they appear in modern versions of the text? Is
Romans, like Paul's other letters, a response to specific circumstances in Paul's ministry or the life of the Roman
Christian communities, or is Romans some type of "timeless"
summary of Paul's theology? If the former is the case, was
Paul moved to compose this letter (a) owing to problems

---

[3]In addition to the commentaries of Fitzmyer and Dunn, see
especially Karl P. Donfried, "Introduction 1977: The Nature and Scope
of the Romans Debate," and "Introduction 1991: The Romans Debate
Since 1977," in *The Romans Debate*, xli–xlvii and xlix–lxxii; L. Ann
Jervis, *The Purpose of Romans. A Comparative Letter Structure Investigation*, JSNTSup, vol. 55 (Sheffield: JSOT Press, 1991), 11–28; Neil
Elliott, *The Rhetoric of Romans: Argumentative Constraint and Strategy
and Paul's Dialogue with Judaism*, JSNTSup, vol. 45 (Sheffield: JSOT
Press, 1990), 9–43; J. Christiaan Beker, *Paul the Apostle: The Triumph
of God in Life and Thought* (Philadelphia: Fortress Press, 1980), 59–74;
for greater coverage of German scholarship see A. J. M. Wedderburn,
The Reasons for Romans (Minneapolis: Fortress Press, 1991), 1–65;
Ernst Käsemann, *Commentary on Romans*, trans. and ed. Geoffrey W.
Bromiley (Grand Rapids: William B. Eerdmans, 1980), 402–06; and
Dieter Zeller, *Juden und Heiden in der Mission des Paulus: Studien zum
Römerbrief*, 2d aufl., FB, bd. 8 (Stuttgart: Verlag Katholisches Bibel-
werk, 1976), 38–44.

among the Christians in Rome which he wanted to resolve, (b) out of concerns for his own future ministry either in Spain or Jerusalem, or (c) some combination of the two? And finally, can one combine into a single, coherent historical reconstruction Paul's brief statements of his purposes and plans at the beginning and end of the letter (1:1–13; 15:14–16:27) with the entire content of the body of the letter (1:14–15:13)? This dissertation argues that this last issue is the important one in the Romans Debate.

Uniting the letter's frame with its body has proved difficult because large sections of the body seem unrelated to either Paul's circumstances or those of the Roman Christians, circumstances known from information provided in the letter-frame. We learn from the letter's opening and closing sections that Paul cannot come to Rome at the time he writes because he must soon travel to Jerusalem with the collection "for the poor among the saints" there (15:26). He did, however, plan to visit Rome on his way to Spain after completing his work in Jerusalem (15:22–29). He requests prayer for his venture to Jerusalem (15:30–32) and greets a long list of friends and coworkers (16:1–16).

Of the Roman Christians we learn little other than that they were apparently mostly gentile (1:6, 13) and that Paul knew many of them (16:3–16). Yet, while the audience appears to be mostly of gentile birth, the argument of the letter-body seems directed to Jewish concerns (e.g., circumcision, the role of Mosaic Law, and God's faithfulness in dealing with Israel). Other than 11:13–24 and 14:1–15:7, little appears to be directly addressed to circumstances that prevail in Rome. Even with this limited amount of information, a satisfactory solution will account for why Paul wrote about these particular issues (the body) to these Christians (known from both body and frame) at this particular time in his ministry (known from the frame).[4]

---

[4]Similarly, Wedderburn, *Reasons for Romans*, 1. According to Sam K. Williams, "The apostle says quite clearly why he writes (Rom 1:9–15, 15:22–28); what is not clear is why he writes *what* he writes"

Furthermore, numerous studies have documented that Paul both highlights key themes in his letters and indicates his purpose in writing in the formulaic elements of the opening and closing sections of the letter.[5] Not all of these elements are present in the same way in every letter nor can they always be carefully delineated. Nevertheless, Paul's own indicators of his reason(s) for writing and signals of key themes must be sought out in these sections and given their full weight.[6] In what follows, therefore, the frame of the letter will be examined closely for both indicators of purpose and statements of issues that are emphasized or recur as themes in the body. These are Paul's own signals to his hearers of what he considers important.

The key problem in the Romans Debate can therefore be stated as follows:

> How does one unite the information found in the frame of the letter with the particular contents of the body in such a way that it provides a rationale for why Paul wrote about these specific issues (and not others) to these particular Christians

---

("The 'Righteousness of God' in Romans," *JBL* 99 [1980], 245; emph. original).

[5]Robert W. Funk, *Language, Hermeneutic, and Word of God: The Problem of Language in the New Testament and Contemporary Theology* (New York: Harper & Row, 1966), 257; Jeffrey A. D. Weima, *Neglected Endings: The Significance of the Pauline Letter Closings*, JSNTSup, vol. 101 (Sheffield: JSOT Press, 1994), 238–39; William G. Doty, *Letters in Primitive Christianity*, GBS, New Testament Series, ed. Dan O. Via, Jr. (Philadelphia: Fortress Press, 1973), 33; G. P. Wiles, *Paul's Intercessory Prayers*, SNTSMS, vol. 24 (Cambridge: Cambridge University Press, 1974), 68, 173, 293–94; John L. White, *Light from Ancient Letters*, FFNT (Philadelphia: Fortress Press, 1986), 19; Jervis, *Purpose of Romans*, 42; Thomas R. Schreiner, *Interpreting the Pauline Epistles*, Guides to New Testament Exegesis, ed. Scot McKnight (Grand Rapids: Baker, 1990), 29; Paul Schubert, *Form and Function of Pauline Thanksgivings*, BZNW, vol. 20 (Berlin: Alfred Töpelmann, 1939), 77.

[6]See the perceptive comments by L. Ann Jervis, quoted on p. 9 below, regarding the significance of the letter-frame for ascertaining the letter's purpose.

at this time in his ministry?[7] Any attempt to answer this
question will take seriously Paul's own signals of key themes
and his purpose(s) in the frame of the letter, while aligning
that information with the argument of the entire body.

Examples of proposals that fail to meet this standard
abound. A brief summary of several proposals will illustrate
the problem and justify the claim made above regarding the
chief problem in the Romans Debate.

Solutions to the Romans Debate:
Four Proposals

Four approaches to the Romans Debate are analyzed
below. The first two, by Anders Nygren and L. Ann Jervis,
illustrate the danger of ignoring either the body or the frame
of the letter. The third, by Douglas A. Campbell, recognizes
the need to account for both body and frame, but fails to deal
with the entire body in his reconstruction. The final proposal,
by A. J. M. Wedderburn, also considers the need to deal with
both the body and the frame, as well as the necessity to
account for the entire body of the letter. Wedderburn,
however, despairs of uniting the disparate evidence in the
letter into a singular motive for Paul's writing it. Instead, he
proposes that Paul had multiple reasons for writing to the
Roman Christians.

---

[7]See also Harry Gamble, Jr., *The Textual History of the Letter to
the Romans*, SD, vol. 42 (Grand Rapids: William B. Eerdmans, 1977),
136. He writes, ". . . like the other letters, it (Romans) presents only aspects of Paul's thought. But why these particular concerns and aspects?
What 'principle of selection,' what specific aim, dictated that the letter
should have the substance it does?"

A Body without a Frame Anders Nygren

Romans has traditionally been viewed as a summary of Paul's theology.[8] Invariably, such a view devalues the importance of the frame of the letter. Anders Nygren, for example, asserts that Romans "impresses one as a doctrinal writing, a theological treatise, which is only externally clad with the form of a letter."[9] He goes on to state that seeking a purpose of the letter in either the situation in Rome or Paul's need to justify himself to the Roman Christians "does not contribute to the deeper understanding of its contents; but quite the contrary."[10] According to Nygren, Paul explains "the great problem of his life" which "is at the same time the great problem of all Christendom," namely, the relationship between walking in the new way of faith in Christ and the old way of works.[11] Nygren asserts that this was a problem for Paul but not for the Roman Christians, who only needed knowledge of Paul's views on the matter. Paul had always wanted to explain this position to them, but as he was unable

---

[8]Among the more explicit recent treatments are T. W. Manson, "St. Paul's Letter to the Romans—and Others," in *The Romans Debate*, 3–15; Günther Bornkamm, "The Letter to the Romans as Paul's Last Will and Testament," in ibid., 16–28; Philip R. Williams, "Paul's Purpose in Writing Romans," *BSac* 128 (1971): 62–67. Douglas J. Moo wants to acknowledge that Romans is a genuine letter, but succumbs to the temptation to universalize its content and thereby remove the letter from its particular historical circumstances. He writes,

> The legitimate desire to pin down as precisely as possible the historical background and purpose of the letter should not obscure the degree to which Romans deals with theological issues raised by the nature of God's revelation itself. That Paul was dealing in Romans with immediate concerns in the early church we do not doubt. But, especially in Romans, these issues are ultimately those of the church—and the world—of all ages.

The Epistle to the Romans, NICNT (Grand Rapids: William B. Eerdmans, 1996), 21–22. But this still does not explain why Paul should write about these issues (and not others) to these particular Christians.

[9]*Commentary on Romans*, trans. by Carl C. Rasmussen (Philadelphia: Muhlenberg Press, 1949), 7.

[10]Ibid., 7.

[11]Ibid., 8.

to get to Rome himself, he sent the letter to accomplish the task in his absence.[12]

Despite Nygren's desire to locate this letter in the particular circumstances of Paul's life, he cannot resist the tendency to dehistoricize its content and thereby turn it into abstract theologizing.[13] For example, why should Paul feel constrained to write to the Roman Christians[14] (or want to visit them) to tell them about his personal struggles relating the old way of the law and the new way of the Spirit? Nygren never really answers this question other than to say that Paul wanted to do it and that his own struggle was a universal Christian problem. Nygren denies these were issues the Roman Christians struggled with, yet claims they "greatly needed the answer to them."[15] As a result, Nygren prioritizes the content of 1:16–11:36 to the neglect of the rest of the letter and elevates the content of the body of the letter as "the great problem of all Christendom."

---

[12]Nygren's explanation for Paul's reason for writing is riddled with contradictions. The problems Paul confronts in Romans are Paul's problems. Yet the Romans "greatly needed the answer to them" (8). Romans is a real letter rather than a doctrinal treatise, yet it treats a matter that is a problem for "all Christendom" (8). In spite of Nygren's denials, he interprets the letter as a piece of Christian theologizing abstracted from its context as a letter to a specific Christian community.

[13]"The abstract nature of the discussion in the letter body seems to tempt interpreters to conclude that they don't have to go through all the trouble of contextualizing this letter within a particular situation." Douglas A. Campbell, "Determining the Gospel Through Rhetorical Analysis in Paul's Letter to the Roman Christians," in *Gospel in Paul: Studies on Corinthians, Galatians and Romans for Richard N. Longenecker*, eds. L. Ann Jervis and Peter Richardson, JSNTSup, vol. 108 (Sheffield: Sheffield Academic Press, 1994), 317. See also Ulrich Wilckens' summary of Nygren's approach in "Über Abfassungszweck und Aufbau des Römerbrief," in *Rechtfertigung als Freiheit: Paulusstudien* (Neukirchener-Vluyn: Neukirchener Verlag, 1974), 111.

[14]See, for example, the criticisms by Wilckens of Ulrich Luz (and, by implication, of Nygren as well) on this point in "Abfassungszweck und Aufbau," 112–13.

[15]Nygren, *Romans*, 8.

Nygren demonstrates a lack of concern for the frame of the letter by devoting only six pages of his 457-page commentary to the concluding section, 15:14–16:27.[16] In doing so, he effectively ignores vital information about Paul's circumstances, his reason(s) for writing, and the Roman Christians.

Attempts to include the letter-frame within such a "theological" reading of Romans typically view the letter as Paul's self-introduction to the Roman Christians. The conjecture is that if Paul expected the support of those Christians for his future mission to Spain, they needed a summary of his gospel for approval. But this presupposes that since Paul had never visited Rome, the Roman believers did not know of him or the gospel he preached. As shall be seen, that is a false assumption. Furthermore, if Paul intended to summarize his theology for the Romans, why did he write in detail about these specific issues while leaving other vital matters largely untouched (such as Christology and eschatology)?[17]

A Frame without a Body: L. Ann Jervis

L. Ann Jervis reconstructs Paul's purpose in writing from a comparative study of formal aspects of Paul's letters.[18] Following an extensive survey of research on the form of ancient Greek and Pauline letters, she concludes that Paul's letters have six structural components: "the opening formula,

---

[16]Likewise, Karl Barth devotes only eleven pages to 15:14–16:27 out of 511 total pages of commentary on the text of Romans. See *The Epistle to the Romans*, trans, Edwyn C. Hoskyns (New York: Oxford University Press, 1968).

[17]"If this understanding of Romans can explain why Paul wrote *a* letter to Rome, it offers no reason why he wrote *this* letter, which is far more than an introduction" (Harry Gamble, Jr., *Textual History*, 134 [emphasis original]). Gamble offers a thorough justification for reading Romans as a letter to a specific community and not as a summary of Paul's theology (132–137). Critics of the theological reading of Romans often include ecclesiology as one of the neglected topics. Ecclesiology, however, stands at the heart of Paul's concern in Romans, as the final chapter of this dissertation will demonstrate.

[18]*Purpose of Romans.*

the thanksgiving period, the body, the apostolic parousia, the paraenesis and the conclusion."[19] She then comments,

> All of the structural sections of a Pauline letter are not, however, of equal value in this quest for understanding the letter's function. . . . For even though it is the letter-body that conveys the specific reasons for writing, the function intended by the information in the letter-body is indicated in the opening and closing sections. The opening and closing sections of Paul's letters serve to reaffirm Paul's relationship with his readers and to direct their attention to the main themes of the letters. It is, therefore, in the opening and closing of Paul's letters that their functional characteristics are most clearly seen.
>
> Much of the letter-body will, therefore, be eliminated from the investigation.[20]

Jervis correctly notes the importance of the opening and closing sections of Paul's letters for determining their purpose, but it does not follow that the letter-body can therefore be ignored. Although she states "much of the letter-body" will not be considered, her study gives no substantial consideration to it at all. The index of her book lists only ten references to the body of Romans with several of those involving multiple chapters (indicating they do not involve close examination of the text of the letter). Although the opening and closing sections must be given their proper place, whatever one finds in the opening and closing of the letter must be correlated with the actual content of the body. If not, the investigator closes her eyes to vital evidence.

The results of Jervis's study demonstrate the weakness inherent in her method. She concludes that Paul wrote to proclaim his gospel to the Roman Christians so that they would come under his apostolic authority, as part of his offering of obedient Gentiles.[21] The body of the letter is a summary of Paul's gospel, an example of Paul's "preaching

---

[19]Ibid., 42.
[20]Ibid., 42–43.
[21]Ibid., 163.

the gospel in writing."[22] Although Jervis qualifies this characterization by stating that this presentation of the gospel is not an "abstract" of his message nor is it "complete,"[23] she provides no rationale for why Paul would write such a specialized, incomplete version of his gospel to the Roman Christians.[24] For example, why should Paul write to a largely gentile audience about such "Jewish" matters as observance of the Mosaic Law, the fatherhood of Abraham, and the faithfulness of God to Israel in 1:18–11:36?[25] She also fails to explain why Paul would include specific advice on such issues as taxes (13:1–7) and problems between the "strong" and "weak" (14:1–15:6) as part of communicating his understanding of the gospel. In sum, in both her methodology and conclusions, she relegates the particular contours of the longest sustained argument in Paul's surviving letters to the level of irrelevance for determining what Paul wanted to accomplish by that argument.

---

[22]Ibid., quoting Nils A. Dahl, "The Missionary Theology in the Epistle to the Romans," in *Studies in Paul* (Minneapolis: Augsburg, 1977), 75.

[23]Jervis, *Purpose of Romans*, 161.

[24]Ulrich Wilckens says Paul must have a special reason for writing such an "extensive and carefully thought out" ("ausführlichen und wohldurchdachten") argument (*Der Brief and die Römer [Röm 1–5]*, 3d aufl., EKKNT, bd. 6.1 [Neukirchener-Vluyn: Neukirchener Verlag, 1997], 34.

[25]Within this dissertation, phrases such as the "'Jewish' matters" or the "'Jewish' argument" of the letter refer to topics such as those listed above that concern the Jewish scripture and traditions. These topics predominate in the letter. Additional issues include those regarding Scripture, the prophets, David, and the Messiah all found in 1:1–7 (see Robert Morgan, *Romans*, NTG [Sheffield: JSOT Press, 1995], 17). Campbell provides a longer list of such issues in the letter-body. These include circumcision, the last judgment, Israel within the plan of God. See, "Determining the Gospel," 321.

A Frame, but Only Part of a Body: Douglas A. Campbell

In contrast to both Nygren and Jervis, Douglas A. Campbell recognizes the need to unite the frame of the letter and its body, and attacks the problem head on.[26] Campbell believes Paul's "Jewish" arguments in a letter addressed to an audience of gentile Christians can only be explained by positing the presence of Jewish-Christian opponents threatening to turn the Roman Christians against Paul. If these opponents succeed before he can get to Rome himself, Paul could lose the support he needs from them in order to carry out his mission to Spain.[27] Paul writes Romans, therefore, to defend his view on issues that had proved controversial during his ministry in the East.[28] It would be on these issues that Jewish-Christian opponents would continue to challenge him in Rome.[29] In Campbell's view, only the threat of such opponents in Rome unites Paul's statements about his future travel plans expressed in the letter-frame with what can be reconstructed about the Roman Christians from the letter-frame and body, and the peculiar "Jewish" content of the letter-body.

Campbell's argument successfully accounts for the opening and closing sections of the letter as well as Paul's argument in 1:16–11:36, but he makes no mention of how the paraenesis from 12:1–15:13 fits within this purpose. It is interesting that the most thorough defense of this "apologetic" thesis also says little on this same section of the letter.[30]

---

[26]"The fundamental problem of Romans' contingency is how to fit these two broad components of the letter together within a single plausible explanation of why Paul wrote as he did." Campbell, "Determining the Gospel," 317.

[27]Ibid., 321–23.

[28]Because Paul writes to "defend" his interpretation of the gospel, this view of the letter's purpose will be called the "apologetic" thesis.

[29]This accounts for the parallels between the subject matter of Romans 1–11 and portions of Galatians and Philippians (ibid., 324). "The letter to the Romans is therefore something of a pre-emptive strike in that important strategic arena" (ibid., 322).

[30]Markku Kettunen, *Der Abfassungszweck des Römerbriefes* (Annales Academiae scientarum Fennicae: dissertationes humanarum

Consequently, this explanation also remains incomplete and therefore unsatisfactory.

Multiple Reasons: A. J. M. Wedderburn

In the most thorough, sustained treatment of the Romans Debate in English, A. J. M. Wedderburn (*Reasons*)[31] posits that no single reason for Paul's writing of Romans can successfully integrate all the diverse evidence in the letter. Instead, Wedderburn claims, Paul had several motivations for writing Romans (hence the plural in the title of his monograph, Reasons). Wedderburn's approach has won numerous followers.[32]

Wedderburn holds that the church in Rome was gentile, and was therefore one of the churches for which Paul felt himself responsible as apostle to the gentiles.[33] These Christian gentiles, however, were divided by differing views regarding Paul's Law-free gentile mission. Believers on both sides of the argument misunderstood Paul in significant ways. On the one hand, those agreeing with Paul's Law-free position took that viewpoint further than Paul himself did, rejecting Israel and all things Jewish. On the other hand, those Christians in Rome with strong Jewish loyalties were both offended by Paul's interpretation of Israel's story and fearful

---

literarum, bd. 18; Helsinki: Suomalainen Tiedeakatemia, 1979). Kettunen treats 13:1–7, but gives no more than passing attention to the rest of 12:1–15:13.

[31]*The Reasons for Romans* (Minneapolis: Fortress Press, 1991); hereafter cited in the text as *Reasons*.

[32]The fact that several views can be supported from evidence in the text proves that "Paul had not simply one but several purposes in view when he wrote. . . . No single suggested reason on its own can explain the full sweep of the document." James D. G. Dunn, "Romans, Letter to the," in *DPL*, eds. Gerald F. Hawthorne and Ralph P. Martin (Downers Grove, Ill.: InterVarsity Press, 1993), 840. See also Joseph A. Fitzmyer, *Romans*, AB, vol. 33 (New York: Doubleday, 1992), 80; Moo, *Romans*, 20.

[33]This synthesis of Wedderburn's argument follows closely his own summary in *Reasons for Romans*, 140–42.

that his Law-free gospel would encourage sinful behavior (*Reasons*, 140–141).

Paul wrote because he wanted the Roman Christians' support both for his visit to Jerusalem with the collection and for his planned ministry in the West. Because his collection from the gentiles brought to a head existing tensions among the believers, and because his planned visit to Rome would only further exacerbate those tensions, Paul feared he could lose the Roman Christians' backing for both projects. He therefore wrote to explain and defend his preaching to those on both sides of the controversy (*Reasons*, 141).

To those loyal to the Jewish roots of their faith, Paul demonstrates how his gospel proclaims that God has acted in a way consonant with Israel's scriptures. To those more sympathetic to Paul's Law-free mission, he demonstrates the essential Jewish roots of their Christian faith. Paul argues that the Roman believers need to have their minds "renewed" (12:2) and thereby see each other in a new light. If they do so, they will "receive one another" (15:7) and consequently heal the divisions exacerbated by Paul and his gospel. Only then can Paul hope to gain the assistance he needs for his ventures to both Jerusalem and Spain (*Reasons*, 141–142).

Wedderburn concludes, therefore, that the confluence of several factors (divisions among the Roman Christians and the particular contours of the contentious issues, Paul's pending visit to Jerusalem and his planned visit to Rome) produces this particular letter from Paul to the Roman believers. As a result, one must speak of the reason*s* for Romans in the plural rather than the singular (*Reasons*, 142).

Wedderburn's thesis possesses several strengths.[34] He correctly recognizes that a complex set of issues motivates Paul to write. In addition, his reconstruction provides an explanation for the entirety of the letter, integrating the circumstances of both Paul and the Roman Christians with

---

[34]A thorough engagement with Wedderburn's wide-ranging argument cannot be undertaken at this point. Numerous aspects of it will be dealt with as necessary in the course of the argument below.

the argument of the letter. Furthermore, Wedderburn rightly acknowledges that Paul must defend his gospel against "misunderstandings and misapprehensions" (*Reasons*, 142) from those loyal to the Mosaic Law and that Paul displays an evident concern for relationships within the Christian community in Rome.

Yet, two telling criticisms can be raised regarding his argument. The first can be succinctly stated, the second requires more lengthy treatment. First, one must distinguish between the circumstances that led to the letter's writing and the aim(s) Paul had in writing it. Wedderburn is correct that several issues converged and prompted Paul to write. But those issues are not the same thing as what Paul hoped would happen as a result of his letter. One must also recognize that multiple causes do not necessarily require multiple aims. Although several matters impelled Paul to write, understanding Paul to have a single aim in the letter provides a better reading of the evidence than Wedderburn offers.

Second, Wedderburn posits that Paul had two basic aims. On the one hand, he sought support for his trip to Jerusalem with the collection. On the other hand, he hoped to lay the foundation for his later visit to Rome and thereby gain the necessary support for his planned mission to Spain. Wedderburn's explanation of the second objective makes clear sense. Paul must quiet the controversies surrounding his gospel and his person before he arrives on the scene if he wants to gather the community's support for Spain. But Wedderburn's first proposed aim vastly overstates the evidence in Romans regarding the importance of the collection.

Wedderburn bases his interpretation of the twofold aim of the letter upon the work of C. J. Bjerkelund.[35] According to Wedderburn, Bjerkelund traces Paul's use of the verb "I urge"

---

[35]C. J. Bjerkelund's *Parakalô: Form, Funktion and Sinn der parakalô-Sätze in den paulinischen Briefen*. Bibliotheca theologica norvegica 1 (Oslo: Universitetsforlaget, 1967). Wedderburn's use and extension of Bjerkelund's thesis is found in chapter 4 of *Reasons for Romans*.

($\pi\alpha\rho\alpha\kappa\alpha\lambda\hat{\omega}$) in his letters. The word typically appears in first
person singular or plural, followed by a conjunction ($o\hat{\upsilon}\nu$ or $\delta\acute{\epsilon}$)
and then the object "you" ($\acute{\upsilon}\mu\hat{\alpha}s$). This formula often followed
the thanksgiving section in the letter-opening in order to
introduce a request.

This formula appears twice in Romans, at 12:1 and
15:30. Bjerkelund claims, Wedderburn says, that the key to
Paul's purpose in Romans is found with the $\pi\alpha\rho\alpha\kappa\alpha\lambda\hat{\omega}$-
formula in 15:30, where Paul urges the Romans to support his
trip to Jerusalem with the collection by praying for Paul's
safety in Jerusalem and the successful reception of the
collection. Wedderburn asserts, however, that the $\pi\alpha\rho\alpha\kappa\alpha\lambda\hat{\omega}$-
formulas of 12:1 and 15:30 provide the two keys for locating
Paul's purposes in Romans.

In Wedderburn's view, on the basis of Paul's argument
in 1:16–11:36, Paul appeals in 12:1–15:13 for the differing
groups in Rome to overcome their differences. The second appeal calls for the Roman believers to support Paul's delivery of
the collection to Jerusalem in prayer (since it is too late for
them to contribute materially). The second appeal is not
possible without the first, for the issue of the offering brings
to the fore the place of the gentiles in Paul's gospel, the very
matter that divided the Christians in Rome.

Still, whereas Wedderburn correctly recognizes that
Bjerkelund places more weight on the issue of the collection
than the actual content of Romans will bear, Wedderburn
himself reasserts the importance of the collection on other
grounds for which there is only hypothetical evidence.
According to Wedderburn, Paul's collection was controversial
in Rome because it involved the place of the gentiles in his
gospel. Yet, where does one find evidence that Paul's gospel
was controversial at this time in Rome?[36] And how is one to

---

[36]The only evidence would be in 3:8. Yet even there, any dispute
in Rome on this matter appears to be relatively minor, according to
Paul's perception, at the time he writes. This issue will be examined in
chapter four below. Although one may agree that Paul's gospel had the
potential to foster controversy in Rome, the reconstruction of the
situation in Rome offered in this dissertation posits a different (and

know that the collection was a disputed issue for the Christians in Rome?

In 15:31 Paul mentions the collection rather opaquely as "my service in Jerusalem." Evidently, the Roman Christians already knew about the collection since Paul did not have to explain it or even mention it in a more explicit manner. If the collection was controversial, would Paul ask for their prayers that he be delivered from "unbelievers" in Jerusalem? If a number of Christians in Rome opposed the collection-project, Paul's description of those who opposed it in Jerusalem as "unbelievers" would hardly be a diplomatic move (and it would certainly violate the spirit of Paul's instructions in 14:1–15:6).

Wedderburn overrates the importance of the παρακαλῶ-formula for understanding Paul's purpose in this letter. As a result, he must assign more significance to 15:30–32 and the issue of the collection than the evidence will allow. Consequently, Wedderburn's overall argument becomes skewed. Nevertheless, Wedderburn's study remains on target in many respects. He will be a frequent dialogue partner as the argument of this dissertation progresses.[37]

Summary

This brief review of the work of four scholars illustrates the main avenues of approach to the issue of the purpose of Romans. Nygren and Jervis exemplify two primary means of addressing the problem that both fail because they neglect

---

more satisfactory) reading of the evidence than that provided by Wedderburn.

[37]One other major criticism of Wedderburn's argument should also be mentioned at this point. Wedderburn relies heavily on the Emperor Claudius' expulsion of the Jews from Rome in 49 CE and their subsequent return after Claudius' death as a shaping factor in Roman Christianity. This "Claudius thesis," however, has now been rendered untenable. See Wolfgang Wiefel, "The Jewish Community in Ancient Rome and the Origins of Roman Christianity," in *The Romans Debate*, 85–101 for an original and influential argument for the Claudian proposal. For criticism of this reconstruction, see the literature cited in chapter four below.

either the letter-frame or the letter-body. Campbell and Wedderburn represent recent attempts to account for both frame and body. Yet, Campbell fails to consider the entire body of the letter. As a result, his reconstruction explains only part of the evidence. Wedderburn mistakenly assumes that the multiple factors prompting Paul to write necessitate multiple aims for the letter as well. Furthermore, although his argument satisfies the need to take the entire letter into account, his overdependence on the significance of the παρακαλῶ-formula distorts his conclusions. In other words, Wedderburn correctly recognizes the scope of information that needs to be accounted for, but offers an unsatisfactory reading of that information.

Thesis

Paul's motivation for writing Romans emerged from his desire to travel on to Spain and there to evangelize among the gentiles. In order for that ministry to become reality, Paul needed the help of the Christians in Rome. Yet, at the time he wrote, he knew it would be at least six months (and likely longer) before he could get to Rome[38] and personally secure that assistance. Aware that reports of controversies surrounding his preaching in the East were known in Rome (3:8), Paul feared that opponents would arrive there and begin speaking against him and his gospel before he could get there himself (16:17–19). If that happened, the Roman Christians could be turned against him or become sharply divided regarding Paul and his gospel. In either event, Paul's aim to gain the necessary support for a Spanish mission, and therefore the Spanish mission itself, would evaporate.

The thesis of this dissertation is that Paul wrote Romans in order to shape a "community of the new age"[39] and

---

[38]See chapter four below.

[39]In this dissertation, the "community of the new age" will be used interchangeably with the "eschatological people of God."

thereby head off opposition to his gospel before it could take root among the Roman Christians during his absence. A "community of the new age" was an obedient, Spirit-led community characterized first and foremost by Jew and gentile receiving one another just as Christ had received them (15:7). This was the appropriate expression of the people of God now that the anticipated new age had been inaugurated by the death and resurrection of Jesus the Christ, and the gentiles were joining the Jews in the worship of God. Although establishing such communities was at the heart of Paul's call, in Romans that task takes on additional importance since it was precisely a community of this character that would prove resistant to the expected criticisms from Paul's opponents. For the Christian community in Rome was vulnerable along the theological and ethnic fault lines where tensions among Roman believers already existed. Paul's opponents could exploit those tensions (as they had done in the East) in order to turn some or most against him.

Paul employs a twofold strategy to achieve his goal. First, he seeks to strengthen the Roman Christians' adherence to his interpretation of the gospel specifically at the points where he anticipates it will be challenged (1:18–11:36). In doing so, he lays the necessary groundwork for his second tactic, describing how that gospel should work itself out in the life of the community (12:1–15:13). In other words, Paul's so-called "theological" arguments of the first eleven chapters, while addressing disputed issues, at the same time concern very practical matters for the formation of a community worthy of the age begun by Jesus' resurrection from the dead. In this sense, Paul's argument is "practical" throughout.[40]

---

[40]As mentioned above, contrary to those who insist that Paul does not treat ecclesiology in Romans, the letter is "ecclesiological" through and through. At its very core, Romans is concerned with questions like, "Who are the people of God now that the second Adam has been raised from the dead? What are the similarities and differences between the people of God under the old covenant and those 'in Christ' under the new one?"

In summary, Paul's missionary plans, his historical situation, events he anticipates taking place in Rome in the near future, and the broad contours of charges he expected to be leveled against him—all these factors combined to determine the content, shape, and purpose of Paul's argument throughout Romans.[41] Instead of a broad summary of Paul's theology, Romans served a strategic purpose in the furtherance of Paul's missionary plans. Specifically, Romans was intended to shape a community of the new age where Jew and gentile dwelt in unity. Only such an obedient, Spirit-led community would prove resistant to the charges Paul anticipates will be made against him and his gospel, thereby preserving the assistance Paul needed to carry out his ministry in Spain.

Outline

In view of the definition of the primary problem in the Romans Debate and thesis proposed as a solution to that problem in chapter one, I will argue for this thesis in the following manner.

On the basis of an analysis of the frame of the letter, chapter two concludes that Paul intended the letter to have the same effect upon the Roman Christians as his intended visit, that is, to "strengthen" their faith. This chapter also highlights Paul's emphasis on the theme of "the obedience of faith" in the letter's opening and closing sections.

Taking Romans as a genuine letter to the Christian communities in Rome, chapter three asks, "What particular obedience does Paul hope to foster in Rome?" I contend that 15:7 serves as the capstone for Paul's argument in the letter. The primary "obedience" Paul wants to occur among the Roman Christians is that they receive one another just as Christ received them to the glory of God.

---

[41]This position agrees with Wedderburn that multiple circumstances together prompt Paul to write. His *aim* in response to that confluence of circumstances is another matter.

Chapters four, five and six address the issues of why Paul wrote to these particular people at this point in his ministry about these specific issues (and not some others). Chapter four gleans what can be known about Paul's circumstances at the time he writes the letter and the identity of the Christians in Rome. Paul sees his preaching ministry in the East as completed. He plans to go to Spain to proclaim the gospel there, and needs the help of the Roman Christians to do so. First, however, he must travel with the collection to Jerusalem, where he knows he will face opposition to his inclusion of gentiles, as gentiles, into the people of God.

The Roman Christians were numerous, well-instructed in the faith, and met in house groups in several sections of the city. There were also some divisions among them owing to varying degrees of adherence to Jewish traditions. The chapter concludes that Paul was aware of circumstances prevailing among the Christians in Rome and that the Roman Christians were at least somewhat familiar with Paul and the content of his preaching.

In light of this reconstruction, chapter five examines why Paul would write about the specific issues he includes in the body of the letter. Based on what can be known from Paul's other letters about opposition to Paul and his preaching in the East, the content of the letter-body in chapters 1–11 can be elucidated as a defense against similar opposition.[42] An examination of Romans 3:8, 16:17–20a and 15:31, indicates that Paul believes criticisms of his preaching are known in Rome and that he expects opponents to arrive in Rome soon.

The above analysis accounts for Romans 1–11 and most of chs. 15–16, but not for Romans 12:1–15:6. Chapter six examines this latter section, arguing that it demonstrates clear concern by Paul for relationships among community members. Paul outlines general instructions regarding relationships (chs. 12–13), and then applies these instructions to the specific disagreements between the "strong" and the

---

[42]This stands, of course, in agreement with the positions of Douglas A. Campbell (and Markku Kettunen) outlined above.

"weak" in Rome. The application section culminates in the exhortation in 15:7 for the Roman Christians to "receive one another."

The focal point of the differences between the "strong" and the "weak" in 14:1–15:6 is the question of the place of the Jewish Law in the life of the eschatological people of God. Paul was attacked in the East for his views on this very issue. He is aware that should such criticisms reach Rome, his reputation with the church there as well as the unity of the believers would crumble. This is of particular concern to him since his planned mission to Spain will depend on the support of the Roman Christians.

The convergence of these factors, therefore, prompts Paul to write "boldly" at this time in order to "remind" (15:15) them of specific issues where they could be susceptible to influence by Paul's critics. He seeks to "strengthen" (1:11) them against this eventuality by imparting to them the "obedience of faith" (1:5; 15:18; 16:26) by which he means specifically the obedience of welcoming one another after the model of Christ to the glory of God (15:7).

This understanding of Paul's purpose resolves the key issue in the Romans Debate. It not only takes seriously important signals of Paul's intent in the framework of Romans, it also provides a coherent rationale for the entire content of the letter.

The dissertation concludes with a brief summary chapter, recapitulating the thesis along with its supporting arguments and delineating the specific contributions made as a result.

Chapter Two

EVIDENCE FROM THE LETTER-FRAME: THE "OBEDIENCE OF FAITH" IN ROMANS

This chapter investigates statements made in the frame of the letter that provide indications of Paul's intent in writing. It then traces one theme found in the letter-frame throughout Romans and interprets its significance for understanding Paul's purpose.

Three passages in the letter-frame will be examined. First, I analyze 1:11–15 where Paul says he writes in order that the Roman believers may be strengthened, that he might have fruit among them, and that he might evangelize in Rome. Second, I consider Paul's statement in 15:15 that he writes this letter as a "reminder" to them. Third, I examine Paul's statements, primarily in 1:5, but also in 15:18 and 16:26, that the purpose of his apostolic ministry is to bring about "the obedience of faith" among the gentiles. Recognizing the fact that Paul calls special attention to the theme of obedience in the frame of the letter, the chapter then explores this theme in Romans.

Statements Related To Purpose In The Letter-Frame

Three passages serve as the focus of the following discussion: 1:11–15; 15:15; and 1:5 (15:18; 16:26). They serve as Paul's own indicators of what he considered important in the letter as well as why he wrote it. Together these passages lay the initial groundwork for resolving the Romans Debate.

Romans 1:11–15

Beginning in 1:8, Paul relates his long felt desire to visit the Roman believers. He states his intended purpose for this visit using two parallel clauses of purpose (ἵνα), one in v. 11 and the other in v. 13. In v. 15 he adds a third statement using an infinitive of purpose. First, Paul wants to impart some spiritual gift to them. That gift, in turn, would result[1] in the Roman Christians being strengthened (v. 11). Second, Paul believes he will have some fruit (καρπὸν) among them as a result of his visit (v. 13). Finally, Paul says he desires "to evangelize" (v. 15; εὐαγγελίσασθαι) in Rome. These statements will be examined in the order in which they occur in the text.

Romans 1:11. Paul hopes through his visit "to impart some spiritual gift" (ἵνα τι μεταδῶ χάρισμα ὑμῖν πνευματικὸν) to his hearers. Determining the specific referent of the gift here becomes complicated because of Paul's use of the indefinite adjective "some" (τι). This indefiniteness leads many commentators to conclude that a precise referent cannot be known.[2] Within this context, however, one can ascertain the

---

[1]εἰς τὸ with the infinitive may indicate purpose or result. *BDF* §402(2); Stanley E. Porter, *Idioms of the Greek New Testament*, 2d ed., Biblical Languages: Greek, vol. 2 (Sheffield: JSOT Press, 1994), §11.2.2. Here, following Paul's statement of purpose "in order that I may impart a spiritual gift to you," the "strengthening" is better understood as the result of the imparting of the gift.

[2]John Murray, *The Epistle to the Romans*, NICNT (Grand Rapids: William B. Eerdmans, 1968), 1:22; H. P. Liddon, *Explanatory Analysis of St. Paul's Epistle to the Romans* (London: Longmans, Green, and Co.,

general thrust of Paul's words. Certainly, Paul does not mean
that he will impart a gift such as those he cites in Romans
12:6–8 and 1 Corinthians 12. Rather, he expresses "his confidence that . . . God will minister through him in a particular
way."[3] God will manifest gracious acts through Paul, God's
servant.[4] Hence, the gift will be a "spiritual" gift, the work of
the Holy Spirit.[5]

That gift will result in the Romans being
"strengthened."[6] Paul uses the word in a similar fashion in

---

1893), 11; Adolf Schlatter, *Romans: The Righteousness of God*, trans.
Siegfried S. Schatzmann (Peabody, Mass.: Hendrickson Publishers,
1995), 15; C. K. Barrett, *A Commentary on the Epistle to the Romans*,
HNTC (Peabody, Mass.: Hendrickson, 1987), 25.

[3]James D. G. Dunn, *Jesus and the Spirit* (Grand Rapids: William
B. Eerdmans, 1997; reprint London: SCM Press, 1975), 207.

[4]James D. G. Dunn, *Romans 1–8*, WBC, vol. 38A (Milton Keynes,
England: Word, 1988), 30.

[5]Cranfield's contention that Paul is intentionally indefinite because "he has not yet learned by personal encounter what blessing they
particularly stand in need of" misses the mark. C. E. B. Cranfield, *The
Epistle to the Romans*, vol. 1, ICC (Edinburgh: T & T Clark, 1975), 79;
followed by Douglas Moo, *The Epistle to the Romans*, NICNT (Grand
Rapids: William B. Eerdmans, 1996), 60. Certainly 11:13–32, 13:1–7,
and 14:1–15:7 indicate that Paul knows details of their need. It is better
to see this "gift" as a general reference to the working of God through
Paul.

Markku Kettunen finds the key to understanding the "gift"
referred to here in the verb μεταδῶ. In contrast to giving a simple gift
such as would be indicated by the verb δῶ, μεταδῶ indicates Paul plans
to "impart" something of what he already has himself. Kettunen believes
this refers to his gospel which is the subject of the letter (1:1, 9; *Der
Abfassungszweck des Römerbriefes*, Annales Academiae scientiarum
Fennicai, dissertationes humanarum litterarum, bd. 18 [Helsinki:
Suomalainen Tiedeakatemia, 1979], 146). Although there is an element
of truth in this, Kettunen makes an overly fine identification of the
referent of χάρισμα. Yes, Paul wants to impart the gospel to them (cf. 1
Thess. 2:8), but his concern is more for what the Spirit will do among
the Romans through Paul's activity. Kettunen offers a partial correction
on p. 148 of *Abfassungszweck*.

[6]The passive infinitive, στηριχθῆναι, is a divine passive indicating
that it is God who will do the strengthening.

the concluding doxology of Romans (16:25).[7] There he expresses confidence that God will strengthen the hearers through his gospel and the preaching of Jesus Christ. Paul also uses this word in 1 Thessalonians (3:2, 13) to express his hope for the Christians to be strengthened there (similarly in 2 Thess. 2:17; 3:3). In fact, Dieter Zeller calls it "already an almost technical expression for the apostolic work."[8]

Consistent with Paul's commendation of the faith of the Roman Christians elsewhere in the letter (1:8; 15:14), Paul's desire to "strengthen" his hearers indicates that Paul finds no fault with their spiritual health. He envisions his ministry among the Romans not as correcting deficiencies in their faith but as making stronger what is already there.[9]

Romans 1:13. In v. 13, Paul tells the Roman Christians that he often longed to come to them "in order that I might also have some fruit among you" (ἵνα τινὰ καρπὸν σχῶ καὶ ἐν ὑμῖν). Paul uses the term "fruit" (καρπός) figuratively in several ways throughout his letters. First, he employs it to

---

[7] "Τῷ δὲ δυναμένῳ ὑμᾶς στηρίξαι κατὰ τὸ εὐαγγέλιόν μου καὶ τὸ κήρυγμα Ἰησοῦ Χριστοῦ" The textual problems with 16:25–27 are dealt with in the Appendix.

[8] "ein schon fast technischer Ausdruck für die apostolische Nacharbeit," *Juden und Heiden in der Mission des Paulus: Studien zum Römerbrief*, 2d aufl., FB, bd. 8 (Stuttgart: Verlag Katholisches Bibelwerk, 1976), 53.

[9] "To strengthen, is not to turn one into another way, it is to make him walk firmly on that on which he is already" (F. Godet, *Commentary on St. Paul's Epistle to the Romans*, vol. 1, trans. A. Cusin [Edinburgh: T & T Clark, 1886], 144); similarly, Joseph A. Fitzmyer, *Romans*, AB, vol. 33 (New York: Doubleday, 1993), 248; Luke Timothy Johnson, *Reading Romans: A Literary and Theological Commentary* (New York: Crossroad, 1997), 23–24. Contra Mark D. Nanos, who believes that the Romans' faith lacked an apostolic foundation. He therefore translates the term here as "established" rather than strengthened, indicating Paul's ministry would provide such a needed foundation (*The Mystery of Romans: The Jewish Context of Paul's Letter* [Minneapolis: Fortress Press, 1996], 239). The letter offers no indication that the Romans' faith was lacking in any way due the absence of an apostolic basis for their communities.

describe the outcome of differing manners of life (Rom. 6:21, 22; Gal. 5:22; Phil. 1:22). He also utilizes the term in describing the general results of his missionary labors (Phil. 1:22; 4:17).[10] Finally, in one instance, he refers to the collection he plans to carry to Jerusalem as "the fruit" (Rom. 15:28).[11]

In 1:13, this "fruit" is the purpose (ἵνα with the subjunctive) of his coming visit. The "fruit" Paul speaks of consists of the intended outcome of his missionary work in Rome (usage 2). Paul's statement regarding this result in v. 13 therefore stands in parallel to the "strengthening" of v. 11. The "fruit" Paul hopes will become reality in Rome is that believers will be made stronger. In this sense, v. 13 refers to the outcome of Paul's ministry in Rome, but that outcome (usage 2) only becomes tangible in the manner of life of the Roman Christians (usage 1) as they are built up.

Paul employs the indefinite adjective τινὰ ("some") with "fruit" in 1:13 just as he used it in 1:11 when speaking of a "spiritual gift." C. E. B. Cranfield states that the adjective may "express a certain reserve and circumspection felt to be appropriate in speaking of fruit to be obtained by him in a church he has not founded."[12] In 1:11, however, the adjective qualifies "gift" by showing that the gift in question was a general reference to the work of God through Paul (rather than to a specific spiritual gift). Here it has the same function. Paul hopes to have "some" fruit among them. What, in particular, that fruit might consist of, other than strengthening the Christians, he does not specify at this point in the letter. One may, however, legitimately ask whether Paul did have any specific hopes in mind. An answer to that inquiry demands further study of the letter itself.

---

[10]Referring to the work of an apostle, Friedrich Hauck writes (citing Romans 1:13), "The results of the missionary are his fruit" ("καρπός", *TDNT* 3:615).

[11]The fact that Paul uses the term in this manner in 15:28 in no way requires that it carry the same sense in 1:13, contra Keith F. Nickle, *The Collection: A Study in Paul's Strategy*, SBT, vol. 48 (London: SCM Press, 1966), 70, and Luke T. Johnson, *Reading Romans*, 24.

[12]*Romans*, 1:82.

Romans 1:15. "That I might have . . . fruit" could also mean that Paul hopes to see new converts made in Rome. In verse 15, he speaks of his desire to come to Rome in order "to evangelize" (εὐαγγελίσασθαι) among them. Paul's use of εὐαγγελίζεσθαι here in Romans has created difficulties for interpreters. He states in 15:20 that he made it his practice to "evangelize" (εὐαγγελίζεσθαι) only where Christ had not been named. Why, then, would he come to the Christian communities in Rome? Two responses are in order. First, Paul did not intend to evangelize the Roman Christians as if they were unbelievers themselves. The terms Paul has already used of his hearers in Rome make it clear they are part of the people of God. If he hopes to evangelize in the sense of proclaiming his message to non-believers in Rome, he could possibly do so among the non-Christian gentile God-fearers in their synagogues or house churches.[13] In this sense, Paul could have evangelistic fruit "among the gentiles," but that would not refer to his work among Roman Christians.

Second, Paul uses the term εὐαγγελίζεσθαι in a broad sense not only to designate his missionary work of preaching so as to garner new converts, but also to refer to the work of strengthening existing believers.[14] Gerhard Friedrich notes that Paul

> can use εὐαγγελίζεσθαι to describe his whole activity as an apostle (1 C. 1:17). . . . But the message is also addressed to Christians (R. 1:15, cf. 11; 1 C. 9:12–18; Gl. 4:13; 2 Tm. 4:5, cf. 2). The same gospel is proclaimed in both missionary and congregational preaching. Paul makes no distinction.[15]

---

[13]That activity could also take place in the workshops of Rome where Paul could ply his tentmaking trade as a means of evangelism. See Ronald Hock, *The Social Context of Paul's Ministry: Tentmaking and Apostleship* (Philadelphia: Fortress Press, 1980), esp. 37–42.

[14]Cranfield, *Romans*, 1:86; Neil Elliott, *The Rhetoric of Romans: Argumentative Constraint and Strategy and Paul's Dialogue with Judaism*, JSNTSup, vol. 45 (Sheffield: JSOT Press, 1990), 85.

[15]"εὐαγγελίζομαι" *TDNT* 2:719–720.

Although one cannot rule out that Paul had evangelism among non-believers in mind, his mention of evangelizing in Romans 1:15 appears directed to the believers in Rome and therefore refers broadly to his work as an apostle. He may well have intended to gain new converts in Rome. But in this context Paul has addressed these people as mature believers[16] and stated that he wants to strengthen their existing faith. Paul's claim of wanting "to evangelize" in Rome should be understood as another way of saying what he has already stated in 1:11: he wants to come to Rome "to strengthen" the followers of Christ there.

In summary, Paul planned to travel to Rome in order to strengthen the believers there by building up their faith.[17] The results of that strengthening would be "fruit" that Paul would have as a result of his visit.

Apostolic Parousia. If this is Paul's hope for an intended visit to Rome, how is this hope related to his letter? In an article published in 1967,[18] Robert W. Funk (*"Parousia"*) argued that Paul's letters functioned as substitutes for his personal presence and authority. Because of its significance for understanding Paul's purpose in Romans, this thesis warrants brief summary and application.

On the basis of his analysis of Paul's letters, Funk claimed that Paul "thought of his presence as the bearer of charismatic, one might even say, eschatological, power" (*"Parousia,"* 265). Recognizing that groups of believers want-

---

[16]1:7–8. Note also the terms and concepts that Paul assumes his hearers already understand in 1:1–6.

[17]With reference to the "strengthening" mentioned in 1:11, Paul Bowers states, "Here Paul discloses the heart of his proposed role for the Roman Christians within his divine assignment. It is an edificatory function that he expressly envisages" ("Fulfilling the Gospel: The Scope of the Pauline Mission," *JETS* 30 [1987], 195).

[18]"The Apostolic *Parousia*: Form and Significance," in *Christian History and Interpretation: Studies Presented to John Knox*, eds. W. R. Farmer, C. F. D. Moule, and R. R. Niebuhr (Cambridge: Cambridge University Press, 1967), 249–268; hereafter cited in the text as *"Parousia."*

ed, or needed, that presence when Paul could not be among
them, Paul sent letters or emissaries to effect his personal
presence (*"Parousia"*) among the recipients. Funk identified
sections of Paul's letters where Paul was especially concerned
with his presence. It was through these sections of his letters,
Funk claimed, that Paul exerted his authority.

Funk identified five elements of these sections based on
an examination of Romans 15:14–33.[19] L. Ann Jervis has sim-
plified Funk's analysis by isolating three categories distinguished on the basis of their content, form, and function.[20]
Jervis's analysis is employed here. These passages concern:

(1) "Paul's writing of the letter." Paul will include a
phrase containing the verb "I write" (γράφω) and speak of his
manner of writing. The section will also include some reference to Paul's apostolic authority and possibly a request to
obey that authority.

(2) "Paul's dispatch of an emissary." The main verb in
this section is "I send" (πέμπω). Paul makes mention of the
emissary's credentials and describes the his or her task.

----

[19]These can be summarized as: (1) a γράφω ("I write") clause
specifying Paul's manner of writing the letter, typically with some
reference to Paul's apostolic authority to write and his mindset as he
writes; (2) a statement of Paul's relation as an apostle to the recipients;
(3) an expression of Paul's desire to see the hearers, causes of hindrance
or delay, mention of an emissary and that emissary's credentials, and an
announcement of Paul's plan to visit; (4) an "invocation of divine
approval and support for the apostolic *parousia*;" (ibid., 252); (5) a
statement of benefits of the *parousia* to Paul and his hearers (ibid., 252–
253).

[20]*The Purpose of Romans: A Comparative Letter Structure Investigation*, JSNTSup, vol. 55 (Sheffield: JSOT Press, 1991), 113–114. Jeffrey
A. D. Weima claims that it is better to focus on content rather than
form. "It would seem better to speak of the apostolic parousia as a
distinct epistolary convention that exhibits a rather loose form or
structure in which certain words or expressions are often found."
"Preaching the Gospel in Rome: A Study of the Epistolary Framework of
Romans," in *Gospel in Paul: Studies on Corinthians, Galatians and
Romans for Richard N. Longenecker*, eds. L. Ann Jervis and Peter
Richardson, JSNT Sup, vol. 108 (Sheffield: Sheffield Academic Press,
1994), 354.

(3) "Paul's visit." This includes either an announcement of a planned visit or an expression of Paul's desire to visit, including a statement of the purpose of the visit.

These features are readily recognizable in Romans 15:14–16:2.[21] In 15:14–15, Paul restates for the readers his manner of writing and reminds them of his authority (vv. 15b–21). He then (vv. 22–29) outlines his plans for coming to Rome.[22] Finally, in 16:1–2, Paul commends Phoebe, states her qualifications for the task he has assigned her, and makes a mild request that the Roman believers do whatever she asks.

Although not as complete as 15:14–16:2, Romans 1:1–15 includes features of Jervis's first and third categories. This passage does not contain a specific "I write" clause, but Paul mentions his mindset as he writes (1:8–9) and asserts his apostolic authority (1:1–5). Furthermore, he emphasizes that he desires to come to Rome personally (1:10–15).

Through the use of several means (calling attention to his apostolic authority and citing his reasons for writing a letter, commending an emissary and explaining the task Paul has given him or her, and announcing his plans or hopes to visit the recipients personally) Paul asserts his authoritative presence among his hearers. Jeffrey A. D. Weima aptly summarizes Paul's intent as follows.

> For Paul is not simply informing his readers about his future travel plans so as to satisfy their curiosity or to provide details about himself for their general interest. Rather, this epistolary convention serves as an effective literary device by which Paul can exert his apostolic authority and power over his letter recipients. This should not be interpreted as a power-hungry, ego trip by Paul but as a pragmatic means to place his readers under his apostolic authority such that they will accept and obey the contents of the letter.[23]

---

[21]This section is extended beyond the conclusion of ch. 15 (where Funk and Jervis end it) in order to include the recommendation of Phoebe, Paul's emissary with this letter.

[22]Jervis offers a more detailed analysis of 15:14–32 as a *parousia* section in *Purpose of Romans*, 114–27.

[23]"Preaching the Gospel," 354.

Thus, what Paul hoped to accomplish through his physical presence in Rome at a later date, he seeks to accomplish before that time through this letter and the presence of Phoebe, its bearer (16:1–2).[24] In other words, he seeks to have some fruit among them by strengthening their faith. Romans 1:11 and 1:13, therefore, provide clear indication of Paul's intention in writing the letter.[25]

In light of Paul's lengthy, detailed argument that follows in the rest of the letter, one must ask in what specific ways he wanted them strengthened. Surely, Paul would not write at such length and in such detail if his intentions were so undefined. A resolution to this question must await further analysis of the text. Nevertheless, one further observation must be made at this point. Whatever "strengthening" will occur among the Roman believers through this letter will be the work of the Spirit.[26] Paul emphasizes this point by separating the adjective "spiritual" (πνευματικὸν) from the noun it modifies, "gift" (χάρισμα), in 1:11.[27]

---

[24]Similarly, Kettunen, *Abfassungszweck*, 146–47.

[25]Klyne Snodgrass is one of the few who clearly catch the connection between the intended purpose of Paul's visit and the verb στηριχθῆναι. See "The Gospel in Romans: A Theology of Revelation," in *Gospel in Paul: Studies on Corinthians, Galatians and Romans for Richard N. Longenecker*, JSNTSup, vol. 108 (Sheffield: Sheffield Academic Press, 1994), 294. Although one cannot agree with all the details of their statements on this point, see also John Paul Heil, *Romans— Paul's Letter of Hope*, AnBib, vol. 112 (Rome: Biblical Institute Press, 1987), 12, and Nils A. Dahl, *Studies in Paul* (Minneapolis: Augsburg Publishing House, 1977), 77.

[26]". . . was die Römer brauchen, sei nur etwas von der Gabe des Geistes" ("what the Romans need, would only be something from the gift of the Spirit") (Kettunen, *Abfassungszweck*, 146).

[27]See also Hans Wilhelm Schmidt, *Der Brief des Paulus an die Römer*, THKNT, bd. 6 (Berlin: Evangelische Verlagsanstalt, 1962), 25 (citing E. Kühl, *Der Brief des Paulus and die Römer*, Leipzig: Quelle & Meyer, 1913), n.p.. The grammar of Blass, Debrunner, and Funk states,

> Closely related elements in the sentence . . . are usually placed together in simple speech. Poetic language and that rhetorically stylized in any way frequently pulls them apart in order to give greater effect to the separated elements by

Likewise, Ulrich Wilckens recognizes that the "fruit" mentioned in this passage, as it pertains to the outworking of Paul's ministry in the lives of the believers, was the work of the Spirit. He notes, "The word, however, can also be used of the effects of the Spirit in the behavior of the Christian; compare Gal. 5:22; Eph. 5:9; furthermore Phil. 1:11; 4:17."[28]

An inquiry regarding the work of the Spirit as Paul explains it in Romans and as it pertains to the Roman Christians will be necesary. At this point, it is sufficient to note that Paul calls attention to the fact that the strengthening he envisions among the Romans and the fruit he hopes to have among them as a result of this letter will both be the work of the Spirit.

Romans 15:15

In discussions on the purpose of Romans, Paul's description of his letter as a "way of reminding" the Romans (15:15) often gets overlooked. For example, the index to Karl P. Donfried's (ed.) *The Romans Debate*[29] lists only four references to this verse in the collection of articles and none of these references relate 15:15 to the purpose of the letter. Paul's own description of the letter, however, should not so easily be dismissed.[30]

---

their isolation. Such a word, torn out of its natural context and made more independent, is emphatic . . . (*BDF*, §473).

The authors cite these words in Romans 1:11 as an example. Dunn makes a similar point, *Romans 1–8,* 1:30.

[28]"Doch kann das Wort auch von der Wirkungen des Geistes im Wandel der Christen gebraucht werden, vgl. Gal 5,22; Eph 5,9; ferner Phil 1,11; 4,17." *Der Brief an die Römer (Röm. 1–5),* 3d aufl., EKKNT, bd. 6.1 (Neukirchener-Vluyn: Neukirchener Verlag, 1997), 79, n. 85.

[29]Rev. and expanded ed. (Peabody, Mass.: Hendrickson, 1991).

[30]Romans 15:14–15 is "a primary index of Paul's purposes in the intervening chapters because it is Paul's own attempt to tell the Romans what he has intended." J. Paul Sampley, "Romans in a Different Light: A Response to Robert Jewett," in *Pauline Theology,* vol. 3, *Romans* (Minneapolis: Fortress Press, 1995), 129. Markku Kettunen also emphasizes this point (*Abfassungszweck,* 150).

Two observations regarding this verse in its context warrant mention at the outset. Both will become significant as the argument progresses. First, after drawing the body of the letter to a close in 15:7–13, Paul moves on to the epistolary conclusion (15:14–16:27). In the previous section of this chapter, it was shown that the first part of 15:14–16:2 contains the elements of an apostolic *parousia*. In fact, Paul makes specific mention of his apostolic authority in 15:15, citing it as his motive for writing. As he concludes the letter, Paul wants to remind his hearers of his apostolic authority.[31]

Second, Paul begins this closing section by restating his confidence in the maturity of the Romans believers (15:14; cf. 1:8). Paul is convinced that the Christians there are "full of goodness, having been filled with all knowledge, and able to admonish one another." Stanley N. Olson has noted that such expressions of confidence in one's hearers function to reinforce the purpose of a letter by increasing the potential for gaining a receptive hearing.[32] One must be alert, therefore, to statements of purpose in this context.

Turning to the main concern of the following analysis, Paul writes, "Because of the grace given to me by God, I have written to you rather boldly at some points as a reminder to you."[33] Two issues require special attention in this statement. First, what does Paul mean by the phrase "at some points" (ἀπὸ μέρους)?. Second, how does this letter function as a "reminder" (ἐπαναμιμνῄσκων) for his hearers?

----

[31]A. J. M. Wedderburn cites the connection between Paul's calling and his manner of writing as unmistakable evidence that Paul asserts his authority. He comments, "Otherwise it is hard to explain why the grace of his calling to be an apostle to the gentiles should be offered as an explanation for his boldness in writing to them." *The Reasons for Romans* (Minneapolis: Fortress Press, 1991), 99.

[32]"Pauline Expressions of Confidence in His Addressees," *CBQ* 47 (1985): 295.

[33]τολμηρότερον δὲ ἔγραψα ὑμῖν ἀπὸ μέρους ὡς ἐπαναμιμνῄσκων ὑμᾶς διὰ τὴν χάριν τὴν δοθεῖσάν μοι ὑπὸ τοῦ θεοῦ

ἀπὸ μέρους. How one understands the sense of the prepositional phrase ἀπὸ μέρους determines to a significant extent how one understands Paul's point in the verse. The phrase has been construed in three ways. First, it can refer to all or parts of the letter where Paul has "reminded" them strongly. In this case, Paul is trying to soften the impact of his words in order to lessen any offense they may have given. Paul would then be saying, "Nevertheless *on some points* I have written to you . . ." (NRSV; emphasis added). On the other hand, it could specify one reason (among others) why Paul writes to them—"Yet I write to you quite boldly, *partly* to remind . . ."[34] Finally, it could merely qualify the degree of Paul's boldness, as in *"somewhat* boldly."[35]

The phrase lies between Paul's statement "I have written" and the adverbial clause "as a way of reminding," linking it more naturally with either of these phrases rather than with the adverb "boldly" (τολμηρότερον;[36] option three), making the last option less likely.[37] Paul also does not seem to restrict his reasons for writing at this point in the letter (option two) since he makes no comments about additional purposes in this context other than that he writes as a "way of reminding" to his hearers. Following upon his commendation of the Romans in v. 14, the phrase is best taken in an apologetic tone, recalling all or parts of the letter where Paul has spoken boldly. The NRSV correctly captures this sense by translating the conjunction δέ in an adversative sense, "never-

---

[34]Fitzmyer, *Romans*, 709 (emphasis added); also Barrett, *Romans*, 275. Even though this is Fitzmyer's translation, his comments on p. 711 indicate he takes the phrase in the first sense outlined above.

[35]John Murray renders the phrase "partly," as in "I partly write to you as . . ." Here he agrees with the American Standard Version (1901) translation on which his commentary is based, "in some measure" (*Romans*, 2:209, n. 19). See also Heinrich Schlier, *Der Römerbrief*, HTKNT, bd. 6 (Freiburg: Herder, 1977), 428.

[36]The textual witnesses for τολμηρότερον (p[46], ℵ, C, 33, 1739, 1881) outweigh those for the variant τολμηροτέρως (A, B).

[37]It would also be odd for Paul to further qualify a comparative adverb (τολμηρότερον is an comparative adjective used adverbially). It is almost as if Paul is saying, "I write to boldly, sort of . . ."

theless." Even though the Roman Christians are mature, Paul
has still had the boldness to address them on certain issues.

Taking the phrase in this sense, one still must ask
whether it refers to all or only parts of the letter. James D. G.
Dunn asserts that the parallels of mood and content between
this section of the letter and the opening section in 1:8–15
may well indicate Paul has the whole letter in mind.[38] Yet,
the fact that Paul recognizes that the Roman believers
already basically know what he has said in the letter (see
below) indicates that Paul has particular sections of the letter
in mind where he presses his case.

I identify the "bold" sections as those where he applies
his theological arguments to specific issues in Rome in the
form of exhortation (11:11–32; 12:1–15:13). This is not to deny
that in his "theological" arguments which dominate the letter-
body in chapters 1–11, Paul may push his viewpoint on
certain issues. Yet, several factors favor understanding the
phrase as primarily referring to Paul's exhortations. First,
Paul may be considered most "bold" when he applies that
teaching to the life of the Roman community of believers. Paul
did not found the Christian communities in Rome, yet he
asserts his apostolic authority and instructs the believers on
how they should live. Second, Paul claims he speaks through
this letter "boldly." Boldness is a theme often associated with
exhortation.[39] Finally, expressions of confidence in one's

---

[38]*Romans 9–16*, WBC, vol. 38B (Milton Keynes, England: Word,
1991), 859.

[39]Abraham J. Malherbe, "Exhortation in 1 Thessalonians," in
Paul and the Popular Philosophers (Minneapolis: Fortress Press, 1989),
58–59; Elliott, *Rhetoric of Romans*, 89. Although Paul uses the comparative adverb τολμηρότερον here rather than the term παρρησία of
which Malherbe speaks, the terms are virtually synonymous in
meaning. See Johannes P. Louw and Eugene A. Nida eds. *Greek–
English Lexicon of the New Testament Based on Semantic Domains*, vol.
1, *Introduction and Domains* (New York: United Bible Societies, 1988),
§25.159, §25:161, and §25:162; Gottfried Fitzer, "τολμάω," *TDNT* 8:184–
185; Heinrich Schlier, "παρρησία," *TDNT* 5:882–884.

hearers, like the one that directly precedes this verse (15:14), also characterize paraenesis.[40]

ἐπαναμιμνῄσκων. The word ἐπαναμιμνῄσκω occurs only here in biblical literature. In fact, the word is seldom found in the extant literature of the period. The term is used of reminding someone of something repeatedly.[41] The double prepositional prefix ἐπανα- gives the verb a specific focus.[42] Used here with ὡς ("as") and γράφω ("I write"), it indicates the manner of Paul's writing: "by way of reminder" (NRSV).[43]

"Remembering" was not just a mental exercise for Paul and the early Christians. Recalling something stimulated thought in such a way that it shaped attitudes and actions.[44] In this regard, Nils A. Dahl cites the example of Colossians 4:18, "remember my chains." He writes, "The meaning is either: 'Pray for me, I who am imprisoned' or 'Consider that I write as a prisoner for the sake of the gospel and heed my words.'"[45] Paul's use of the term in Romans can be summarized as follows: confident that they have already been "filled with all knowledge and are able to admonish one another" (15:14), Paul now writes to "remind" them of that knowledge so that they can apply it to their communal life.[46] He then backs up that statement of purpose with an assertion

---

[40]Elliott, *Rhetoric of Romans*, 88–89.

[41]*BAG(D)*, 282. Also *LSJ*, 607.

[42]James Hope Moulton and Wilbert Francis Howard, *A Grammar of New Testament Greek*, vol. 2, *Accidence and Word-Formation* (Edinburgh: T & T Clark, 1929), 312. Determining what specifically Paul wanted to remind his auditors of requires further analysis below.

[43]Moo, *Romans*, 888, n. 25; citing *BAG(D)*, I.2.a (p. 897 in *BAG[D]*).

[44]Nils A. Dahl, "Anamnesis: Memory and Commemoration in Early Christianity," in *Jesus in the Memory of the Early Church* (Minneapolis: Augsburg, 1976), 13.

[45]Ibid, 12, n. 6.

[46]Douglas Moo captures this idea nicely, "The things he has taught them and exhorted to do all derive from the faith that they hold in common with Paul. In his letter Paul has done nothing but to explicate, for them in their circumstances, the implications of the gospel" (*Romans*, 889).

of his apostolic authority. That authority stands behind what they are to recall and act upon.

Paul considered "reminding" to be an integral part of his ministry.[47] It has already been noted that "reminding" played an important role in moral exhortation.[48] According to Otto Michel, within early Christianity, "The verb is typical for the passing on of a fixed halacha."[49] For example, during the late New Testament era, Clement of Rome prefaces exhortations to the Corinthians by saying, "We are not only writing these things to you, beloved, for your admonition, but also to remind (ὑπομιμνήσκοντες) ourselves (1 Clem. 7:1)."[50] By describing his mode of writing as one of reminding, Paul in no way diminishes its importance.[51] Instead, Paul highlights the significance he attached to what he had written.

---

[47]ἀναμιμνήσκω, 1 Cor. 4:17; γνωρίζω, 1 Cor. 15:1; see also Phil. 3:1b; 1 Thess. 1:5, 4:1.

[48]This gives further evidence for understanding ἀπὸ μέρους as a reference especially to paraenetic parts of the letter.

[49]"Das Verbum ist typisch für die Weitergabe einer bestimmten Hallacha" (*Der Brief an die Römer*, 10 aufl., KEK [Göttingen: Vandenhoeck & Ruprecht, 1955], 327, n. 2). Although one must use the adjective "fixed" with caution with regard to the content of Romans, one can still agree with Michel that "reminder" was employed with the passing on of tradition. See also David E. Aune, "Romans as a *Logos Protreptikos*," in *The Romans Debate*, 295.

[50]*The Apostolic Fathers*, trans. Kirsopp Lake, *LCL* (Cambridge, Mass.: Harvard University Press, 1935), 21.

[51]Francis Watson regards it a "fiction" that Paul describes his letter as a "reminder," thereby implying that the Roman Christians are already familiar with its contents (*Paul, Judaism and the Gentiles: A Sociological Approach* [Cambridge: Cambridge University Press, 1986], 211, n. 63). In chapter four, evidence will be marshaled demonstrating the likelihood that the Roman Christians *did* know much of Paul's teaching found in the letter.

Summary. Paul knows that much of the content of this letter is not new to the recipients.[52] He assumes they are aware of at least the broad contours of much of it. His application of it to the situation of the Roman Christians, however, may be perceived by some in Rome as a bit too bold since Paul had not founded a Christian community there. Yet, Paul's apostolic authority stands behind what he writes. His hearers are expected to heed his admonitions.

Still, as Markku Kettunen notes, if the Romans' faith is healthy (and Paul gives every indication it is), why does he need to write such an extensive letter to "remind" them again of what they already largely know? Paul is about to depart for Jerusalem, yet feels compelled to write a long and detailed argument to a church he has not established.[53] Whatever his intentions were in writing, they were obviously important to Paul. The question posed as the key issue in to Romans Debate comes to the fore once again, "Why does Paul write this letter to these Christians at this point in his life?"

An answer to that question requires additional analysis of the letter and the circumstances that surrounded its production. Yet, the information Paul provides in 15:15 cannot be overlooked in the Romans Debate. It will play a significant role in the argument which follows below.

---

[52]Hans-Werner Bartsch aptly notes that Paul's label 'reminder' "is not understandable if his letter is a treatise about his own theology written in order to introduce himself" ("The Concept of Faith in Paul's Letter to the Romans," *BR* 13 [1968]: 44).

[53]Kettunen, *Abfassungszweck*, 151–152, 154. Moo notes how Paul's statement here raises this issue of why he wrote such an extensive letter. Yet, Moo fails to follow through on the implications of his questions, electing to dismiss Paul's characterization of the letter as largely rhetorical. Moo therefore understands the content of Romans to be new information based upon their common faith. Although some of what Paul argues in the letter is undoubtedly new to the Roman Christians, Moo's interpretation goes beyond what Paul states in 15:15. Why should Paul say he is "reminding" his auditors if the content is so new to them? (*Romans*, 888–89).

Romans 1:5

The study of 1:11–15 and 15:15 demonstrated that Paul's apostolic authority stands behind and motivates what he writes. Furthermore, the activities he describes in those verses, strengthening and reminding, were ways in which Paul carried out his apostolic responsibilities. The clear implication is that Paul wants to exercise his apostolic calling by performing both activities through his letter to the Romans. Since Paul's apostolic call plays an important role in the writing of this letter, it is significant that in 1:5 he provides a description of the purpose of that call: "for the obedience of faith among all the nations to the honor of his name."

Two additional factors also indicate the importance of this "obedience of faith." First, initially stated in 1:5, the theme of "obedience of faith" is echoed in 15:18 and repeated verbatim in 16:26. As mentioned in chapter one, Paul typically signaled for his hearers important themes in his letters by highlighting them in the opening and closing sections. Second, both obedience and faith serve as important motifs in the letter-body. Clearly, Paul's summary of his apostolic responsibility in 1:5 serves as a key indicator of what Paul hoped to accomplish among the Roman Christians through this letter.[54]

This portion of the chapter will first analyze 1:5 in the context of the opening section of Romans, giving special attention to the disputed genitive construction "obedience of faith"

---

[54]This verse often gets overlooked in the Romans Debate. For example, though Jervis focuses exclusively on the letter-frame in determining the purpose of Romans, Paul's obvious highlighting of the "obedience of faith" plays no role in her conclusions. Perhaps, her neglect of the letter body in her study allowed her to overlook its significance. The index to *The Romans Debate*, lists six references to 1:5, none of which deals with the purpose of the letter. Don B. Garlington, however, correctly observes, "Rom 1:5 can be looked upon as a programmatic statement of the main purpose of Romans" (*Faith, Obedience and Perseverance: Aspects of Paul's Letter to the Romans*, WUNT, vol. 79 [Tübingen: J. C. B. Mohr {Paul Siebeck}, 1994], 10. Matthew Black offers the same opinion on the basis of 15:18 (*Romans*, 2d ed., NCBC [Grand Rapids: William B. Eerdmans, 1989], 203).

(ὑπακοὴν πίστεως). The theme of obedience will then be
examined in the entire letter in order to demonstrate that
obedience is one of Paul's key concerns.

Context. Paul opened his letter using the formal elements typical of a letter in his time, namely, an identification
of the sender, an identification of the recipient(s), and a
greeting. Romans 1:5 concludes the identification of sender
unit, drawing this section to a close by returning to the issue
with which he opened the letter, his apostolic call. Each
element of the verse is examined separately below.

Call. Paul makes clear that he received this call through
the agency of the resurrected Lord Jesus Christ.[55] He
describes what he received[56] as "grace and apostleship" (χάριν
καὶ ἀποστολὴν). The two terms stand in hendiadys, where two
words describing one idea are joined by a conjunction rather
than by one word plus an adjectival genitive.[57] In this
instance, the second term "apostleship" modifies the first.
Paul received a divine grace[58] which consists of the call to
serve as apostle. The phrase could therefore be translated
"grace which is apostleship." Paul uses χάρις ("grace" or

---

[55]James D. G. Dunn notes that this call from the resurrected Lord
shows that Jesus Christ is still active in the ongoing work of redemption
(*Romans 1–8*, 16).

[56]Paul's use of the first person plural "we received" here is either
an example of an epistolary plural (so Cranfield *Romans*, 1:65; M.-J.
Lagrange, *St. Paul: Epitre aux Romains*, 6th ed., Etudes Bibliques
[Paris: Gabalds, 1950], 10; Franz J. Leenhardt, *The Epistle to the
Romans: A Commentary*, trans. Harold Knight [London: Lutterworth
Press, 1961], 38, n. §; see also C. F. D. Moule, *An Idiom Book of New
Testament Greek*, 2nd ed. [Cambridge: Cambridge University Press,
1959], 118–119) or a reference to the fact that Paul does not consider
himself as the only apostle (Dunn, *Romans 1–8*, 16). The matter has no
bearing on the argument here.

[57]"The co-ordination of two ideas, one of which is dependent on
the other (hendiadys), serves in the NT to avoid a series of dependent
genitives." *BDF*, §442 (16).

[58]Aptly described by Dunn as an "effective divine power in the
experience of men and women" (*Romans 1–8*, 17).

"gift") in relation to his apostolic call elsewhere in Romans (12:3: 15:15) as well.

Obedience of Faith. The purpose of this apostleship was to bring about the "obedience of faith" among all the nations. The sense of the genitive πίστεως ("of faith") and therefore of the phrase as a whole has generated no little discussion.[59] The list of proposed interpretations can be reduced to four viable options.

1. objective genitive: "obedience to the faith" or "obedience to God's faithfulness"
2. subjective genitive: "obedience which faith works"
3. genitive of apposition/epexegetical genitive: "obedience which consists in faith"
4. adjectival genitive/genitive of quality: "obedience which is characterized by faith"[60]

The objective genitive reading,[61] while popular in the past, founders on the fact that the word for faith here is not used to refer to a body of teaching without the direct article present—*the* faith.[62] In 1:5, πίστεως lacks the article.

---

[59]Cranfield lays out seven options with characteristic clarity. See *Romans*, 1:66. Don B. Garlington rightly cautions, "It should be clarified, however, that our interest lies not in grammatical labels for their own sake but principally in the complex of ideas suggested by these categories" (*Faith, Obedience and Perseverance*, 15). Likewise, A. B. du Toit warns, "We must remember that language is so subtle and dynamic that often it cannot be neatly squeezed into our reductionary schemes" ("Faith and Obedience in Paul," *Neot* 25 [1991]: 66).

[60]The translation of point 4 is adapted from du Toit, "Faith and Obedience," 66. Du Toit acknowledges the difficulty in finding an English equivalent for this genitive.

[61]See, for example, the commentaries of Liddon, Luther, and Sanday and Headlam.

[62]As in Acts 6:7, ὑπήκουον τῇ πίστει (Geoffrey H. Parke-Taylor, "A Note on 'εἰς ὑπακοὴν πίστεως' in Romans i.5 and xvi.26," *ExpTim* 55 [1943–44]: 305).

C. E. B. Cranfield cites several parallel expressions from Romans where faith in God and obedience to God appear to be synonymous concepts. As such they constitute a strong argument for reading πίστεως in 1:5 as a genitive of apposition.[63] These parallels are worth listing.[64]

1:8   ἡ πίστις ὑμῶν καταγγέλλεται ἐν ὅλῳ τῷ κόσμῳ
16:19 ἡ γὰρ ὑμῶν ὑπακοὴ εἰς πάντας ἀφίκετο

10:16a Ἀλλ' οὐ πάντες ὑπήκουσαν τῷ εὐαγγελίῳ
10:16b Ἡσαΐας γὰρ λέγει· κύριε, τίς ἐπίστευσεν τῇ ἀκοῇ ἡμῶν;

11:23 ἐὰν μὴ ἐπιμένωσιν τῇ ἀπιστίᾳ
11:30 τῇ τούτων ἀπειθείᾳ
11:31 οὕτως καὶ οὗτοι νῦν ἠπείθησαν

1:5   δι' οὗ ἐλάβομεν χάριν καὶ ἀποστολὴν εἰς ὑπακοὴν πίστεως ἐν πᾶσιν τοῖς ἔθνεσιν
15:18 οὐ κατειργάσατο Χριστὸς δι' ἐμοῦ εἰς ὑπακοὴν ἐθνῶν

As persuasive as these parallels are, Mark Nanos argues that some distinction needs to be made between the terms. He asks, "Why bother with the phrase if Paul's point is the faith of the faith?"[65] Likewise, Glenn N. Davies claims that the two concepts certainly overlap, but are not identical. He goes on to argue for a subjective genitive or a genitive of origin, "obedience that springs from faith."[66]

The list of parallels make it apparent that "obedience" and "faith" bear a high degree of overlapping meaning in

---

[63]Among the commentators also opting for apposition (or epexegetical genitive) are Althaus, Calvin, Godet, Johnson, Käsemann, Kuss, Murray, Nygren, Schlier, and Wilckens.

[64]Cranfield, *Romans*, 1:66, n. 3.

[65]*Mystery of Romans*, 224, n. 164.

[66]*Faith and Obedience in Romans: A Study in Romans 1–4*, JSNTSup, vol. 39 (Sheffield: JSOT Press, 1990), 30.

Romans. But all the matched references to these terms are
not entirely parallel. For example, the similarities between
1:5 and 15:18 produce evidence for reading πίστεως in 1:5 as a
subjective genitive. Both verses concern Paul's apostolic
calling and express that calling in nearly identical terms, εἰς
ὑπακοὴν (for obedience). In both cases the noun ὑπακοὴν is
followed by a genitive. Although the sense of πίστεως is disputed in 1:5, the genitive ἐθνῶν in 15:18 is clearly a subjective
genitive; it is an obedience which the nations carry out. If
these verses are truly parallel, would not the genitive of 1:5
(disputed) carry a sense similar to that of 15:18 (undisputed)?
If the parallels are true, in 1:5 Paul is saying "the obedience
that faith works" (subjective genitive).[67] The failure of this
one parallel to support reading πίστεως in 1:5 as a genitive of
apposition does not, however, nullify the strong evidence in
favor of apposition offered by the other examples.

A. B. du Toit highlights the overlapping nature of the
genitive of apposition and the genitive of quality. He understands the genitive of quality to have a more "descriptive
rather than an identifying function." He argues for a genitive
of quality, paraphrasing the expression as "the obedience
which belongs to, is characterized by and goes together with
faith." He also recognizes that this interpretation comes close
to a genitive of origin: "obedience which stems from faith."[68]

How is all this evidence to be sorted out? Nigel Turner
recognizes that context must provide the key for inter-

---

[67]Other evidence reveals the lack of a true parallel here. In both
1:5 and 15:18 the gentiles "obey." In 15:18, Paul demonstrates who
obeys through the use of the subjective genitive ἐθνῶν immediately
following εἰς ὑπακοὴν. The genitive (πίστεως) in question in 1:5,
however, also qualifies the obedience Paul is called to bring about, but
does not do so by specifiying who performs it. In 1:5 Paul indicates who
performs it in the phrase which follows the genitive πίστεως —"among
all the gentiles" (ἐν πᾶσιν τοῖς ἔθνεσιν). In other words, the genitive
πίστεως in 1:5 has a different function than ἐθνῶν in 15:18. Consequently, the use of 15:18 to support reading πίστεως in 1:5 as a
subjective genitive fails.

[68]Ibid., 67.

pretation.[69] On this basis, the genitive πίστεως in 1:5 is best described as standing in apposition to obedience.[70] In 1:5 (and 16:26), Paul emphasizes the inseparability of faith and obedience. Paul called men and women to faith in Jesus Christ as Lord (6:16; 10:9) and lordship necessarily entailed submission, in other words, obedience.[71] The parallel uses of the concepts cited by Cranfield demonstrate how closely Paul understood them.

This does not mean that Paul cannot distinguish between the concepts in other contexts. If the sense of each term could be thought of as circles, the circles would be almost entirely overlapping and inseparable, but not entirely concentric. Yet, in this context Paul is emphasizing their inseparability.[72] Faith in Christ and obedience to Christ are of one cloth. Douglas Moo aptly summarizes Paul's use of faith and obedience in this verse. They are

> mutually interpreting: obedience always involves faith, and faith always involves obedience. They should not be equated, compartmentalized, or made into separate states of Christian experience. Paul called men and women to a faith that was

---

[69]"Indeed, so rich is Paul's compression of language with genitives that the attempt to define too narrowly the various types of genitive is vain; they all denote a relationship which is amplified by the context." *A Grammar of New Testament Greek*, vol. 3 (Edinburgh: T & T Clark, 1963), 212.

[70]The objection from the supposed parallel in 15:18 does not hold. The genitives of 1:5 and 15:18 stand in different relationship to the nouns with which they are joined due to the context in which they are found and the significance of the different nouns in the genitive. In both the gentiles are to be obedient. But in 1:5 Paul expresses the gentiles' role differently in order to make a more emphatic statement about *obedience*.

[71]Ernst Käsemann comments, "When the revelation of Christ is accepted, the rebellious world submits again to its Lord" (*Commentary on Romans* [Grand Rapids: William B. Eerdmans, 1980], 15).

[72]"When one trusts in God one obeys God; faith and works are inextricably woven together in the response of trusting faith" (Nanos, *Mystery of Romans*, 223).

always inseparable from obedience . . . and to an obedience
that could never be divorced from faith.[73]

The interpretive debate over this expression should not
cause one to lose sight of the fact that Paul is emphasizing the
first term in this phrase, "obedience".[74] What all Paul understands obedience to entail must await further examination of
obedience as a theme in Romans (see below).

Among All the Nations. This obedience is to take place
"among all the nations" (ἐν πᾶσιν τοῖς ἔθνεσιν). What is
noteworthy here is that while the phrase "obedience of faith"
(ὑπακοὴν πίστεως) is first attested in Paul, the concept has
deep roots in the Jewish faith. Don B. Garlington summarizes
his study of the concept in the Jewish writings from Paul's
time by saying

> Although the actual phrase ὑπακοὴν πίστεως does not occur
> before Paul, the idea embodied in it is clearly present. The
> obedience of God's people, consisting in their fidelity to his
> covenant with them, is the product of prior belief in his person
> and trust in his word. . . . faith's obedience is the appropriate
> response of Israel, the covenant partner, to the election, grace
> and mercy of God.[75]

In other words, Paul has been charged with bringing about a
Jewish response to God among the non-Jewish peoples.

In the first seven verses of the letter-opening, Paul
describes the gospel he preaches to gentiles in thoroughly
Jewish terms. This gospel was "proclaimed beforehand
through God's prophets in the holy scriptures" (v. 2). This

---

[73]*Romans*, 52–53.

[74]Du Toit emphasizes this fact, citing the Protestant inheritance
of many interpreters as the causal factor leading to the its being overlooked. In other words, Protestants have emphasized faith, but devalued
obedience out of fear of 'works righteousness' ("Faith and Obedience,"
67).

[75]*'The Obedience of Faith': A Pauline Phrase in Historical Context*,
WUNT 2:38 (Tübingen: J. C. B. Mohr [Paul Siebeck], 1991), 233.

gospel concerns God's son, born "of the seed of David" (v. 3). When he turns to describe the Christians in Rome, among whom undoubtedly are a number of gentiles by birth (11:13), he employs concepts drawn from the Jewish scriptures (vv. 6–7) such as "called," "beloved of God" and "called to be saints."[76] The call to the gentiles, in other words, is the same as Israel's call: to become, or (in the case of gentiles) to join (11:17) the obedient people of God (9:24–26).

This inclusion of the gentiles within the people of God carries distinct eschatological overtones.[77] Although the Hebrew Bible and the non-canonical Jewish literature from the Persian through the Roman period reflect a variety of perspectives regarding the non-Jewish peoples, early Christians seized upon strands of thinking that envisioned the nations making pilgrimage to Jerusalem to worship YHWH as part of the coming age.[78] Scholars differ on the specifics of how this incoming of the gentiles influenced Paul's thought, especially with regard to Paul's understanding of the significance of the collection for the church in Jerusalem (15:30–32). Yet, the fact that this concept was linked to future saving acts of YHWH in the Jewish literature from which Paul draws his understanding of his call and mission is seldom questioned.[79]

---

[76]A fuller listing of references can be found in the critical commentaries and in Garlington, ibid., 238–242. Only a brief sampling can be provided here. On "beloved of God" see, for example, Ps. 60:5 [LXX 59:7], 108:6; Rom. 9:25, 11:28. On "called" see, for example, Isa. 49:1, 50:2, 65:12, 66:4; Jer. 7:13. On "saints" (or "holy ones") see, for example, Lev. 17–26; Pss. 16 [LXX 15]:3, 74 [LXX 73]: 3; Isa. 4:3; Tob. 8:15.

[77]Dunn, *Romans 1–8*, 18; Brendan Byrne, *Romans*, SacPag, vol. 6 (Collegeville, Minn.: Liturgical Press, 1996), 40; Nanos, *Mystery*, 229.

[78]"Thus one of the relatively minor themes of the OT became a definitive element for the Christian church because of its conviction that the fulfillment of that hope for the conversion of the nations had begun." Donald E. Gowan, *Eschatology in the Old Testament* (Philadelphia: Fortress Press, 1986), 57.

[79]Among the numerous accounts of this phenomenon see, for example, Johannes Munck, *Paul and the Salvation of Mankind* (London: SCM Press, 1959), 303–305; Gowan, *Eschatology*, 42–57; Ferdinand

In addition to the inclusion of the gentiles, other eschatological concepts appear in 1:3–5 as well. First, in 1:4, Paul
speaks of Jesus as the "son of God." That title recalls passages
from the Old Testament where the royal messiah is also
called the "son of God" (2 Sam. 7:14; Ps. 2:7) as well as those
which speak of a future ruler who would take captive the
nations (Gen. 49:10; Num. 24:17–19; Amos 9:12).[80] According
to Paul, the son of God is now calling the nations into
submission to his reign through Paul's preaching. Paul's call
is not just to announce this significant moment, but to be
instrumental in implementing it. Second, and most signi-
ficantly, Paul speaks of Jesus' resurrection from the dead in
v. 3. Within early Christianity this resurrection was often
understood to be the "first fruits" of the general resurrection
anticipated in the age to come (1 Cor. 15:20, 23).[81]

Further elaboration of the significance of the connection
between obedience, Paul's calling, and eschatology follow
below. For now, it is enough to note the connections between
these issues as they emerge in 1:3–5.

Hahn, *Mission in the New Testament*, SBT, vol. 47 (London: SCM Press,
1965), 19; Dieter Georgi, *Remembering the Poor: The History of Paul's
Collection for Jerusalem* (Nashville: Abingdon Press, 1992), 36–39;
Joachim Jeremias, *Jesus' Promise to the Nations*, trans. by S. H. Hooke
(Philadelphia: Fortress Press, 1982), 56–71.

[80]Garlington, *Obedience of Faith*, 236–237; Dunn, *Romans 1–8*,
18. The eschatological context of Paul's call and gospel can also be seen
in Paul's description of Jesus having been "declared Son of God by the
resurrection from the dead" (1:4). The resurrection of the dead was, of
course, an event of the eschaton (1 Cor. 15:12, 20, 23; 1 Thess. 4:14–17;
Acts 4:2. See also L. J. Kreitzer, "Eschatology," in *DPL*, 257–59 and
George W. E. Nickelsburg, "Resurrection [Early Judaism and Christian-
ity]," in *ABD*, 5:684–691). Paul's concern for the collection (15:25–31)
also appears to be motivated by his view of it as symbolic of the eschatological coming of the nations to worship God.

[81]See, for example, John J. Collins, *The Apocalyptic Imagination:
An Introduction to Jewish Apocalyptic Literature*, 2d ed. (Grand Rapids:
William B. Eerdmans, 1998), 264.

"*For His Name's Sake.*" Finally, the gentiles' coming to the obedience of faith was to lead "to the honor of his [Jesus'] name."[82] When Paul's call, received through Jesus Christ the Lord, bears fruit in this way, this same Jesus[83] will receive glory and honor. Though Paul does not use the term "glory" (δόξα) here, the idea is clearly present.[84]

The point of Paul's preaching is not just the winning of gentiles to obedience to God. Above all, Paul's preaching was to result in the glorification of Christ.[85] With this allusion to the topic of the glory of Christ or God, we find Paul once again mentioning in this verse a theme that will prove central in this letter to follow.

"Obedience" In Romans

Although it is widely recognized that "the obedience of faith" plays an important role in Paul's argument and that Paul signals its significance by his repetition of that phrase in the letter-frame, the concept has received too little attention in reference to Paul's purpose in writing.[86] In addition, much has been made of the importance of faith in Romans,[87] yet

---

[82]"ὑπὲρ τοῦ ὀνόματος αὐτοῦ." The translation supplied here is from *BAG(D)*, 573, "ὄνομα" 4.q.

[83]The antecedent of the pronoun in the phrase is certainly "Jesus Christ our Lord" at the end of verse four, who is also referred to by the relative pronoun in the opening clause of v. 5.

[84]Gerhard Kittel defines δόξα in the NT using overlapping concepts of "'divine honour,' 'divine splendour,' 'divine power'" ("δόξα," *TDNT*, 2:247). Divine honor readily catches the sense here.

[85]Cranfield, *Romans*, 1:67. Similarly, Dunn, *Romans 1–8*, 18; Moo, *Romans*, 53; Byrne, *Romans*, 40.

[86]Paul Minear entitled his monograph on Paul's purpose in Romans "The Obedience of Faith" (SBT, second series, vol. 19, London: SCM Press, 1971). Yet, he never engages the phrase in any depth, exerting almost all his effort to identify numerous parties among the Roman Christians.

[87]For example, Dunn says, "To clarify what faith is and its importance to his gospel is one of Paul's chief objectives in this letter."

little has been said about the crucial role that the related idea obedience serves in the letter.[88]

Obedience plays a far more important role in what Paul hoped to effect through this letter than has been previously recognized.[89] In order to support this assertion and define precisely what that role is, this study makes several further probes of Romans based upon the conclusions reached above. (1) It will define "obedience"/"to obey" in general. (2) It will demonstrate the centrality of obedience in the argument of Romans. (3) It will place Paul's understanding of obedience within in its eschatological context in the letter.

Definition

The noun "obedience" (ὑπακοή) was not a common term in the New Testament era, probably becoming established through Christian usage.[90] As the form of the word suggests, obedience indicates the proper response to hearing.

Romans 1–8, 17. Dunn, however, does recognize the centrality of the theme "obedience of faith" in the letter (ibid., 17–18).

[88]The noun "obedience" occurs four time outside of Romans in the undisputed letters of Paul (2 Cor. 7:15; 10:5, 6; Phlm. 21) while the verb "obey" appears once (Phil. 2:12). The noun can serve as a general characterization of the Christian lifestyle (2 Cor. 7:15) or of submission to the Lordship or Christ (2 Cor. 10:5–6), or even of a proper response to Paul's appeal to an individual (Phlm. 21). This study is limited to Paul's use of the terminology in Romans because (1) its significance thematically in Romans (a role it does not have in any other letter), and (2) its use elsewhere in Paul's letters does not contribute to an understanding of how it functions in Paul's argument in Romans.

[89]Mark D. Nanos serves as an exception. See his comments regarding the phrase 'obedience of faith' in Romans in *Mystery of Romans*, 219–220 (quoted on p. 55 below). Although Nanos's interpretation of the phrase and his understanding of Paul's purpose in Romans differ from what is offered here, his observation about the importance of this phrase in Romans is right on target. See also Garlington, *Faith, Obedience and Perseverance*, 10, and Black, *Romans*, 203.

[90]Dunn, *Romans 1–8*, 17. See *LSJ*, 851 and *MM*, 650 for the limited evidence of its use.

The use of two terms together in Hebrews 2:2 (also in Romans 5:12–21) illustrates what obedience is not, and therefore what it is, as well. The writer states, "and every transgression (παράβασις) and disobedience (παρακοή) received its just reward." B. F. Westcott summarizes the author's use of these terms by saying, "παράβασις describes the actual transgression, a positive offence (the overt act); παρακοή describes properly the disobedience which fails to fulfill an injunction, and so includes negative offences."[91] The writer therefore encapsulates both the doing of the overt wrong act (transgression) and the failure to do the right (disobedience).[92] The choice of παρακοή was obviously determined by the warning in Hebrews 2:1 to "pay closest attention to what we have *heard*" (ἀκουσθεῖσιν),[93] meaning to act upon what was heard. Failure to respond constitutes παρακοή.

Obedience, therefore, indicates the proper response to what is heard. In Paul's case, the "obedience of faith" involves proper response to the hearing of his gospel. Paul says, "faith comes from what is heard, and what is heard comes through the word of Christ" (10:17; NRSV). Taking the final phrase as a genitive of reference, "the word about Christ," Paul is claiming faith comes through hearing the gospel he preaches.

"Obedience" in Romans

Paul employs the verb "to obey" (ὑπακούω) only four times in Romans and the noun "obedience" (ὑπακοή) in seven instances. Yet, obedience is closely intertwined with other key themes in the letter. These thematic connections reveal that

---

[91]*The Epistle to the Hebrews* (Grand Rapids: William B. Eerdmans, 1984 [n. d. for original]), 38. See also Ceslas Spicq, *L'Épître aux Hébreux*, vol. 2 (Paris: Librairie Lecoffre, 1952), 26.

[92]Gerhard Kittel ("παρακοή," *TDNT*, 1:223) observes that παρακοή "in the NT always means 'bad hearing' in consequence of unwillingness to hear, and therefore in the guilty sense of disobedience which does not and will not proceed to the action by which hearing becomes genuine hearing."

[93]William Lane, *Hebrews 1–8*, WBC 47A (Dallas: Word, 1991), 38. The translation is Lane's (emphasis added).

obedience plays a more significant role in Paul's argument than a mere word count suggests. This section therefore examines "obedience" in relation to issues that permeate Paul's argument.

Disobedience. Of course, obedience cannot be separated from its opposite, disobedience (παρακοή). Paul contrasts the two most clearly in his discussion of the one act of Adam and the one act of Christ in 5:12–21. In 5:19, Paul describes Adam's act as disobedience. Up to this point in the passage he has already described Adam's act as sin (ἁμαρτία, v. 12), transgression (παράβασις, v. 14),[94] and trespass (παράπτωμα, vv. 15, 17, 18). All of these terms serve as meaningful components of vital themes running through the letter. Although transgression and trespass are found less often,[95] Paul uses "sin" over forty times in chs. 3–14. The verb "to sin" (3:23) summarizes Paul's indictment of all humanity outside of Christ, both Jew and gentile, in 1:18–3:20. Furthermore, the categories Paul establishes in 5:12–21 of "under sin" (with its parallel "under law") and "under grace" and their corresponding "reigns" (βασιλεύω, 5:21; cf. 3:9, 6:14) establish the two groupings under which all humanity can be placed. These two categories form the basic salvation-historical paradigm within which all that Paul argues in the letter must be understood.

Paul also speaks of disobedience using the term ἀπείθεια. In 11:30–32, Paul summarizes his argument in chs. 9–11 in terms reminiscent of 1:18–3:20. All humanity has been bound together in disobedience (εἰς ἀπείθειαν, 11:32). Using Paul's terms from ch. 5, one could say, "bound under the reign of Adam." Once again, the relationship of obedience to a broad theme in Paul's argument becomes apparent.

---

[94]In Hebrews 2:2, παρακοή and παράβασις are used in hendiadys.
[95]Transgression, 2:23, 4:15, 5:14; transgressor, 2:25, 27; trespass, 4:25, 5:15–20 [5x], 11:1,2.

Righteousness. In contrast to Adam's act of disobedience (5:19), Paul describes Christ's act as one of obedience (διὰ τῆς ὑπακοῆς, 5:19). As with disobedience, Paul employs several terms synonymously to refer to the same phenomenon. In this case, he uses four interchangeable terms for "gift" to describe Christ's obedience.[96] For example, this gift exhibits God's righteousness, "the gift which is righteousness" (τῆς δωρεᾶς τῆς δικαιοσύνης, 5:17),[97] and can be described as a "righteous deed" (δικαιώματος, 5:18). James D. G. Dunn notes the parallels between "the gift of grace" of v. 15 and the "gift of righteousness" cited above in v. 17. He claims that through this repetition Paul can "recall the principal theme of 1:17–5:21."[98] 'Righteousness,' however, also serves as the 'principal theme' of chs. 9–11[99] and, in light of 1:17 and 15:8[100] should be recognized as a central theme of the letter as a whole.

Faith. In the discussion of the "obedience of faith" in 1:5, I argued that obedience and faith stand in apposition. With this link to faith, obedience once again becomes joined to a theme at the forefront of Paul's "reminder" to the Romans. Faith linked to God's act of righteousness in Christ constitutes the pivotal point of Paul's gospel (1:16–17; 3:22; 4:3, 16, 22–24; 9:30–32; 10:4). Of the numerous examples one could cite here, perhaps 9:30–10:4 makes this point most distinctly. Unbelieving Israel has not received God's eschatological offer of righteousness because they did not pursue it by faith.

---

[96]χάρισμα, vs. 15, 16; χάρις, vs. 15, 17; δωρεά, vs. 15, 17; δώρημα, v. 16.

[97] The second genitive is epexegetical (Moo, *Romans*, 339, n. 116).

[98]*Romans 1–8*, 281.

[99]This view understands these three chapters as Paul's defense against the charge that his gospel entails a failure of God's word (9:6a), meaning God's "covenant faithfulness" or "righteousness."

[100]"Christ has become a servant on behalf of the truth of God [which is another way of referring to the righteousness of God; cf. 3:4] in order to confirm the promises made to the fathers" (Χριστὸν διάκονον γεγενῆσθαι περιτομῆς ὑπὲρ ἀληθείας θεοῦ, εἰς τὸ βεβαιῶσαι τὰς ἐπαγγελίας τῶν πατέρων).

Believing gentiles, on the other hand, have received this righteousness precisely because they did pursue it by faith.

Unbelief. As obedience can be linked to faith (10:16), so also disobedience can be linked to unbelief. In 10:16a Paul states that not all "obeyed" the gospel. He then quotes Isaiah in order to confirm the prophetic (1:2) proclamation of this fact by calling that disobedience failure to believe (10:16b; Isa. 53:1). Paul then quotes a litany of scriptural passages to confirm that judgment (10:17–20). He concludes with yet another word of judgment against Israel from Isaiah which characterizes them as "a disobedient (ἀπειθοῦντα) and obstinate people" (10:21; Isa. 65:2). Paul applies these arguments to the large portion of his fellow Jews of that day who do not believe what Paul claims God has done in Christ (an unbelief apparent from 9:30 onward through Paul's own summary of his argument in 10:21). It is noteworthy that Paul characterizes some of these same Jews as disobedient (ἀπειθούντων) in 15:31.

Obedience in 12:1–15:13. Finally, although most of these themes punctuate the body of the letter through 11:36, few are mentioned in the paraenesis of 12:1–15:13. Yet, this fact does not negate the reality that Paul's instructions in 12:1–15:13 characterize the obedience he wants the believers in Rome to undertake.

Two factors make this connection apparent: (1) In 12:1, Paul summons his auditors to "offer" (παραστῆσαι) themselves to God, a clear echo of his call in 6:13, 16, 19 (παρίστημι and παριστάνω) to do the same. Paul is obviously returning to his earlier call to the Roman believers to live out their true identity in Christ.[101] (2) Christ's obedience not only makes Christian obedience possible (8:3–4), it also serves as the

---

[101]For more detailed lists of connections between the exhortations of ch. 6 and 12:1–2, see Victor Paul Furnish, *Theology and Ethics in Paul* (Nashville: Abingdon Press, 1968), 103–04, and Dunn, *Romans 9–16*, 708–09.

model for that obedience (6:4–5, 11–14; 15:7). The lifestyle Paul exhorts Roman believers to embrace in 12:1–15:13 is, therefore, one of obedience to the one to whom they have offered themselves.

In summary, obedience is inextricably linked to other key themes that permeate Paul's letter to the Roman Christians. As a result, one can see that obedience constitutes a central concern of Paul's throughout the letter. Mark D. Nanos summarizes the place of this theme in Romans as follows:

> I suggest that Paul's fascinating programmatic phrase 'obedience of faith' . . , which appears in the midst of these contexts throughout this letter . . . actually knits together and succinctly defines the various strands of this message to Rome.[102]

Without doubt, faith and obedience entail a particular lifestyle emerging out of submission to the lordship of the Son of God, Jesus Christ.

"Eschatological Obedience" in Romans

In order to grasp what Paul thought of as "obedience" in Romans, one must also understand the eschatological context in which Paul understands and uses the idea in the letter.[103] The eschatological concepts that surround the appearance of the expression "obedience of faith" in 1:3–5 have already been noted above. But Paul speaks of obedience elsewhere in Romans in eschatological contexts as well. An analysis of its use in Romans will substantiate this claim.

---

[102]*Mystery of Romans*, 219–20. This study would differ with Nanos's interpretation of the meaning of the obedience of faith in the context of Romans. Nevertheless, Nanos correctly assesses the significance of this phrase for understanding Paul's message in the letter.

[103]This is not to deny that the concept of "obedience of faith" was present among Jewish people before Paul coined the phrase as it appears in Romans. It is merely a claim that *as Paul uses it in Romans,* the concept carries distinct eschatological overtones. See Garlington, *Faith, Obedience and Perseverance*, 13.

The "Two Ages" in 5:12–21. In 5:12–19, Paul develops both contrasts and comparisons between Adam and Christ. Adam's disobedience introduced sin and death into human experience (5:12, 19). From that point on, sin and death "reigned" (5:14, 17, 21), even over those "under" the Mosaic law (5:20; 6:14). Christ's act of obedience (5:19), however, made many righteous, enabling grace to reign just as sin had reigned under Adam (5:21).

Paul here employs the idea of "two ages" found in apocalyptic strands of Judaism.[104] "For apocalyptic Judaism, history is the basic category and everything else is understood in terms of God's plan for his people, now being worked out in the history of the world."[105] That history is divided into two stages: the present evil age and the future age when God will intervene in history and transform all of creation.

In Rom. 5:12–21, Paul describes the first age, initiated by Adam, as characterized by sin and death. The second, begun by Christ, Paul depicts as one of righteousness and life (5:17). Each age exerts power over those under its rule. In the first, sin and death reign. In the second, grace reigns leading to eternal life (5:21). For Paul, however, the age to come has now begun with Christ's death and resurrection.[106]

It is significant that beginning at 6:1 when Paul goes on to defend his gospel against the charge that it promotes sin (an objection first noted in 3:8), he describes the experience of the believer in precisely these same "two age" terms.[107] Paul explains that believers undergo a death to sin (the sinful "reign" of 5:21) like Christ's through baptism (6:3–5). The purpose of that death was that the believer should, like

---

[104]E.g. 4 Ezra 7:[50] "the Most High has made not one world but two" (*OTP*). See also 4 Ezra 7:[113], 8:1; 1 Enoch 71:15.

[105]Paul J. Achtemeier, *Romans*, IBC (Louisville: John Knox Press, 1985), 7.

[106]For explicit statements elsewhere in Paul's letters, see Gal. 1:4; 1 Cor. 11:10; and 2 Cor. 5:17.

[107]In fact, Paul lays out the comparisons and contrasts between Adam and Christ in 5:12–21 in order to define the terms for his discussion of sin and Law in chs. 6–8.

Christ, be raised to a new life lived to God (6:4b–5). Through that death, the believer's existence under sin's reign is destroyed (6:6),[108] freeing him or her from its control (6:7, 9). On this basis, Paul exhorts his hearers to act in accordance with their new life in Christ "under grace" (6:11–14).

At a fundamental level, then, Paul's understanding of who believers are, is framed within this "two age" construct. Believers in Christ have passed from living under the reign of one to living under the reign of another. Life must be lived under one of these two dominions. Paul calls his hearers to "present yourselves to God" (παραστήσατε ἑαυτοὺς τῷ θεῷ, 6:13) so that sin and disobedience will not rule over them (6:14). The implications of all this for the theme of obedience become clearer when we see how Paul relates the Spirit to the lifestyle of those under grace (6:14).

The Role of the Spirit. That the Spirit of God played an important role in the eschatological understanding of Second Temple Judaism and in that of the early Christians, is beyond question.[109] This phenomenon appears in Romans where Paul associates the activity of the Spirit with the new age inaugurated by Christ and with the future work of God in bringing that which has been inaugurated to completion.

Against those who would charge that the Mosiac Law was needed in order to effectively deal with sin, Paul answers that the Law proved unable[110] to provide the answer for the Adamic sin problem due to the power of human sin itself (8:3a; 7:7–25). Yet, what the Law was unable to do, God made

---

[108]ἵνα καταργηθῇ τὸ σῶμα τῆς ἁμαρτίας

[109]For the most recent extensive treatment with regard to eschatological expectations of Paul (pp. 803–26) and intertestamental Judaism (pp. 904–15), see Gordon D. Fee, *God's Empowering Presence: The Holy Spirit in the Letters of Paul* (Peabody, Mass.: Hendrickson Publishers, 1994). See also Terence Paige, "Holy Spirit," *DPL*, 411; James D. G. Dunn, *The Theology of Paul the Apostle* (Grand Rapids: William B. Eerdmans, 1998), 416–19; Fitzmyer, *Romans*, 124.

[110]Τὸ γὰρ ἀδύνατον τοῦ νόμου ἐν ᾧ ἠσθένει διὰ τῆς σαρκός (8:3a).

possible through Jesus Christ (8:2, 3b–4). As a result, the righteous requirements of the Law can be fulfilled among believers who walk according to the Spirit (8:4–5).

The Spirit is clearly associated with the age introduced by Christ. In contrast to the life lived helplessly under the rule of sin described in 7:14–24, under the reign of grace the Spirit enables an obedience not possible under the Law. "By the Spirit" (8:13) the deeds of the body under sin can be put to death. In summary, the obedience to which Paul calls the Romans is one lived under grace, in the age introduced by Christ's death and resurrection, and made possible by the work of the Spirit.

The Spirit is also linked with the completion of the redemption begun in Christ's death and resurrection. Paul claims that those who are led by the Spirit are the true children of God (8:14–17),[111] and they await the future glory coming to God's children (8:18). Until that time, the Spirit has been given as "the first fruit" (τὴν ἀπαρχὴν τοῦ πνεύματος, 8:23). Reversing the traditional order whereby the first-fruits are given to God (Deut. 18:4), here the first-fruits are given by God to human beings, anticipating the completion of their "adoption" (υἱοθεσίαν, 8:23).[112]

Paul's Call to the Gentiles. Finally, Paul's call is to bring about the "obedience of faith" among the gentiles (1:5; 16:26). The purpose of that call identifies it as one to be understood in eschatological terms. Johannes Munck, whose grasp of this particular point has proved influential, states

> With Paul it is not a matter of a call to apostleship in general, but of a clearly defined apostleship in relation to the Gentiles. His personal call coincides with an objective eschatological

---

[111]Paul anticipates this identification in 2:25–29.
[112]Gerhard Delling, "ἀπαρχή," *TDNT*, 1:486.

necessity, namely God's plan that the Gospel is to be preached to the Gentiles before the end of the age.[113]

The obedience Paul was to foster was one belonging to the age to come as the gentiles were summoned to worship the one true God (15:9b–12) along with the Jews.

Summary. "Obedience" is thoroughly integrated with other key themes in Romans. Furthermore, it also forms a key part of the "two age" understanding of salvation-history that creates the backdrop to all of Paul's theological argument. As such, the key role obedience plays in Paul's thought in Romans must be recognized.

Conclusion

When Paul speaks of "fulfilling the righteous requirements of the Law" (8:4), he asserts that something is possible now that was not before. Paul had been commissioned to effect that reality among the gentiles as part of the eschatological activity of God. The claim made here is that this is precisely the "obedience of faith" that Paul speaks of in the letter-frame.[114] Paul calls gentiles to become obedient by the power of the Spirit and thereby be able to fulfill the righteous requirements of the Law in a way that is not possible under reign of the old age. Hence, one may speak of "the new obedience."[115]

---

[113]*Salvation of Mankind*, 41. See also the insightful summary of Munck's understanding of Paul's call and the subsequent influence of Munck on this issue in Paul W. Bowers, "Mission," in *DPL*, 616–18.

[114]Richard B. Hays correctly observes that obedience of faith "evidently describes a particular response to the proclaimed gospel" ("ΠΙΣΤΙΣ and Pauline Christology: What Is at Stake?" in *Pauline Theology*, vol. 4, *Looking Back, Pressing On*, eds. E. Elizabeth Johnson and David M. Hay [Atlanta: Scholars Press, 1997], 40).

[115]The phrase comes from Herman Ridderbos, *Paul: An Outline of His Theology*, trans. John Richard de Witt (Grand Rapids: William B. Eerdmans, 1975), 253. Ridderbos, however, arrives at this title in a

Yet, this obedience is not only for gentiles. Paul makes the case in 2:1–3:20 that apart from Christ, Jews just as much as gentiles live "under sin." In fact, in 6:14 he equates life "under Law" with life "under sin." Paul's fellow Jews are therefore called to submit to the mastery of the Lord Jesus Christ (6:15–23) as well. Failure to do so is not only unbelief, but also disobedience (10:16). So Paul is called to bring the gentiles to the "obedience of faith," but Jews are called to the same obedience.[116]

The "obedience of faith" therefore not only expresses "the design of Paul's apostleship," but also is a "delineation of the eschatological purposes of God."[117] Romans is Paul's attempt to carry out his calling with regard to those in Rome so that those eschatological purposes, summarized by Paul as the "obedience of faith," may become reality there.[118] When that happens, Paul will have some "fruit" (1:13) among them since the Roman believers will be "strengthened" (1:11) in their faith.[119] To that end he writes "as a way of reminding" (15:15; NRSV) them, so that by the Spirit the "obedience of faith" may become reality among them.

---

different manner and gives the concept a different sense than that outlined here.

[116]Against Nanos (*Mystery of Romans*, 224), who sees Paul's call as limited to gentiles, and therefore the "obedience of faith" as limited to gentiles as well. That Paul's call was directed toward the gentiles is obvious. Such a focus should not be used to restrict the scope of those who were to walk in such obedience. Paul makes it clear in Romans 1:18–3:20, 23: his fellow Jews were as steeped in sin as the gentiles.

[117]Don B. Garlington, *Faith, Obedience and Perseverance*, 12.

[118]Ibid., 10; Matthew Black states that "to win obedience from the Gentiles" (NRSV translation of 15:18) is "the main purpose of the Epistle to the Romans" (*Romans*, 203).

[119]"Such obedience, emerging from a strengthened faith, was the goal not only of the letter to Rome but of his anticipated trip there (1.11)" (Minear, *Obedience of Faith*, 1).

Chapter Three

ROMANS 15:7-13 WITHIN THE ARGUMENT OF ROMANS

Several questions were posed in the previous chapter that cannot be answered apart from further examination of the letter. These questions included: In what specific way did Paul want to see the Romans "strengthened?" And what particular "obedience" was this letter intended to foster among Paul's auditors? In order to answer these questions, this chapter investigates the role of Romans 15:7-13 in the letter. The chapter concludes that Paul wrote Romans in order that his Christian recipients would "accept one another just as Christ has accepted you, to the glory of God" (15:7). In obeying the Lord Jesus Christ in this way, the "community of the new age" in Rome would be strengthened.

The role 15:7-13 plays in the argument of the letter is disputed. Its opening exhortation in 15:7 loudly echoes Paul's instructions to the "strong" in 14:1-15:6 (14:1, 3; 15:1), leading many to propose that it summarizes and concludes those instructions alone. Other scholars argue that its position at the end of the extensive section of paraenetical material begun in 12:1 indicates that it summarizes Paul's advice from 12:1-15:6. Still others identify echoes in 15:7-13 of several themes found throughout the letter as evidence that it may summarize Paul's message in the letter as a whole.

These numerous associations with other parts of Romans complicate any attempt to understand the role this pericope plays within the letter. If it can be demonstrated that the passage draws together Paul's argument throughout the letter, then this summary section contains important information regarding what Paul considered central to his argument, and hence, about the letter's purpose.

Romans 15:7–13

The structure and content of the pericope itself must be examined before turning to the larger question of its function within Romans. The following analysis consists of four parts determined by the structure of the passage. The parts are: exhortation and christological example (15:7), christological warrant (15:8–9a), scriptural substantiation (15:9b–12), and benediction (15:13).

Exhortation and Christological Example: 15:7

The opening causal conjunction "therefore" (διὸ) indicates that what follows results from what precedes. As has been shown, whether 15:7–13 portrays the consequences to be drawn from the exhortations beginning in 14:1, from those beginning in 12:1, or from the letter as a whole lies at the heart of the investigation of these verses.

Whereas Paul's instructions were directed to the "strong" in 14:1 and 15:1, here he broadens his admonition to the community in general: "receive one another" (ἀλλήλους). This follows closely on Paul's prayer in 15:5–6 that the community "live in harmony with one another" (ἐν ἀλλήλοις) so that they "may glorify God together in one mind." This enlarging of the scope to include the entire community raises important questions about the relationship of the passage to 14:1–15:6. Does the change of scope indicate that Paul also broadens his perspective beyond the matter dealt with in 14:1–15:6? Or is this merely another way to phrase his admonition as he summarizes the instructions to the strong and the weak? This matter will be taken up in the second half of this chapter.

The mutual receiving that Paul calls for must be model-ed after the manner in which Christ received the members of the Christian communities in Rome (5:6–10). Although some scholars claim the conjunction "just as" (καθώς) should be understood in a causal sense ("receive one another because Christ accepted you"),[1] Paul could easily have chosen another conjunction had he wanted to indicate causation.[2] Instead, Paul offers Christ as the example for his auditors to follow.

Romans 15:3 provides decisive support for this inter-pretation. Romans 15:1–6 displays clear parallels of structure and content to 15:7–13 (which are dealt with in more detail below). Within this parallel structure, 15:3 and the appeal to Christ in 15:7 stand as obvious counterparts. In v. 3, Christ is cited as the example for the "strong" to imitate in their attitude toward themselves and in how that attitude con-sequently works out in action toward the "weak." The impli-cation of this parallel structure is that Christ also serves as the model for imitation in v. 7.[3] Furthermore, the benediction in 15:5 prays that God may give the Roman Christians the same mindset toward one another "in accordance with Jesus Christ" (NRSV; τὸ αὐτὸ φρονεῖν ἐν ἀλλήλοις κατὰ Χρισ-τὸν Ἰησοῦν). Once again, the implication is that the Roman Christians are to imitate the attitude and consequent actions that Christ displayed in his dealings with them, an attitude explained in v. 3. In light of the explicit appeal to Christ's example in two verses in such close context, including one standing in parallel to 15:7, it is evident that Paul is citing Christ as an example in v. 7 as well.

---

[1]Douglas Moo, *The Epistle to the Romans*, NICNT (Grand Rapids: William B. Eerdmans, 1996), 875; against C. E. B. Cranfield, *The Epistle to the Romans*, vol. 2, ICC (Edinburgh: T & T Clark, 1979), 739; Ernst Käsemann, *Commentary on Romans*, trans. and ed. Geoffrey W. Bromiley (Grand Rapids: William B. Eerdmans, 1980), 385.

[2]James D. G. Dunn, *Romans 9–16*, WBC 38B (Milton Keynes, England: Word, 1991), 846.

[3]J. Ross Wagner, "The Christ, Servant of Jew and Gentile: A Fresh Approach to Romans 15:8–9," *JBL* 116 (1997): 474, n. 11.

Scholars remain divided over whether "to the glory of God" in 15:7 refers to the activity of (1) Christ receiving the Roman Christians, (2) the Christians' receiving one another, or, (3) both. In light of the sentence structure, the accent on Christ as example in this context (15:3), and the centrality of Christ's actions (15:8–9a), the phrase most naturally applies to the act of Christ in receiving the Roman Christians. Still, in view of the fact that Paul has just mentioned the community glorifying God in one voice by living in harmony together (15:5–6), he certainly means to include their receiving one another as giving glory to God as well.[4] "To the glory of God" therefore pertains to the actions both of Christ receiving the Roman believers, and of those believers when they receive one another after Christ's model.[5] Paul calls on the Roman Christians to imitate Christ not only in their attitude toward themselves and in the actions that flow from that attitude, but also in the motive underlying their actions toward one another: the glory of God.

---

[4]One of the few commentators to note this connection is James Denney, *St. Paul's Epistle to the Romans*, The Expositor's Greek Testament, vol. 2 (Grand Rapids: William B. Eerdmans, 1979), 709.

[5]Otto Michel captures the sense of the exhortation in this respect. He says with reference to Christ, "Er tat alles 'zur Ehre Gottes', wie sein ganzer Weg unter diesem Ziel stand (Phil 2,11), sollten wir nun die Ehre Gottes verunglimpfen?" ("He did everything 'to the glory of God,' as being in every way placed under this goal, should we now denigrate the glory of God?"). *Der Brief an die Römer*, 10th aufl., KEK (Göttingen: Vandenhoeck & Ruprecht, 1955), 321.

Christological Warrant: 15:8–9a

Paul substantiates ("for"; γὰρ) this exhortation by citing Christ's actions on behalf of Jews and gentiles (vv. 8–9a).[6] The introductory formula, "I say," establishes a solemn tone for what follows. Paul expects his hearers to take his supporting argument seriously.

The statements that follow in vv. 8–9a contain glaring syntactical difficulties. The pericope consists of two statements, v. 8 and v. 9a, that stand in some kind of parallel relationship. Each statement contains an infinitive, an accusative (apparently of reference), plus a prepositional phrase beginning with ὑπὲρ ("on behalf of" or "for the sake of"). Whereas the assertion in v. 8 is straightforward, problems arise in trying to relate it to what follows in v. 9a.[7]

Douglas Moo outlines the two most common interpretive options as follows. The verse numbers appearing below in parentheses in Moo's translation of the verses have been added for the sake of clarity.

(1) Paul might intend most of v. 8 and v. 9a as two parallel assertions dependent on "I say":

---

[6]Michael Thompson claims that λέγω γὰρ "expresses not an additional reason for the imperative in 15:7, but expands and explains Paul's previous assertion" (*Clothed With Christ: The Example and Teaching of Jesus in Romans 12:1–15:13*, JSNTSup, vol. 59 [Sheffield: JSOT Press, 1991], 232). It is difficult, however, to see how what follows "expands and explains" the exhortation in 15:7. Paul clearly provides supporting reasons for his instruction. This will become increasingly clear as the argument progresses below.

[7]Although Ulrich Wilckens can comment that Paul's syntax in vv. 8–9a "ist nicht ganz deutlich" ("is not entirely clear"; *Der Brief an die Römer [Röm. 12–16]*, 2d aufl., EKKNT, bd. 6.3 [Neukirchener: Neukirchener-Vluyn, 1989], 106), the same evaluation applies to many commentators' explanations of the difficulties. For exemplary descriptions of the interpretive problems and options, see especially Moo, *Romans*, 875–77; Wagner, "The Christ," 476–85; Leander E. Keck, "Christology, Soteriology, and the Praise of God (Romans 15:7–13)," in *The Conversation Continues: Studies in Paul and John In Honor of J. Louis Martyn*, eds. Robert T. Fortna and Beverly R. Gaventa (Nashville: Abingdon Press, 1990), 89–91; and Wilckens, *Römer*, 3:106.

I say:
a. that Christ has become a servant of the circumcision for the sake of the truth of God, in order to confirm the promises to the fathers; (8)
b. and that the Gentiles are glorifying God for the sake of his mercy. (9a)

(2) Paul might intend v. 8b and v. 9a as two parallel purpose expressions dependent on v. 8a:

I say that Christ has become a servant of the circumcision for the sake of the truth of God, (8)
a. in order to confirm the promises made to the fathers; (8)
b. and in order that the Gentiles might glorify God for the sake of his mercy.[8] (9a)

The first option emphasizes two clauses dependent on the verb "I say" (λέγω) and separated by an adversative conjunction usually translated "but" (δὲ; Moo translates it "and"). Both clauses begin with accusatives (Χριστὸν, τὰ ἔθνη) and contain parallel prepositional (ὑπέρ) phrases, "for the sake of," set in contrast by the conjunction. On the other hand, the second solution emphasizes the three infinitives (γεγενῆσθαι, βεβαιῶσαι, δοξάσαι). It understands the last two infinitives ("to confirm" and "to glorify") as governed by "in order to" (εἰς τό), thereby making them both explain the first infinitive ("has become").[9]

Most commentators opt for the second interpretation,[10] though neither solution is without serious difficulties.[11] Both options posit a change of subject between v. 8 and v. 9a that appears awkward. Both also make the preposition ὑπὲρ modify the infinitive "to glorify": "glorify *for the sake of* his mercy." Yet, as Ross Wagner notes, "the use of ὑπέρ to express that for which praise is given to someone is otherwise unattested in

---

[8]Moo, *Romans*, 876.

[9]Keck, "Christology," 89–90.

[10]For example, see the commentaries of Barrett, Käsemann, Murray, and Sanday and Headlam.

[11]For a more complete analysis of the options, see Wagner, "The Christ," 477–81, and Cranfield, *Romans*, 2:742–43. The following evaluation of these interpretations largely follows the criticisms of Wagner.

biblical Greek, the prepositions ἐπί or διά being employed instead."[12]

Turning to each proposal individually, the first solution displays parallels between vv. 8 and 9a, yet fails to find a counterpart for the important purpose statement of v. 8. The first solution also portrays a contrast between Christ's work as an act of faithfulness to the Jews and as an act of mercy to the gentiles, an opposition that runs counter to the heart of Paul's argument in the letter.[13]

The second solution posits an ellipsis in Paul's thought that must be supplied by the interpreter. Even if an ellipsis does occur here, determining just what the interpreter needs to supply remains problematic. For example, C. E. B. Cranfield provides an extensive amount of missing information in order to establish a precise balance between the two statements.[14] Supplying the elliptical material in parentheses, his translation is something like, "For I declare that (Jewish Christians ought to glorify God because) Christ has become the minister of the circumcision for the sake of God's faithfulness, in order to establish the promises made to the fathers, but (Christ has called the Gentiles for the sake of his mercy, in order to manifest his kindness, so) the Gentiles (ought to) glorify God for his mercy."[15] As J. Ross Wagner recognizes, in Cranfield's reconstruction, "Paul has left more unspoken than he has said!"[16] Ulrich Wilckens, on the other hand, balances the two parts of the sentence by adding only that Christ became "a

---

[12]Wagner, "The Christ," 479. Wagner based his decision on a search using the *Thesaurus Linguae Graecae* (ibid., 479, n.30).

[13]See, for example, Sam K. Williams, "The 'Righteousness of God' in Romans," *JBL* 99 (1980): 285–86. Williams concludes, "there is no warrant in the text for differentiating between God's mercy to the nations/Gentiles and the fulfillment of his promises to the fathers" (286).

[14]*Romans*, 2:743–44. Cranfield bases his reconstruction of the missing thoughts on an obscure work in Latin, R. Cornely, *Commentarius in s. Pauli Apostoli epistolas I* (Paris: no publisher, 1896), 736–39.

[15]Cranfield's translation is found in *Romans*, 2:699. The parenthetical material is taken from ibid., 743.

[16]Wagner, "The Christ," 481.

servant to (the uncircumcision on behalf of mercy)" to 15:9a.[17]
This approach has the advantage of producing a sensible
counterpart to the statement of 15:8 in 15:9a that involves
supplying only a minimal amount of Paul's unexpressed
thought. Still, the troublesome reading of the prepositional
phrase "on behalf of mercy" remains.

J. Ross Wagner proposes a third solution to this
dilemma.[18] In an attempt to portray the parallels between the
two statements, one can diagram Wagner's proposal as
follows. The translation is Wagner's.[19] The letter notations,
structural arrangement, and verse numbers are added for the
sake of clarity. Wagner's reconstructions of the unexpressed
elements appear in brackets.

For I say that
   a. the Christ has become a servant
      (1) of the circumcision
         (2) on behalf of the truthfulness of God,
            (3) in order to confirm
               (4) the promises made to the
                   patriarchs,
   b. and [a servant]
      (1) with respect to the Gentiles
         (2) on behalf of the mercy [of God]
            (3) in order to glorify
               (4) God.[20]

---

[17]"In der Tat überstürzen sich die Gedanken des Paulus gerade im
Römerbrief häufig; und hier ist es nicht einmal schwer, in V9a διάκονον
δὲ ἀκροβυστίας ὑπὲρ ἐλέους ὥστε o.ä. zu ergänzen" ("Actually, the
thoughts of Paul frequently rush along in Romans; and here it is not
difficult to complete the thought in v. 9a with, 'but a servant to the
uncircumcision on behalf of mercy so that' or something similar."
Wilckens, *Römer*, 3:106).

[18]Wagner, "The Christ," 481–484.

[19]Ibid., 481–482.

[20]Wagner outlines his position, in a manner similar to the way Moo
outlines the other positions, as follows (slightly modified for reasons of
space; ibid., 48):

λέγω γὰρ
  Χριστὸν διάκονον γεγενῆσθαι

This interpretation overcomes the major problems encountered with the two leading proposals. By making Christ the subject of both phrases, the sentence demands no change of focus between the two. Furthermore, the difficulty of modifying "to glorify" with the preposition ὑπέρ is resolved since Christ is the sole subject of 9a. In addition, this reading produces simple, balanced parallels between v. 8 and v. 9a. In particular, key terms from the letter (e.g., Jew and gentile, truth and mercy) stand in clear symmetry. Furthermore, this rendering demands that only a small piece of Paul's thought that is not actually written in the text be supplied. And those additions are posited on the basis of simple parallels in thought found with what Paul did write.[21]

The content of this reading also harmonizes with what Paul has argued throughout the letter. Christ, Paul has claimed, is God's agent of salvation for both the Jew and the gentile who believe (3:22). Through Christ the promises to Abraham are fulfilled (4:16; 9:6) and mercy has now been lavished upon the gentiles (just as it was upon the Jews [9:14–15, 24–25]). Any need to understand the conjunction δέ in an adversative sense is thereby overcome.

Finally, interpreting "the gentiles" (τὰ ἔθνη) as an accusative of respect enables the infinitives "to confirm" and "to glorify" to stand in parallel by allowing each to have the same subject.[22] As noted above, this produces a reading where the two halves show finely balanced parallel components.

περιτομῆς	ὑπὲρ ἀληθείας θεοῦ,
	εἰς τὸ βεβαιῶσαι
	τὰς ἐπαγγελίας τῶν πατέρων,
τὰ δὲ ἔθνη	ὑπὲρ ἐλέους (θεοῦ)
	(εἰς τὸ) δοξάσαι
	τὸν θεόν

[21]Ibid., 482–84.

[22]Hence, overcoming the objection of Williams, "Righteousness," 287, n. 141, that the two cannot stand in parallel since they do not have a subject in the same case.

The primary problem with this reading is that an accusative of respect is a rather unusual usage in the NT, although not in secular Greek. Paul employs the accusative in this sense elsewhere in Romans (7:21; 8:3; 9:5; 12:18; 15:17). He could, therefore, expect his hearers to recognize the sense here. Paul may have wanted to use the accusative of respect rather than the genitive here in order to avoid confusion with the genitive that immediately precedes "the gentiles" (τὰ ἔθνη), "to the patriarchs" (τῶν πατέρων, τὰ δὲ ἔθνη).[23]

Of the proposed solutions, Moo's solution (2) (with Wilckens' addition) and that of Wagner offer the best readings of the passage. Moo's solution (1) exhibits less balance between the two statements and creates further imbalance by making Christ the subject of the first and gentiles alone the subject of the second. Moo's solution (2) makes both parallel clauses express the results of Christ's work, which appears to be Paul's emphasis in this context in Romans. God's action through Christ demonstrated God's truth regarding the promises made to the fathers (cf. 3:4, 7). It also resulted in the gentiles praising God, a matter that is the subject of the quotations in 15:9b–12. Wagner's construal provides even clearer parallels between the statements, including making Christ the subject of both. This obvious advantage to Wagner's interpretation may be offset by the need to interpret the accusative "the gentiles" (τὰ ἔθνη) as an accusative of respect.

In the context of 15:7–13, Paul's point is that Christ's service to the Jews had implications for the gentiles.[24] More specifically, Christ became a servant of the Jews in order to confirm the promises to the patriarchs.[25] Such a ministry

---

[23]Wagner, "The Christ," 482. One must keep in mind the original text would have no punctuation or spacing between letters.

[24]Markku Kettunen notes that it is the Jewish Messiah (1:5) who called Paul to go to the gentiles (*Der Abfassungszweck des Römerbriefes*, Annales Academiae scientiarum Fennicai, dissertationes humanarum litterarum, bd. 18 [Helsinki: Suomalainen Tiedeakatemia, 1979], 98).

[25]By stating Christ's service to the Jews first, Paul is likely affirming his earlier statement (1:16) that the gospel is for the Jew first (H. P. Liddon, *Explanatory Analysis of St. Paul's Epistle to the Romans*

demonstrated God's righteousness, God's covenant faithful-ness.[26] Those promises to the Jews (some of which are cited in 15:9b–12) involve the incorporation of the gentiles into the worship of the eschatological people of God.[27] A statement that Christ's confirmation of God's promises to the fathers involved the merciful inclusion of the gentiles makes sense as a warrant for the exhortation to mutual reception among the Roman Christians found in v. 7. In Christ, God accepted both Jew and gentile. The Jewish and gentile Christians in Rome must follow suit and do the same for one another. The syntax of the statement is scrambled, but the sense of Paul's claim remains apparent.

Scriptural Substantiation: 15:9b–12

Paul follows his assertions about Christ's ministry with a string of four quotations from the Scriptures. The passages are taken from all three components of the Hebrew Bible (Deut. 32:43; Isa. 11:10; Pss. 18:49, 117:1), thereby emphasizing beyond all shadow of doubt that the Scriptures do witness to what Paul has claimed (cf. 1:2; 16:26). Since the Scriptures confirm this point unequivocally, Paul's claim that the gentiles have been received into the people of God is truly God's will, having been part of the plan of God from the beginning.[28]

[London: Longmans, Green, and Co., 1893], 281; C. H. Dodd, *The Epistle of Paul to the Romans*, MNTC [London: Hodder and Stoughton, 1932], 223).

[26]See below on this interpretation of "on behalf of the truth of God."

[27]"Christ accepted the *Gentile* Christians by being a διάκονος of the *Jews*, in order to fulfill promises made in the Jewish scriptures to Jewish patriarchs about Gentiles" (Wayne A. Meeks, "Judgment and the Brother: Romans 14:1–15:13," in *Tradition and Interpretation in the New Testament: Essays in Honor of E. Earle Ellis for His 60th Birthday*, eds. Gerald F. Hawthorne with Otto Betz [Grand Rapids: William B. Eerdmans; Tübingen: J. C. B. Mohr {Paul Siebeck} 1987], 292). Christ's ministry to the circumcision is not a matter that can be separated from the impact of that ministry for the uncircumcision (as Moo's solution [1] implies).

[28]"Und das—das ist ja die Spitze der Schriftzitate—war schon von Anfang an Gottes Plan" ("And that—which is indeed the point of the

The quotations are united by the use of several synonymous terms for praise depicting gentiles glorifying God.[29] Following upon Paul's claim in v. 9a that the ministry of Christ resulted in the gentiles praising God, these passages reinforce that specific point.[30] The gentiles are now praising God, "just as" (καθὼς γέγραπται), the Scriptures said they would. To say with Dieter-Alex Koch that Paul's statements in vv. 8–9a require ("bedarf") the support that the quotations provide overstates the case.[31] Instead, Paul hammers home his point with these Scriptures not because his argument is weak or questioned, but in order to emphasize his point. Matthew Black notes that "invoking the authority of Scripture" is Paul's customary way of "clinching his argument."[32]

In addition, by allowing the introductory διὰ τοῦτο ("because of this") to stand in the first quotation, these passages not only highlight Paul's point in vv. 8–9a, but also show what God's act in Christ has caused.[33] In other words, because of what Christ has done as servant to the Jews (and gentiles in Wagner's reading), what the Scriptures foresaw has now become reality. The eschatological implications are

---

quotations from Scripture—was already part of the plan of God from the beginning") (Gerhard Saß, "Röm 15,7-13 —als Summe des Römerbriefs gelesen," *EvT* 53 [1993]: 518, see also 521).

[29]Richard B. Hays notes that the theme of mercy can also be traced through the wider context from which these passages are quoted (*Echoes of Scripture in the Letters of Paul* [New Haven: Yale University Press, 1989], 71–72).

[30]"Thus, the salvation of the Gentiles . . . is anything but a scissors-and-paste act on God's part. Their salvation was inherent in God's promise to Israel from the beginning!" James R. Edwards, *Romans*, New International Biblical Commentary, vol. 6 (Peabody, Mass.: Hendrickson, 1992), 340–41

[31]*Die Schrift als Zeuge des Evangeliums*, BHT, bd. 69 (Tübingen: J. C. B. Mohr [Paul Siebeck], 1986), 282.

[32]*Romans*, 2d ed., NCBC (Grand Rapids: William B. Eerdmans, 1989), 201. "Why does Paul place this florilegium at the end of his letter to the Romans? Clearly, he has saved his clinchers for the end" (Hays, *Echoes*, 71).

[33]Williams, "Righteousness," 289.

clear: what Moses, David, and Isaiah looked forward to is now taking place.

Although only v. 10 (Deut. 32:43) specifically mentions the gentiles praising God along with Jews, this joint praise can certainly be understood to underlie the other quotations as well. For if the call goes to the gentiles to praise God, they would not do so in a vacuum, but would join the Jewish people already praising. This joint praise would fit the emphasis on Christ's ministry impacting both Jews and gentiles in vv. 8–9a.

Taking the categories of Jew and gentile in this passage as Paul's restatement of the "strong" and the "weak" of 14:1–15:6 (see ch. 4 below), these quotations obviously echo Paul's admonition of 15:5–6 that the "strong" and the "weak" be of one mind and so "glorify God together in one voice." In doing so, they accomplish that which is envisioned in all the Scripture: all people glorifying the one God. Richard B. Hays summarizes the significance of these quotations in this context at the close of the letter-body as follows.

> Paul rests his case on the claim that his churches, in which Gentiles do in fact join Jews in praising God, must be the eschatological fulfillment of the scriptural vision. If so, then God's Gentile-embracing righteousness, proclaimed in Paul's gospel, really is 'promised beforehand through his prophets in holy texts' (Rom. 1:2), and Paul has successfully made his case in defense of the justice of God.[34]

Benediction: 15:13

Finally, Paul concludes with a benediction. Taking its cue from the final word of the last Old Testament quotation in v. 12, the blessing clearly focuses on hope, that the God of

---

[34]*Echoes*, 71. "Thus, the work of Christ (v. 8), as anticipated by the OT (vv. 9b–12), was destined to attain its fruition in the harmonious coexistence of the various factions within the Roman congregations (v. 13)" (Don B. Garlington, *Faith, Obedience, and Perseverance: Aspects of Paul's Letter to the Romans*, WUNT, vol. 79 [Tübingen: J. C. B. Mohr {Paul Siebeck}, 1994], 26).

hope may give them joy and peace, so that they may abound in hope.

Although Romans contains arguments shaped by Paul's past defense and explanation of his gospel in worship settings, the letter is not itself a sermon. Robert Jewett's categorization of this benediction as a homiletical marker, therefore, is incorrect.[35] One can, however, still recognize its function in an oral setting. This concluding benediction serves as an auditory marker for Paul's hearers that he was drawing a portion of his argument to a close and moving on to another.

Yet, the benediction serves not merely as an oral marker of transition. For Paul, this benediction actually imparted divine blessing. In J. L. Austin's terms, it is a "performative utterance" in that it effects something rather than merely says something.[36]

Summary

In 15:7 Paul exhorts his Roman auditors to receive one another in the same manner that Christ received them. When they do so, God will be glorified. Paul substantiates this admonition by appealing to the work of Christ (15:8–9a). Through Christ's ministry of service to the Jews, God demonstrated divine faithfulness to the promises made to their Jewish ancestors. Those promises to the Jews involved a merciful inclusion of the gentiles. Paul supports this Christological warrant by quoting four passages from Scripture that envision gentiles praising God along with the Jews (15:9b–12). When Jews and gentiles glorify God together, this scriptural vision is fulfilled. Paul concludes with a benediction, praying that God may give them joy and peace, so that they may abound in hope (15:13).

---

[35]Robert Jewett, "The Form and Function of the Homiletic Benediction," *ATR* 51 (1969): 18–34.

[36]"Performative Utterances," in *Philosophical Papers*, eds. J. O. Urmson and G. J. Warnock (Oxford: Clarendon Press, 1961), 222.

The Relationship of 15:7–13
to the Rest of the Letter

At the outset of this chapter, questions were posed regarding the relationship of this passage to the rest of the letter. Do these verses serve primarily to summarize and bring to closure the discussion of the weak and strong begun in 14:1? Or does this passage close the hortatory section that commenced with 12:1? Or, finally, does it actually take up key themes found throughout the letter and thereby summarize and conclude Romans as a whole? Each of these positions will be examined below.

Romans 15:7–13 as a Summary of 14:1–15:6

The links between 15:7–13 and Paul's instructions to the "strong" and the "weak" starting in 14:1 are numerous and evident. The exhortation of 15:7 resembles Paul's instructions in 14:1 in that both employ the verb "to receive" (or "accept," προσλαμβάνω, echoed in 14:3). In 14:13, Paul also instructs both groups not to judge "one another" employing the same pronoun, ἀλλήλους, he used in 15:7. This obvious concern for relationships between groups in the community constitutes the strongest link between 15:7–13 and the instructions beginning in 14:1. In addition, both passages show obvious concern that the believers bring glory to God either through the united worship of different groups in the community (vv. 5–6) or through the manner in which they conduct their relationships (v. 7).

Second, not only in content, but also in form, 15:7–13 contains striking parallels to 15:1–6. Both passages begin with an admonition (15:1–2, 7). Furthermore, each supports that admonition by citing the example of Christ (15:3a, 8–9a) and quoting Scripture which Paul regards as speaking of Christ's work (15:3b, 9b–12). Finally, both passages close with a benediction (15:5–6, 13). In form as well as in content, both passages summarize Paul's argument on the matter of the "strong" and the "weak."

In summary, 15:7–13 reflects the concerns of 14:1–15:6. As a result, it can easily be read as bringing Paul's instructions to the strong and weak to a satisfying conclusion.

Romans 15:7–13 as a Summary of 12:1–15:6

Fewer scholars would argue that 15:7–13 summarizes Paul's exhortations beginning in 12:1.[37] Still, the evidence for this position is worth noting. First, 12:1 marks a clear turning point in the letter. Having drawn his argument in chapters 9–11 to a close with the doxology in 11:33–36, Paul begins to admonish the Roman Christians in 12:1. These exhortations continue through 15:13 where Paul signals the completion of another part of his argument with a benediction before launching the closing section of the letter in 15:14. Romans 12:1–15:13, therefore, forms an easily defined section within the letter.

Paul's opening exhortations in 12:1–2 and the closing comments in 15:7–13 are linked in several additional ways. For example, Paul mentions the theme of God's "mercy" in 12:1 and then again in 15:7–13. The general admonitions that Paul makes in 12:1–2 on the basis of his call[38] also stand over the entire paraenetical section that follows. In other words, the specific instructions that follow in 12:3–15:7 are all particular instances of "offering your bodies to God" so as to be "transformed by the renewing of your minds" rather than "conformed to the standards of this age" (12:1–2). Peter Stuhlmacher is therefore correct when he recognizes that the mutual reception of 15:7 is part of the "embodied worship to

---

[37]See, for example, John Ziesler, *Paul's Letter to the Romans*, TPI New Testament Commentaries (Philadelphia: Trinity Press International, 1989), 336–37 (who recognizes nonetheless the connection of the Jew/gentile theme in 15:7–13 with the same theme in "much of the letter"). See also Wilckens, *Römer*, 3:105; Dieter Zeller, *Juden und Heiden in der Mission des Paulus: Studien zum Römerbrief*, 2d aufl., FB, bd. 8 (Stuttgart: Verlag Katholisches Bibelwerk, 1976), 218.

[38]The "mercies" (οἰκτιρμῶν) of God in 12:1 are therefore the same thing as the "grace" (χάρις) of God that refers to Paul's apostolic call elsewhere (1:5).

which they are called (12:1f.), and should thus serve to glorify God."[39] A. J. M. Wedderburn likewise regards mutual reception among Paul's hearers as the product of minds that have been renewed (12:2) after the pattern of Jesus Christ.[40]

Romans 15:7–13 as a Summary of 1:14–15:6

The arguments in favor of reading 15:7–13 as a summary of Paul's argument in the entire letter are twofold. First, there are significant problems with reading this passage as a summary of Paul's argument beginning with either 12:1 or with 14:1. Second, 15:7–13 returns to several key themes that serve an integral role in Paul's argument in chs. 1–11. In almost every case, Paul has not mentioned these themes since the end of ch. 11. The connections of 15:7–13 with Paul's argument from 14:1, from 12:1, and from the beginning of the letter argue persuasively for reading 15:7–13 as the capstone of Paul's argument in the entire letter. These two arguments are treated in depth below.

Arguments against 15:7–13 as a Summary from 14:1 and 12:1. An interpretation of Rom. 15:7–13 as a summary of Paul's argument from 14:1 creates several difficulties. First, in 14:1–15:6 Paul instructs the strong to receive the weak. Again in 15:1, he tells the strong (among whom he identifies himself) to bear the weaknesses of the weak. Yet, in 15:7–13, Paul instructs both groups to receive one another. Why the change of address from the "strong" to the community as a whole?

Second, why does Paul return to the categories of Jew and gentile in 15:8–9a, when the latter designations have not been employed since ch. 11? It is possible that the differences between the "strong" and the "weak" in 14:1–15:6 were largely disagreements between those adhering to the Mosaic Law (mostly Christian Jews) and those not observing the same

---

[39]*Paul's Letter to the Romans*, trans. by Scott J. Hafemann (Louisville: Westminster/John Knox Press, 1994), 232.
[40]*The Reasons for Romans* (Minneapolis: Fortress Press, 1991), 87. Wedderburn's exegesis of this passage runs similar to that offered here.

(predominantly Christian gentiles). But Paul does not describe them as such in that passage. Why the "change of labels" when Paul gets to 15:8?

Finally, one must ask why Paul would want to follow his comments in 15:1–6 with a passage so close to it in form and content. Why not allow 15:1–6 to serve as his summary instructions to the strong and the weak and simply move from 15:6 to the closing section of the letter in 15:14?[41]

The ties between 15:7–13 and 14:1–15:6 are obvious and many. I maintain that Paul deliberately repeats concluding comments and changes his referent in order to widen the scope of his closing argument to include more than 14:1–15:6.[42] Romans 15:7–13 repeats much of 15:1–6 because the instructions in the latter passage lie so close to his chief concerns in the letter as a whole. Paul moves the topic of the discussion to Jews and gentiles for the same reason: to reflect the broader concerns of the letter in its entirety.

Furthermore, Paul's widening the reference of this summary to include more of the letter is the reason he places greater emphasis on Scripture in vv. 7–13. In 15:3b he cites one line from Ps. 69:9 read christologically. He then follows that quotation with an assertion of the importance of the Scripture for the church's instruction. In 15:9b–12, however, Paul piles up four quotations drawn from all three parts of Scripture: the Torah, the Prophets, and the Writings. Romans 15:1–6 and 15:7–13 are therefore alike in that both cite Scripture, but they are dissimilar in that Paul gives much greater emphasis to Scriptural quotations in the latter passage. These four quotations are meant to emphatically hammer home Paul's point: the gentiles are now worshipping God just as the Scriptures foretold. This accent on Scripture and the themes raised by those quotations (see below) also broadens the focus to include content that goes beyond what Paul had

---

[41]Keck, "Christology," 86, citing Koch, *Schrift als Zeuge*, 282.

[42]"Both the connection with what precedes and its extension are incontestable" (Käsemann, *Romans*, 384).

to say in 14:1–15:6.[43] All of this argues for reading 15:7–13 as more than just a summary of Paul's instructions to the strong and the weak begun in 14:1.

Finally, Rom. 15:7–13 can be read as the conclusion to the extensive section of paraenesis begun at 12:1. Yet, the only explicit parallel between 15:7–13 and 12:1–2 consists of the theme of mercy. In light of the limited (but clear) connections between 15:7–13 and 12:1, and the numerous thematic links uniting 15:7–13 and Paul's argument in chs. 1–11 as a whole, 15:7–13 is better understood as a summary of Paul's argument in the entire letter.

Romans 15:7–13 as a Summary of Paul's Argument Throughout the Letter. The most convincing evidence for reading this passage as a summary of Paul's overall argument in the letter is that it brings up several themes at the heart of his discussion that have not explicitly been mentioned since the paraenesis began in 12:1. For the sake of convenience, they are summarized below under four headings.[44] These categories do not exhaust the themes to which Paul returns in 15:7–13, but they do provide explicit evidence of the relation of this passage to the entire letter.

(1) The character of God expressed in saving action.
(2) The recipients of God's saving action.
(3) The human response to this saving action.
(4) The witness of Scripture to all the above.

---

[43]Keck ("Christology," 88) observes a double shift from 15:1–6 to vv. 7–13. In 15:7–13, Paul picks up on the theme of glorifying God from the benediction of vv. 5–6 and makes that the focus of vs. 7–13. Second, the subject of "strong" and "weak" is dropped as the emphasis shifts to Jew/gentile.

[44]These categories are modified from those of Gerhard Saß, "Röm 15,7–13," 515.

(1) *The character of God expressed in saving action*. The text points to three specific issues regarding God's saving action in 15:8–9a: (a) the "truth" of God, (b) the "mercy" of God, and (c) the "promises" of God.

(a) The "truth" of God. In 15:8b, Paul states that Christ has become a servant of the circumcision "on behalf of the truth of God" (ὑπὲρ ἀληθείας θεοῦ). Yet, as Sam K. Williams has demonstrated, to speak of the "truth of God" in Romans is to speak of the "righteousness of God" and the "faithfulness of God" as well.[45] In 15:8 then, Paul recalls a theme in the letter first stated in 1:17, questioned (proleptically) in 3:1–4, and defended at length in chs. 9–11: Paul's gospel proclaims that God has acted in Christ in a manner that demonstrates God's faithfulness to the promises made to the patriarchs. This theme is not confined to these passages, however. The questions enunciated in 3:1–4 regarding God's righteousness arise from his argument in 1:18–2:29. Paul then defends the righteousness of God in 3:21–4:25 where he demonstrates how God's righteousness has been manifested through Christ's atoning death (3:21–26), a righteousness to which the Law bears witness (4:1–23; Gen. 15:6). Paul's most thorough response to these questions occurs in chs. 9–11, a section that

---

[45]In Williams' terms, the three are "virtual equivalents" ("Righteousness," 268). Williams (and most scholars listed below) bases his conclusion on Paul's parallel use of the terms for righteousness (δικαιοσύνη), truth (ἀλήθεια), and faithfulness (πίστις) with reference to God in 3:3–7. Williams also notes that Paul quotes from Pss. 116:11 and 51:4 in Romans 3:4. In both Psalms God's truth (אֱמֶת; LXX ἀλήθεια) and righteousness (צֶדֶק; LXX δικαιοσύνη) stand in parallel (ibid.).

For additional support for equating the truth of God in 15:8 with the righteousness and faithfulness of God, see Brendan Byrne, *Romans*, SacPag, vol. 6 (Collegeville, Minn.: Liturgical Press, 1996), 431; Cranfield, *Romans*, 2:741–42; Dunn, *Romans 9–16*, 847; Käsemann, *Romans*, 385; Keck, "Christology," 90; Franz J. Leenhardt, *The Epistle to the Romans: A Commentary*, trans. Harold Knight (London: Lutterworth Press, 1961), 364–65; Moo, *Romans*, 877, Saß, "Röm 15,7–13," 521; Heinrich Schlier, *Der Römerbrief*, HTKNT, bd. 6 (Freiburg: Herder, 1977), 424; Thomas R. Schreiner, *Romans*, Baker Exegetical Commentary on the New Testament (Grand Rapids: Baker Books, 1998), 754–55; and Wilckens, *Römer*, 3:105.

N. T. Wright labels "the climax of the theological argument" in the letter.[46] Richard B. Hays also finds the theme of righteousness resounding through the Scriptures Paul cites in Romans. He writes

> In surveying the scriptural texts that sound within Paul's discourse in Romans, we have observed an extraordinary—indeed, almost monotonous—thematic consistency. In Romans, Paul cites Scripture not as a repository of miscellaneous wisdom on various topics but as an insistent witness of one great truth: God's righteousness, which has now embraced Gentiles among the people of God, includes the promise of God's unbroken faithfulness to Israel.[47]

Paul has not dealt with the subject of righteousness, however, since the end of ch. 11. Why does he brings it up in 15:8 if 15:7–13 is merely a summary of 14:1–15:6 or of the paraenesis beginning in 12:1? And why does he bring it up in order to substantiate his exhortation for the Roman Christians to receive one another? Surely Paul returns to this theme in 15:8 because he now draws together the argument of the letter as a whole in order to forcefully substantiate the exhortation of 15:7.

(b) The "mercy" of God. Paul's discussion of the truth of God is inextricably tied to the mercy of God. Paul claims "Christ has become a servant of the circumcision on behalf of the truth of God" in 15:8 and speaks of the "mercy" of God with regard to the gentiles in 15:9a. "Mercy" and "truth" (ἔλεος/ἀλήθεια; אֱמֶת/חֶסֶד) are a well-known pairing of terms describing God in the Old Testament.[48] As with the "truth of God," God's mercy plays a key role in Paul's argument. God's mercy has been showered on the gentiles (9:15–18, 23; 11:30–32), yet that is the same mercy that made the Jews God's

---

[46]*Climax of the Covenant* (Minneapolis: Fortress Press, 1992), 234 (citing Morna Hooker, *From Adam to Christ: Essays on Paul* [Cambridge: Cambridge University Press, 1990], 3).

[47]*Echoes*, 73.

[48]In the LXX, Pss. 39:1; 84:11; 88:15, 25; 137:2.

people earlier in salvation-history (9:24–25 quoting Hosea 2:23). Once again, this key theme plays no role in 12:1–15:6.[49]

As with the theme of the truth of God, one must ask why Paul brings up God's mercy at this point in the letter after laying it aside for so long. The answer must be that he draws upon a larger context than just his instructions to the strong and weak or to the paraenesis begun in 12:1 in order to reinforce his exhortation in 15:7.

(c) The "promises" of God. God's righteousness has been demonstrated in Christ precisely because Christ's ministry of service to the Jews confirmed "the promises to the fathers" (15:8). Up to this point in Romans, Paul's discussion of God's promise has been limited to chs. 4 and 9. That limitation, however, cannot minimize its importance in Paul's overall argument. In all but one case (9:4), Paul uses[50] the term with reference to the promise to Abraham. In both chs. 4 and 9, the discussion of Abraham and promise lies at the heart of Paul's defense of his gospel as expressing the righteousness of God. Paul claims the "promise" of God to Abraham is not limited to Israel alone, but "has to do with the mysterious outworking of God's purpose as He creates descendants of Abraham and children of God on the basis of faith."[51] In 15:8, when Paul speaks of Christ's work confirming the promises (plural), he refers to both the promise to Abraham and its repetition in

---

[49]Paul speaks of the "mercies of God" (οἰκτιρμῶν) in his appeal to the Romans in 12:1. This, however, is a reference to the mercy shown to Paul by God in calling him to be an apostle (see Victor Paul Furnish, *Theology & Ethics in Paul* [Nashville: Abingdon Press, 1968], 102). "By the mercies of God" (διὰ τῶν οἰκτιρμῶν) is to be understood instrumentally ("through" the mercies of God) and is therefore another way of saying "by the grace [διὰ τῆς χάριτος] given to me I say to you" as in 12:3. The use of the participle "the one who has the gift of mercy" (ὁ ἐλεῶν) in 12:8 obviously does not refer to the mercy of God as spoken of in chs. 9–11 and 15:9a.

[50]Williams ("Righteousness," 286) argues, correctly so, that the "promises" of 9:4 also refer to God's promise to Abraham. That reference is not immediately clear unless one catches the sweep of Paul's references to God's promise in the letter.

[51]Williams, "Righteousness," 286.

other places in Scripture. The string of Old Testament quotations in 15:9b–12 demonstrates this very point. Together they point to the people of God, consisting of gentiles along with Jews, giving united praise to God.[52]

In 15:8, then, Paul returns to an important theme in the letter with his reference to the "promises" made to the fathers. The promise of God to Abraham is tightly bound up with Paul's discussion of God's righteousness. The multiple witnesses to this promise found throughout the Scripture constitute the "promises" to which Paul refers. Furthermore, these promises concern the recipients of God's mercy, another important theme in Paul's argument and one to which attention must now be turned.

(2) *The recipients of God's saving action.* No matter how one construes the syntax of 15:8–9a, it is evident that Paul was making a statement about Christ's work for both Jews and gentiles. By bringing up the subject of Jew and gentile in 15:8–9a, Paul once again returns to the primary theme of the letter first stated in 1:14–16 and at the heart of his argument in chs. 1–4 and 9–11.

Paul first mentions the categories "nations" or "gentiles" in 1:5 in his description of the scope of his apostolic call "to all the nations." Then in the transition from the letter-opening to the letter-body in 1:14–18,[53] Paul specifies the scope of his call

---

[52]Gerhard Saß includes a referent not only to the effect of the work of Christ, but also to the work itself. For example, the promises speak of Christ coming from the seed of David (1:3) and coming as the redeemer of Israel (11:26). The promises of 15:8 include, therefore, those in relation to Christ, those in relation to Jews and gentiles, and those that continue applying to Israel (9:4). As Paul employs the term "promise" in Romans, however, it concerns God's promise to Abraham regarding descendants that include τὰ ἔθνη, and the echoes of that promise found elsewhere in Scripture. See Saß, "Röm 15,7–13," 520.

[53]Paul J. Achtemeier correctly points out that vv. 16–17 cannot be separated grammatically from vv. 14–15, 18–19 (*Romans*, IBC [Louisville: John Knox Press, 1988], 35). This continuity highlights the problem of posing divisions between sections of Paul's letter at precise points (in this case, usually between vv. 15 and 16 or vv. 17 and 18). In many

by pairing Greeks and barbarians, wise and foolish (1:14), and Jews and gentiles (1:16).[54] His eschatological gospel is for all who believe (παντὶ τῷ πιστεύοντι; 1:16; cf. 3:22).

Themes such as righteousness and faith in 1:16–17 have been rightly recognized as central to Paul's argument. When one views Paul's opening thematic statement as spanning at least 1:14–18, the issue of all people becomes even more prominent.[55] In addition to the evidence just cited, Paul employs the adjective "all" (πᾶς) once again in v. 18 in order to describe universal human godlessness and wickedness.[56] In light of Paul's emphasis on this point in his opening thematic statement, the centrality of the theme of the universality of the eschatological people of God in Romans has not properly been recognized.[57]

The association of Jews and gentiles/Greeks pervades Paul's argument in 1:18–4:25 where he demonstrates that God will make no distinction at judgment between Jew and gentile (2:11), because sin has destroyed any differences between the two (3:9, 23). Since all alike are "under sin" (ὑφ' ἁμαρτίαν, 3:9 anticipating 5:12–21), both have access alike (οὐ γάρ ἐστιν διαστολή, 3:22, also 3:30) by grace through faith to justification (3:24). Because of this, no room exists for

---

places such as this in Romans, Paul makes transitions in his argument over the course of several verses, with themes from what precedes overlapping with those he will take up in what follows.

[54]James D. G. Dunn points out that the pairing Ἰουδαίῳ and Ἕλληνι in v. 16 reflects the same distinction as Jew and gentile (ἔθνη). See *Romans 1–8*, WBC, vol. 38A (Milton Keynes, England: Word, 1988), 40. Contra Christopher D. Stanley, "'Neither Jew nor Greek': Ethnic Conflict in Graeco-Roman Society," *JSNT* 64 (1996): 101–24.

[55]I owe this observation to Paul J. Achtemeier.

[56]Note that these actions suppress the "truth" (v. 18) in what surely must be a reference to the "truth of God" (cf. 15:18).

[57]Noteable exeptions include J. Christiaan Beker, *Paul the Apostle: The Triumph of God in Life and Thought* (Philadelphia: Fortress Press, 1980), 71; William L. Lane, "Social Perspectives on Roman Christianity during the Formative Years from Nero to Nerva: Romans, Hebrews, *1 Clement*," in *Judaism and Christianity in First-Century Rome*, eds. Karl P. Donfried and Peter Richardson (Grand Rapids: William B. Eerdmans, 1998), 201–02.

Jewish boasting of privilege before God (3:27); God is not God of the Jews alone (3:29), but is also God of the gentiles (3:30).

The Jew/gentile association is then assumed in the discussion of chs. 5–8. Paul begins ch. 5 by stating, "Having been justified (Δικαιωθέντες) by faith we have peace with God through our Lord Jesus Christ." The causal participle δικαιωθέντες indicates he now takes for granted the argument of 1:18–4:25 regarding Jew and gentile before God. He therefore employs the first person plural "we," meaning both Jew and gentile. The discussion of chs. 5–8 no longer requires any differentiation between the two.

Paul returns to this theme again in chs. 9–11 as he takes up the questions posed in 3:1–8 regarding the righteousness of God. Paul anticipates these questions in response to his argument in 1:18–2:29 that placed Jew and gentile in the same position before God at judgment (2:11; Paul's argument is summarized in 3:9, 23). Once again, Paul raises a theme in 15:7–13 that plays an important role in chs. 9–11, yet which receives no explicit mention in 12:1–15:6.[58]

(3) *The human response to this saving action.* In 15:7–13, Paul depicts two responses that result from God's saving action in Christ. These responses go to the heart of Paul's purpose in writing the letter.

First, Paul exhorts the community to "receive one another just as Christ also received you" (v. 7). Paul substantiates (γὰρ) this exhortation with his twofold assertion about the work of Christ for Jews and gentiles in 15:8–9a. In other words, the exhortation finds its legitimacy in the twofold scope of Christ's redeeming work. Jew and gentile as well as strong and weak should receive one another because God in Christ received Jew and gentile as well as strong and weak. Paul calls his hearers back to the argument of chs. 1–11 in order to make his point in 15:7. Without that argument, his exhortation has no basis.

---

[58]In other words, Paul's discussion of Jew and gentile cannot be separated from his arguments regarding the righteousness of God.

Second, Paul states that believers are to receive one another "to the glory of God" (15:7). Summarizing a shrewd observation by Martin Luther, James R. Edwards comments on this point, "how strange . . . is the glory of God, for God is glorified when believers of differing persuasions accept one another and when the strong bear the burdens of the weak!"[59] If Paul is merely summarizing his instructions for the strong to receive the weak in 15:7, Luther's assessment of God's glory as surprising is correct. Viewed, on the other hand, in the context of the theme of God's glory within the whole of Romans, mutual reception among believers of Jewish and gentile backgrounds resulting in God's glory is not strange at all. A brief review of the "glory" theme in Romans will make this apparent.

In 1:21, Paul summarizes Adamic sin as a refusal to glorify God (οὐχ ἐδόξασαν) or give God thanks. Such a refusal, in other words, epitomizes sin under the Adamic reign. As a result, the glory of the immortal God is exchanged for idolatry (1:23) and all humanity, Jew and gentile, falls short of sharing God's glory (3:23).

When Paul describes an appropriate response to God's promise[60] (and thereby to God), Paul says Abraham grew strong in faith and gave glory to God (4:20). Later, Paul's describes the basic response of faith for those under the reign of Christ as a response of worship. Believers "offer" themselves to God (παριστάνετε/παραστήσατε 6:13). In 12:1, Paul is even more explicit. Believers "present" (παραστῆσαι) their bodies "as living sacrifices, holy and acceptable to God, which is your reasonable act of worship."[61] The theme of worship and glorifying God therefore finds clear ties to the behavior of those "under grace" throughout the letter.

---

[59]*Romans*, 339–40, citing *Luther: Lectures on Romans*, trans. and ed. Wilhelm Pauck, LCC, vol. 15 (Philadelphia: Westminster Press, 1961), 411.

[60]The "promise" theme recurs in 15:8.

[61]παραστῆσαι τὰ σώματα ὑμῶν θυσίαν ζῶσαν ἁγίαν εὐάρεστον τῷ θεῷ, τὴν λογικὴν λατρείαν ὑμῶν

"To glorify God," therefore, serves as the polar opposite of actions carried out under the reign of sin introduced by Adam.[62] For Jew and gentile to glorify God together[63] (15:6–12) reverses the rule of sin and embodies the eschatological will of God for God's people.[64] Leander E. Keck summarizes the point succinctly. He writes, "The theme of the universal praise of God is, in Paul's view, much more than a rhetorical flourish. It is the actual material soteriological alternative to the root problem of humanity: not giving praise to God or honoring God."[65]

(4) *The witness of Scripture to all the above.* Finally, Paul emphasizes that his assertion in 15:8–9a is the fulfillment of Scripture. First, he says that Christ's ministry of service confirmed the promises to the ancestors (v. 8). Second, he hammers home his point about the gentiles praising God together with the Jews in vv. 9b–12 with four quotations drawn from the Law, prophets, and writings.

Paul underscores the role of Scripture in his gospel from the very opening of the letter when he states that his gospel was "proclaimed beforehand by God's prophets in the scriptures" (1:2). The letter closes on the same note (16:26). As is often observed, Paul quotes more Scripture in Romans than in

---

[62]"Worship is the first obligation of the believer and therefore comes first in this section that spells out the obligations of the new covenant community" (Mark Reasoner, "The Theology of Romans 12:1–15:13," in *Pauline Theology*, vol. 3, *Romans* [Minneapolis: Fortress Press, 1995], 294). See also Konrad Weiß, Der doxologische Charakter der paulinischen Soteriologie, in *Theologische Versuche*, bd. 11 (Berlin: Evangelische Verlagsanstalt, 1979), 67–70.

[63]"For the mutuality required from them is a part of the embodied worship of God to which they are called (12:1f.), and should thus serve to glorify God" (Stuhlmacher, *Romans*, 232).

[64]"Paul has now completed the reversal of idolatry's measure of reality on the gauge of the creature (1:19–21). Reality is to be measured not by the creature but by the creator" (Luke T. Johnson, *Reading Romans: A Literary and Theological Commentary* [New York: Crossroad, 1997], 205).

[65]"Christology," 94; see also Byrne, *Romans*, 40.

any of his other letters.[66] In fact, the heart of his theological argument in chs. 9–11 contains the highest density of quotations in all of Paul's letters.[67]

It must also be noted here that the final quotation (15:12; Isa. 11:10) speaks of the "root of Jesse," recalling the opening confession in 1:2–4 where Christ comes from the seed of David (1:3). These messianic references form an *inclusio* around Paul's argument from the beginning.[68]

Summary. Additional evidence could be supplied in support of the claim made here that 15:7–13 stands as Paul's summary[69] and conclusion to the letter's argument.[70] For example, the final prayer wish in v. 13 emphasizes the issue

---

[66]D. Moody Smith, for example, notes that "fully half" of Paul's explicit quotations of the Old Testament (in the seven usually uncontested letters) are found in Romans. "The Pauline Literature," in *It Is Written. Scripture Citing Scripture: Essays in Honour of Barnabas Lindars*, eds. D. A. Carson and H. G. M. Williamson (Cambridge: Cambridge University Press, 1988), 274.

[67]Smith notes that half of the quotations in Romans come from these three chapters (ibid., 274–275).

[68]Richard B. Hays, "Christ Prays the Psalms: Paul's Use of an Early Christian Exegetical Convention," in *The Future of Christology: Essays in Honor of Leander E. Keck*, eds. Abraham J. Malherbe and Wayne A. Meeks (Minneapolis: Fortress Press, 1993), 135, and Johnson, *Reading Romans*, 207.

[69]Romans 15:7–13 is "a passage that functions as a *peroratio*, a summation of the letter's themes" (Hays, *Echoes*, 70).

[70]Douglas Moo reasons that because certain key themes do not find mention here (he cites justification, victory over sin, the law, and death), Paul appeals to other themes in 15:7–13 only "as a means of buttressing his final appeal to the 'strong' and the 'weak.'" In light of the amount of evidence gathered here, that comment is puzzling. Furthermore, Moo claims that relationships among the believers in Rome is one of the main motivations Paul had for writing the letter. Yet, Moo separates relationships among believers from Paul's theological arguments in the letter body. One must therefore ask why the theological arguments of chs. 1–11 and the summary (of 14:1–15:6 for Moo) appeal in 15:7 fit so closely together. It is far better to recognize that Paul's argument throughout the letter is all of one cloth, rather than dividing it into separate, only loosely related pieces. See Moo, *Romans*, 874.

of hope[71] as well as mentioning believing and the Holy Spirit. Each of these matters could be traced in some detail throughout the letter.

The issues discussed above, however, provide evidence not only of extensive and explicit ties between 15:7–13 and the argument of chs. 1–11, but also a dependency of Paul's point in 15:7–13 on those chapters. Without doubt, Paul intends these verses to draw together his argument in the letter.[72] This does not mean those who claim the passage summarizes his argument from 14:1 or from 12:1 are wrong. The passage brings to a close phases of Paul's argument begun at both places. Yet the passage summarizes far more, it concludes Paul's argument for the letter as a whole.

---

[71]J. Christiaan Beker sees hope as the primary theme of the letter and the doxology of 15:13 as the letter's climax ("Conversations with a Friend about Romans," in *Faith and History: Essays in Honor of Paul W. Meyer*, eds. John T. Carroll, Charles H. Cosgrove and E. Elizabeth Johnson [Atlanta: Scholars Press, 1990], 97). Although hope is not the "basic carrier of the argument in Romans" (ibid.), Beker's insight regarding how 15:13 brings up a key theme is accurate. Franz J. Leenhardt observes that hope provides (and one could add the other issues in the doxology) the perspective from which the Roman Christians should view Paul's instructions to them (*Romans*, 365).

[72]Richard B. Hays sees the "fundamental message of Romans . . . encapsulated in 15:8–9a" ("Adam, Israel, Christ: The Question of Covenant in the Theology of Romans: A Response to Leander E. Keck and N. T. Wright," in *Pauline Theology*, 3:84. Hays is commending the view of N. T. Wright, "Romans and the Theology of Paul," in *Pauline Theology*, 3:62. See also Steve Mason, "'For I am not Ashamed of the Gospel' (Rom. 1:16): The Gospel and the First Readers of Romans," in *Gospel in Paul: Studies on Corinthians, Galatians and Romans for Richard N. Longenecker*, eds. L. Ann Jervis and Peter Richardson, JSNTSup, vol. 108 (Sheffield: Sheffield Academic Press, 1994), 276.

The Significance of 15:7–13
for the Argument of Romans

In 15:7, Paul broadens the scope of his address from the "strong" and the "weak" to include the entire community: "receive one another." By doing this, and by drawing upon themes argued throughout the letter as well as Scripture to substantiate this exhortation, he places the full force of that argument and of the authority of Scripture behind his call for mutual reception. By supporting the exhortation in 15:7 in this manner, Paul makes it clear that his chief concern for his Roman audience is that they receive one another in the same way Christ received them. Several additional factors corroborate this contention.

As warrant for that reception, he summarizes the work of Christ as one of service to the Jews, thereby demonstrating God's faithfulness to the promises made to the patriarchs. Yet, that ministry to the Jews also results in the gentiles giving glory to God. Paul emphasizes this second point by quoting four passages from the Scriptures calling on the gentiles to glorify God, implying that Christ's ministry to the Jews has brought this scriptural vision to fruition.

In both the Christological warrant of 15:8–9a and its supporting quotations in vv. 9b–12, one can see Paul's argument throughout the letter come into play. The gentiles have now been mercifully grafted on to the olive tree of Israel (11:17), becoming full members of the people of God in the age inaugurated by Christ. The believers in Rome, whatever their ethnic and religious origins, have now been united into that one people of God (5:1), what one could appropriately call the "community of the new age."[73] The community members

---

[73]"The mutual acceptance between Jewish and Gentile Christians in Rome, together with their common praise of God, . . . , anticipate in a certain sense the song of praise of the eschatological, salvific community made up of Jews and Gentiles" (Stuhlmacher, *Romans*, 233). Although one senses a note of anticipation in Paul's call for mutual acceptance in this passage, the overriding sense is more one of a call to active

must receive one another, therefore, for God in Christ has received them (15:7).[74]

Paul makes the necessity for mutual reception clear in his instructions to the "strong" and the "weak." He writes, "Why do you pass judgment on your brother or sister? Or you, why do you despise your brother or sister?" (14:10; NRSV). Those in the community, Jew or gentile, strong or weak, have their relationships with one another fundamentally redefined because of the eschatological, Scripture-fulfilling work of Christ. For the Jewish Christian, the gentile follower of Christ is now a brother or sister; for the gentile believer, the Christian Jew is a fellow child of God.[75]

In "putting on the Lord Jesus Christ" (13:13a) they will imitate Christ's example of receiving one another (15:7). This behavior is made possible by not making provision for the flesh to satisfy its desires (13:13b). Not to receive one another becomes tantamount to returning to life lived under the reign of sin (6:12–13a). In contrast, the Roman believers are to present themselves to God as those alive from the dead (6:13b; 12:1), living under the reign of grace.

All of the logic of Paul's argument in the letter drives towards this precise point in 15:7. The new age has begun

---

participation in the eschatological work God taking place among the Roman believers.

[74]Jesus' "resurrection signifies God's eschatological intention to create a messianic *community* of those who know themselves summoned to welcome one another, as the Messiah has welcomed them, for the glory of God" (Hays, "Christ Prays the Psalms," 136).

[75]Norman R. Petersen's analysis of symbolic universes and the language of social relations in Philemon applies equally to Paul's language here in Romans. Petersen writes,

> Being 'in Christ' thus represents a comprehensive reality whose principal coordinates are Christ's lordship over them, which entails their faithful enslavement to him, and God's fatherhood, in relation to which they are all brothers and sisters of one another. . . . Their relations with God and Christ therefore define their ultimate social identities, limit and motivate their behavior.

Rediscovering Paul: Philemon and the Sociology of Paul's Narrative World (Philadelphia: Fortress Press, 1985), 200–01.

with the death and resurrection of Jesus Christ, yet the old
still persists. The believers must put on the new life, pre-
senting themselves to God. They do not do this as isolated
individuals. In light of the new realities involving God's long-
promised intentions concerning Jews and gentiles, that new
life involves embodying the eschatological oneness as the
people of God in which believers from Jewish and gentile
backgrounds now exist in Christ. Leander E. Keck captures
this point nicely when he says,

> Romans 15:7–13, then, expands this unity by showing that it is
> not simply a mutual, intramural accommodation to be reached
> in Rome, but *a local instance of God's saving purpose in Christ—*
> the eschatological unity of all people, concretely Jew and
> Gentile. By coming back to this theme, Paul draws a thread
> through the entire letter and shows that in Scripture God has
> indeed promised in advance the gospel for all humanity (1:2).[76]

One further piece of evidence bolsters this claim
regarding the role of 15:7–13 in Paul's argument. In 15:7,
Paul asserts that if his auditors receive one another after the
manner of Christ's reception of them, God will be glorified.
That Paul draws upon a key motif in the letter at this point
has already been demonstrated earlier in the chapter, but a
brief restatement will be helpful. According to Paul's argument in Romans, an act that glorifies God is the opposite of
the one made by Adam and characteristic of the age of sin
and death. On the other hand, an act that glorifies God is the
product of a mind unconformed to the ways of the age of sin
introduced by Adam (12:2). An act that glorifies God is an act
springing from the renewed mind of a person whose life has
been offered to God. It is an act of faith, like that of Abraham
(4:20). Mutual reception is what Paul calls the Roman
Christians to embrace in attitude and action. In doing so, they
will glorify God.

Here one must also note that Paul's commission as
apostle is to bring about the obedience of faith among all the

---

[76]"Christology," 93–94 (emphasis added).

nations on behalf of his name.[77] As shown in the treatment of Rom. 1:5, "on behalf of his name" is another way of saying "to his glory." When the Roman believers carry out Paul's injunction to "receive one another to the glory of God," they are exemplifying the kind of obedience that belongs to the new age, an obedience that gives glory to God.[78] It is this obedience that Paul has been divinely commissioned to bring about among the "community of the new age" in Rome.[79]

Summary and Implications

In Romans, Paul carries out his apostolic call, seeking to bring about the "obedience of faith" among the Roman Christians. That purpose finds its focal point in the letter at 15:7, where Paul draws upon his argument throughout the

---

[77]C. E. B. Cranfield (*The Epistle to the Romans*, vol. 1, ICC [Edinburgh: T & T Clark, 1975], 67) makes explicit identification of the glory of Christ in 1:5 and the glory of God, though without any explanatory comment. As a good Jew, Paul knows glory belongs to God alone. Believers will share in that glory in the future (8:28), but the glory is still God's. In the context of 1:5, Christ's "glory" is likely a reference to Christ's glory as the resurrected Son of God and Lord (1:4). As such, it is difficult to find any distinction between God's glory and Christ's glory. If the believers in Rome obey Paul's injunction in 15:7 to "receive one another," God will be glorified. Yet, when that happens, Paul will have also successfully carried out his commission and Christ will be glorified.

[78]Several commentators connect 1:5 with the theme of the "glory of God" in the letter but fail to exploit that connection for understanding the significance of Paul's call in 15:7 to "receive one another . . . to the glory of God." For example, in his comments on 1:5, Cranfield (*Romans*, 1:67, n. 6) notes the relationship between 1:5, 1:21 (they did not "glorify" God as God) and 15:7, but says nothing of the import of that relationship for interpreting the letter. His treatment of 15:9a deals with the syntactical difficulties, but says nothing regarding the "glory" theme.

[79]"The eschatological revelation of the righteousness of God (1:17; 3:21) can hardly be divorced from the formation of a righteous community modeled on the obedience of Jesus Christ, the last Adam (5:12–19). One may say that the latter-day realization of the δικαιοσύνη θεοῦ has as its intention a covenant-keeping community in the truest sense" (Garlington, *Faith, Obedience, and Perseverance*, 19).

letter up to that point in order to exhort his hearers to "receive one another" to the glory of God.[80] This mutual reception is an act of the "new obedience," made by Jews and gentiles who have been identified with Christ's death to sin and his resurrection to a new life. Empowered by the Spirit to "put off the deeds of darkness" (13:12), those "under grace" (6:14) will be transformed by the renewing of their minds (12:2) so that they can recognize God's mercy extended to the gentiles in the very act that demonstrated God's faithfulness to the Jews (15:8–9a): Christ's death and resurrection (4:25). Cognizant that God is now bringing together the eschatological people of God, the "community of the new age" where Jew and gentile are united in common worship, believers in Rome will "receive one another" in a manner that brings glory to God. When that event becomes reality, Paul will have successfully carried out his apostolic commission through this letter.

Two implications emerge from this reading that bear upon the interpretation of Romans. First, Paul is primarily concerned to form a community of the eschatological people of God in Rome. His argument throughout drives toward this point. Second, viewed in this perspective, chs. 1–11 are hardly abstract, contextless theology. Paul argues for eschatological realities that express God's faithfulness to the Jewish people, yet include the nations in that same action. The entirety of Paul's argument in chs. 1–11 therefore carries implications for

---

[80]"The unification of Jews and Gentiles in the praise of God is the goal toward which the whole letter drives" (Hays, "Adam, Israel, Christ," 81). See also Robert Jewett, "Following the Argument of Romans," in Karl P. Donfried, ed., *The Romans Debate*, rev. and expanded ed. (Peabody, Mass.: Hendrickson, 1991), 276.

community life in Rome, meaning Romans is "practical" not just in chs. 12–15, but throughout.[81] These implications will influence the reading of Romans in the rest of this study.

---

[81]"Life and theology are one for Paul, and to understand them in different terms is simply to misunderstand Paul." Paul J. Achtemeier, *The Quest For Unity in the New Testament Church* (Philadelphia: Fortress Press, 1987), 81. Meeks weaves chs. 1–11 and 12–15 together as follows ("Judgment and the Brother," 290),

> Paul's advice about behavior in the Christian groups cannot be rightly understood until we see that the great themes of chapters 1–11 here receive their denouement. And we do not grasp their epistolary context unless we see how Paul wants them to work out in the everyday life of the Roman house communities.

Chapter Four

PAUL AND THE ROMAN CHRISTIANS

A satisfactory resolution to the Romans Debate must explain why Paul wrote to these people at this time in his life. This chapter reconstructs a picture of what can be known about Paul, Paul's Roman audience, and what Paul and the Roman Christians knew about one another.

Paul

Place and Date of Composition

Although Paul nowhere says he writes from Corinth, the almost unanimous opinion of scholars holds that he sent the letter from that city.[1] This judgment rests on the following line of reasoning. Paul informs the Romans he is about to embark on a journey to Jerusalem with the collection "for the poor among the saints" (15:25–27). In Acts 20:3, Luke places Paul in "Greece" for three months prior to his departure for Jerusalem with the collection.[2] Several factors make Corinth

---

[1]For a list of scholars who locate Paul elsewhere when he composed Romans, see Joseph A. Fitzmyer, *Romans*, AB, vol. 33 (New York: Doubleday, 1993), 85.

[2]Although scholars are skeptical about Luke's historical accuracy, few question Luke's account of Paul's movements as he prepared to travel to Jerusalem (Acts 20–21). See Joseph A. Fitzmyer, *According to*

the most likely location in Greece for that stay, and hence for the place of composition of Romans. First, Paul sends the letter with Phoebe, who is described as "a deacon of the church of Cenchreae" (16:1). Cenchreae was one of the ports of Corinth on the isthmus connecting the Peloponnese with the rest of Greece. Furthermore, in Rom. 16:23, Paul (or Tertius; cf. 16:22) states that both Gaius and Erastus send greetings to the Roman Christians. In 1 Cor. 1:14, Paul speaks of a Gaius who was one of the people Paul baptized in Corinth.[3] It is almost certain that this is the same person mentioned in Romans. Several factors link Erastus with Corinth as well. Paul says that Erastus is the "city treasurer" (NRSV; ὁ οἰκονόμος τῆς πόλεως). The meaning of this designation is uncertain.[4] An inscription dated to the mid-first century C.E. has been found in Corinth identifying a person named Erastus as an *aedilis*.[5] The οἰκονόμος and *aedilis* were probably different offices.[6] But Gerd Theissen has argued that Erastus could have been the city οἰκονόμος when Paul wrote Romans and later risen to become *aedilis*.[7] An Erastus is also associated with Paul as a traveling companion in Acts 19:22 and 2 Tim. 4:20 (which places Erastus in Corinth). The

---

Paul: Studies in the Theology of the Apostle (New York: Paulist Press, 1993), 36–46.

[3]Fitzmyer concludes that this is "undoubtedly" the same person (*Romans*, 85).

[4]Gerd Theissen provides a thorough examination of the title οἰκονόμος as well as the arguments for and against identifying the Erastus in Rom. 16 with the other Erastus' in the NT. See *The Social Setting of Pauline Christianity: Essays on Corinth*, trans. and ed. John H. Schütz (Philadelphia: Fortress Press, 1982), 79–83. See also Florence Morgan Gillman, "Erastus," *ABD*, 2:571.

[5]According to Theissen, two *aediles* served in Corinth concurrently. Their responsibilities included "maintenance and oversight of public places and buildings, the provisioning of grain, and staging of games" (*Social Setting*, 79).

[6]The social role and function of the οἰκονόμος varied by time and place. See Gillman, "Erastus." Theissen does not rule out the possibility that the two terms refer to the same office in Corinth (*Social Setting*, 81).

[7]Theissen, *Social Setting*, 83.

combined weight of these factors makes it likely that the Erastus referred to in Rom. 16:23 resides in Corinth.

None of this evidence conclusively places Paul in Corinth when Romans was composed. Still, it does provide a series of links between Paul and the city that has led to the formation of a general consensus among scholars that Romans was written from Corinth. No other city fits the available evidence so well. Within this study, therefore, Paul is assumed to be in Corinth as he dictates the letter to Tertius.

The precise date when Romans was written remains debated, though scholars agree it was written during the late 50's. For the purpose of this dissertation, the exact year is not important, although an estimate of the time of year in which the epistle was composed is helpful. Placing the time of writing during the winter months (Acts 20:3) enables one to make a rough estimate of how much time Paul would allow for his journey to Jerusalem and then on to Rome (Rom. 15:28–29). Since I argue that Paul fears opponents will arrive in Rome before he can get there himself, some idea of how much time would elapse before he could anticipate getting to Rome is important. Such an estimate can only be approximate for several reasons. Owing to the vagaries of weather as well as the type and availability of ships, travel time on the Mediterranean could vary. Paul also gives no indication of which route he plans to take (by land? by sea?) nor of the amount of time he anticipates spending in Jerusalem. The following reconstruction assumes a best case scenario regarding weather and that Paul would conduct as much of the journey as possible by sea. Nevertheless, it remains a rough approximation at best.

Sea travel largely ceased[8] during the winter owing to rough seas, cloudy skies,[9] and fog that blanketed coastlines[10] (the two latter issues making navigation difficult if not impossible). The seas were open for travel roughly from mid-March until mid-September.[11] If Paul sailed from Corinth in mid-March, westerly winds would enable him to sail to Caesarea and travel from there up to Jerusalem in a few weeks, arriving in mid-April. If he could make his stay in Jerusalem brief, he could hope to make it to Rome during that same summer by departing in mid-May. Prevailing winds made westward sea travel much slower.[12] Lionel Casson estimates that travel from Caesarea to Rhodes would take ten days plus another 45–63 days from Rhodes to Rome.[13] If one figures 65 days for sea travel plus two weeks for land travel and time in ports to locate suitable ships, the journey would take approximately 80 days. Paul could hope to arrive at Rome, therefore, in August. Should events in Jerusalem hold him up, a possibility he feared (15:30–32), his arrival in Rome could be delayed by the wait for the next sailing season or by the additional time required for a land trip (which winter weather also affected). If Paul sent the letter to Rome at the

---

[8]Pliny the Elder mentions that "not even the fury of the storms closes the sea; pirates first compelled men by the threat of death to rush into death and venture on the winter seas, but now avarice exercises the same compulsion" (*Natural History*, 2.47.125). Translation by H. Rackham, *Pliny: Natural History*, vol. 1, *LCL* (Cambridge: Harvard University Press, 1938), 267.

[9]Robert Jewett, *A Chronology of Paul's Life* (Philadelphia: Fortress Press, 1979), 56.

[10]Lionel Casson, *Ships and Seamanship in the Ancient World* (Princeton: Princeton University Press, 1971), 271–72.

[11]See F. F. Bruce, "Travel and Communication (NT World)," *ABD*, 6:650, and evidence cited there.

[12]Lionel Casson estimates that a voyage from Rome to Rhodes took 7–11 days whereas the return trip to anywhere from 45–63 days ("Speed Under Sail of Ancient Ships," in *TAPA*, 82 [1951]: 146).

[13]Ibid. William M. Ramsey estimates that travel from Jerusalem to Rome and back by sea would "occupy the whole summer and part of the autumn" (*Pauline and Other Studies in Early Christian History* [London: Hodder and Stoughton, 1906], 355).

beginning of February and believed he could limit his stay in Jerusalem to only a few weeks, and if his sea travel plans came off without any complications, he could arrive in Rome before the sailing season closed in mid-September. One could estimate, therefore, that if Paul sent the letter to Rome in late February, he would expect that at minimum six months time would elapse before he arrived in Rome. In view of the uncertainties surrounding extensive travel plus potential difficulties Paul might face in Jerusalem, Paul likely anticipated his journey to Rome would take longer.

Paul's Circumstances

Paul explains his situation in Rom. 15:22–32. Specific items will be mentioned in the order in which they occur in the text.

(1) Having preached his gospel "from Jerusalem around to Illyricum" (15:19), Paul feels he has covered the territory for his ministry in the eastern Mediterranean (v. 23a).[14]

(2) Paul now plans to go to Spain and evangelize, passing through Rome on his way. Paul makes three statements about his planned visit with the Roman Christians. First, he wishes to enjoy their company (v. 24) after a successful delivery of the collection. Second, he hopes to be sent on by them to Spain (ὑφ' ὑμῶν προπεμφθῆναι ἐκεῖ; v. 24). James D. G. Dunn notes that the verb Paul uses here, προπέμπω ("send on one's way"; *BAG[D]*, 709), "becomes almost a technical term

---

[14]Paul J. Achtemeier argues that the phrase νυνὶ δὲ μηκέτι τόπον ἔχων in 15:23 may refer to the fact that Paul has lost the battle with opponents in the East and, consequently, no longer has any place for further ministry there. See *The Quest for Unity in the New Testament Church* (Philadelphia: Fortress Press, 1987), 61. According to Acts, Paul maintains good relations with Christians in several cities in the East. That he may be seeking territory where he can proclaim the gospel without continued harassment, as Achtemeier maintains, is possible. Yet, if Paul had been totally defeated in the East, one would expect the Christians in Rome to have some inkling of that information. One would also expect such a defeat to color the tone of this letter, which it does not.

for the provision made by a church for missionary support."[15] Paul used churches in the East, notably Antioch, as support bases for his work. Apparently Paul plans on continuing this practice for his mission to Spain, with the Roman Christians making this new venture possible.[16] Such support could take on any number of forms including money, contacts, means of travel, traveling companions, food, and translators. Paul could not to go to Spain on his own. The assistance of the Roman Christians would be required. Finally, Paul desires that they be mutually refreshed[17] as a result of their time together (15:32).

(3) Before Paul can fulfill his plans to pass through Rome, however, he must travel East to Jerusalem with the collection for "the poor among the saints who are in Jerusalem" (15:25–28).[18]

---

[15]*Romans 9–16*, WBC, vol. 38B (Milton Keynes, England: Word, 1991), 872. See also Heinrich Schlier, *Der Römerbrief*, HTKNT, bd. 6 (Freiburg: Herder, 1977), 434; Bengt Holmberg, *Paul and Power: The Structure of Authority in the Primitive Church as Reflected in the Pauline Epistles* (Philadelphia: Fortress Press, 1978), 86–87; C. E. B. Cranfield, *The Epistle to the Romans*, vol. 2, ICC (Edinburgh: T & T Clark, 1979), 769, n. 4; Ulrich Wilckens, *Der Brief an die Römer*, 2d aufl., EKKNT, bd. 6.3 (Neukirchener-Vluyn: Neukirchener Verlag, 1989), 124.

[16]In addition to the sources listed in footnote 14, see *BAG(D)*, 709 for various ways one could be "sent on one's way."

[17]συναναπαύομαι. This could possibly echo the mutual encouragement of 1:12.

[18]The debate surrounding the purpose of the delivery of the collection goes beyond the scope of this study. The pending journey to Jerusalem and the collection, however, do not serve as the focal point of the letter (as argued by Jacob Jervell, "The Letter to Jerusalem," in *The Romans Debate*, rev. and expanded ed., ed. Karl P. Donfried [Peabody, Mass.: Hendrickson, 1991], 53–64). That the collection played a major role in Paul's conception of his own ministry is certain. That it played a pivotal role in causing Paul to write Romans exaggerates its importance in the letter. In these verses, Paul is informing the Romans of his plans so that they may know when he will come and what to expect when he arrives. He also requests that they pray for the successful delivery of the collection and for Paul's safety in Jerusalem (15:31). These are not issues the letter has been building toward all along.

(4) Finally, Paul anticipates serious opposition from "unbelievers" in Jerusalem and fears possible rejection of the collection. The identity of these opponents will be taken up in the next chapter.

In summary, Paul writes from Corinth where he is spending the winter. He believes his ministry in the East has been completed, except for the delivery of the collection. Once more favorable weather arrives, he will travel to Jerusalem where he anticipates stiff opposition. Following the delivery of the collection, he will set off for new ministry in Spain. He plans to spend time in Rome on his way to Spain, so that he may be refreshed and encouraged by their company, but also to gain the assistance he needs for the Spanish mission.

Roman Christians

Because Paul informs his hearers of his situation and plans, reconstructing his circumstances as he writes is relatively simple. Putting together a picture of the Roman Christians, on the other hand, is not so easy. This section attempts to reconstruct what can be known about Paul's audience. It is organized into three parts. First, it treats general matters regarding the Roman believers and their organization. It then engages the two most controversial issues regarding Roman Christianity. These are (a) the question of whether Paul's hearers were Christians from a Jewish background, a gentile background, or some mixture of the two; and (b) what insight Paul's instructions to the "strong" and "weak" in Romans 14–15 provide or do not provide about the Christians in Rome.

General Information

Paul's letter to the Romans is the earliest witness to Christianity in Rome. The origins of the Christian movement there and many of the details regarding the Roman believers at the time the letter was written remain obscure. A few basic factors, however, can be stated with reasonable confidence.[19]

Paul's list of greetings in ch. 16 indicates that the Christians met in several house groups (ἐκκλησίαι).[20] Like the Jewish communities in Rome, these were likely organized geographically, in different sections of the city. In light of the number of Christians in the city (see below), one can safely

---

[19]For recent, often conflicting, reconstructions of Roman Christianity in the late 50's C.E., see Wolfgang Wiefel, "The Jewish Community in Ancient Rome and the Origins of Roman Christianity," in *The Romans Debate*, 85–101; Raymond E. Brown and John P. Meier, *Antioch and Rome: New Testament Cradles of Catholic Christianity* (New York: Paulist Press, 1983), 92–127; Francis Watson, *Paul, Judaism and the Gentiles: A Sociological Approach*, SNTSMS, vol. 56 (Cambridge: Cambridge University Press, 1986), 88–105; Peter Lampe, *Die stadtrömischen Christen in den ersten beiden Jahrhunderten*, WUNT, reihe 2, bd. 18 (Tübingen: J. C. B. Mohr [Paul Siebeck], 1987); Raymond E. Brown, "Further Reflections on the Origins of the Church of Rome," in *The Conversation Continues: Studies in Paul & John in Honor of J. Louis Martyn*, eds. Robert T. Fortna and Beverly R. Gaventa (Nashville: Abingdon Press, 1990), 98–115; James C. Walters, *Ethnic Issues in Paul's Letter to the Romans: Changing Self-Definitions in Earliest Roman Christianity* (Valley Forge, Penn.: Trinity Press International, 1993), 56–66; idem, "Romans, Jews, and Christians: The Impact of the Romans on Jewish/Christian Relations in First-Century Rome," in *Judaism and Christianity in First-Century Rome*, eds. Karl P. Donfried and Peter Richardson (Grand Rapids: William B. Eerdmans, 1998), 175–95; Mark D. Nanos, *The Mystery of Romans: The Jewish Context of Paul's Letter* (Minneapolis: Fortress Press, 1996), 41–165; Rudolf Brändle and Ekkehard W. Stegemann, "The Formation of the First 'Christian Congregations' in Rome in the Context of the Jewish Congregations," in *Judaism and Christianity*, eds. Donfried and Richardson, 117–27; William L. Lane, "Social Perspectives on Roman Christianity during the Formative Years from Nero to Nerva: Romans, Hebrews, *1 Clement*," in *Judaism and Christianity*, eds. Donfried and Richardson, 196–244.

[20]Regarding Prisca and Aquila, Paul greets Prisca and Aquila and τὴν κατ᾽ οἶκον αὐτῶν ἐκκλησίαν (16:5). In vv. 10–11, Paul greets separately those of the household of Aristobulus and Narcissus (e.g. τοὺς ἐκ τῶν Ἀριστοβούλου), a reference to those who met in their house. Finally, in vv. 14–15 Paul twice greets people "and those with them," again a reference to those who met together.

assume some diversity of practice and belief among these various groups.[21]

In addition, Tacitus, writing early in the second century, reports a fire that destroyed parts of Rome in 64 C.E. In order to squelch rumors that Nero himself had started the fire, the emperor selected Christians as scapegoats. Tacitus writes,

> Therefore, to scotch the rumour, Nero substituted as culprits, and punished with the utmost refinements of cruelty, a class of men, loathed for their vices, whom the crowd styled Christians. Christus, the founder of the name, had undergone the death penalty in the reign of Tiberius, by sentence of the procurator Pontius Pilatus, and the pernicious superstition was checked for a moment, only to break out once more, not merely in Judea, the home of the disease, but in the capital itself, where all things horrible or shameful in the world collect and find vogue.[22]

Raymond E. Brown derives three conclusions from this report about Roman Christianity within a few years of Paul's letter. First, since there is no record of attacks on Jews, Romans were able to distinguish between Christians and Jews. Second, Tacitus describes the torture and killing of large number of Christians, indicating the Christian movement had attracted a significant following.[23] Third, Roman pagans were aware that Christianity had its origins in Judea.[24] Only the first of these contentions requires qualification. Christians could have been viewed as a sect within Judaism rather than as a totally separate movement. Although Tacitus does not describe them as a "Jewish" group, he does connect this "disease" with Judea.[25] Even if the Christians were considered

---

[21]F. F. Bruce, "The Romans Debate—Continued," in *The Romans Debate*, 186.

[22]*Annals* 15.44. This translation by Clifford H. Moore, *Tacitus*, vol. 4, *LCL* (Cambridge: Harvard University Press, 1937), 283.

[23]A large number of Christians also means the Christian movement must have been active in Rome for some time.

[24]*Antioch and Rome*, 99.

[25]See Nanos, *Mystery of Romans*, 385, n. 46 (citing Stephen Benko, *Pagan Rome and the Early Christians* [London: B. T. Batsford, 1985], 16,

one variety of Judaism, they could be identified as a distinct entity within it.

Finally, Paul presupposes a familiarity either with the Jewish Scriptures, Christian tradition, or both, in multiple places in Romans. Robert Morgan notes that several un-explained ideas appear in the letter-opening.

> They know who Christ (Messiah) Jesus is, and what an apostle is, what the Scriptures are, and that God is an agent who has made promises through the prophets. These prophets are said to refer to a person who is called God's Son, and Paul himself has a God-given role to spread a message about him which is described (without explanation) as gospel of God. . . . God's Son is then described and identified in a couplet which contains ideas and phrases not found elsewhere in Paul's writings, and so looks like a quotation from some early Christian creed or confession used in worship. Jesus is descended from David as regards his human origin, and appointed or designated Son of God . . .[26]

In each case (and the list goes on), Morgan writes, "Paul can assume they understand his insider language."[27] One can ascertain, therefore, that many of the Roman Christians are not neophytes in their faith. Paul believes that they are well-instructed in the Scriptures and early Christian tradition (cf. 1:8; 6:17; 16:17).

On the basis of these conclusions, one can suppose that Paul is aware of several different Christian groups meeting in separate homes around Rome. These groups include well-instructed believers. Given the large number of Christians in the city and that Paul greets groups that meet in homes (indicating they are not large meetings), it is likely that these groups make up only a part of the Christians in the city. Paul intends the letter to circulate among the house gatherings with whom he and those listed in 16:3–16 have connections.

---

20); contra Brendan Byrne, *Romans*, SacPag, vol. 6 (Collegeville, Minn.: Liturgical Press, 1996), 11.

[26]*Romans*, NTG (Sheffield: Sheffield Academic Press, 1995), 17.

[27]Ibid. See also Neil Elliott, *The Rhetoric of Romans: Argumentative Constraint and Strategy and Paul's Dialogue with Judaism,* JSNTSup, vol. 45 (Sheffield: JSOT Press, 1990), 76.

Jewish and Gentile Christians in Rome

In several places in Romans, Paul either addresses gentile listeners directly (11:13, 17–18, 24, 28–31) or includes his auditors among the gentiles (1:5–6, 13; 15:15–16).[28] Without question, Paul believes at least some of his audience will be gentile believers. The more difficult matter concerns whether there were also Jewish believers among the Christians in Rome. If there were believers of both Jewish and gentile birth, which group was in the majority and how did that ethnic majority shape Christian movement in the city?

Jewish Christians. The few scholars who argue for a majority of Jewish believers among Paul's audience do so on the basis of the fact that Paul counters Jewish objections to his Law-free gospel in the letter.[29] If one believes the audience

---

[28]Not all of these references are as clear-cut as scholars often want to make them. In 1:6, Paul addresses his hearers "among [the nations] you are also called of Jesus Christ" (1:6; ἐν οἷς ἐστε καὶ ὑμεῖς κλητοὶ ᾽Ιησοῦ Χριστοῦ). This phrase could indicate the geographical location rather than the ethnic make-up of the Roman Christians (see Anthony J. Guerra, *Romans and the Apologetic Tradition: The Purpose, Genre and Audience of Paul's Letter*, SNTSMS, vol. 81 (Cambridge: Cambridge University Press, 1995), 26; C. E. B. Cranfield, *The Epistle to the Romans*, vol. 1, ICC (Edinburgh: T & T Clark, 1975), 68). In 6:17–22, Paul speaks of his auditors' former way of life as one of sin. This is not necessarily a reference to gentile pagan lifestyles, since Paul considers Jews to be under the reign of sin apart from Christ. Furthermore, the references in 9:3–4, 10:1–2; and 11:23, 28, 31 speak of the Jews in third person ("them") leading some to conclude that Paul here addresses gentile Christians about Jews. In these verses, however, Paul speaks of non-believing Jews. These verses cannot be used to argue against the presence of Jewish believers among Paul's audience. For the contrary viewpoint, see Fitzmyer, *Romans*, 33; Peter Lampe, "The Roman Christians of Romans 16," in *The Romans Debate*, 225, n. 37.

[29]See Fitzmyer, *Romans*, 32 for a list of scholars. To this list can be added the following: Steve Mason, "'For I am not Ashamed of the Gospel' (Rom. 1.16): The Gospel and the First Readers of Romans," in *Gospel in Paul: Studies on Corinthians, Galatians and Romans for Richard N. Longenecker*, eds. L. Ann Jervis and Peter Richardson, JSNTSup, vol. 108 (Sheffield: Sheffield Academic Press, 1994), 254–87. Mason argues for a Jewish-Christian audience on other grounds as well.

was made up of gentile Christians, the question then becomes, "Why would Paul write about such Jewish issues to Christian gentiles in Rome?"[30] This approach falsely assumes that people from a gentile background (meaning, in this view, they were not familiar with the Jewish Scriptures) could join a Jewish movement proclaiming "Jesus is Lord," yet remain outside the community of discourse that makes that commitment not only meaningful, but possible in the first place.[31] The Jewish argument of the letter, therefore, does not demand a Jewish audience in Rome.[32]

Paul nowhere addresses Jewish believers in the letter as he does gentile Christians. There are reasons to believe, however, that Paul's audience included believers of Jewish origin. These reasons include:

(1) In Rom. 16:3–16, Paul greets three people he describes as "fellow-country(wo)men" (συγγενής ; *BAG[D]*, 772): Andronicus (v. 3), Junia (v. 3), and Herodion (v. 11). Paul uses this term συγγενής to refer to his fellow Jews (cf. 9:3). Prisca and Aquila (v. 3) are also Jews (Acts 18:2). Other Jews may appear among the names in ch. 16 as well, but the names themselves do not enable one to know if the person is from a Jewish or gentile background.[33] The names and

---

Francis Watson believes Paul directs Romans to separate gentile and Jewish congregations in Rome. But on the basis of the argument of the letter, Watson views Paul's primary task as winning the Jewish Christians over to his point of view (*Paul, Judaism and the Gentiles*, 97–98).

[30]See p. 11, n. 25 for a list of these "Jewish issues."

[31]One envisions something akin to much modern Christianity where the Jewish roots of the faith have become lost. That may be possible in the late 20th century. It would not be comprehensible during the late 50's of the first century.

[32]Contra Mason, "Ashamed of the Gospel," 261.

[33]Lampe, "Roman Christians," 224. Lampe cites three additional names that appear among Jewish inscriptions from Rome: Maria, Rufus, and Julia (ibid., 225).

descriptions that do appear, however, demonstrate that Christian Jews were among Paul's hearers.[34]

(2) Although Paul addresses gentile Christians directly, this does not necessitate limiting the audience to gentile Christians. Paul could easily direct specific remarks within the letter to segments of his audience. Yet, in a letter circulated among Christian groups meeting in houses around the city, he could not limit the letter to only gentile-Christian hearers if Jewish Christians were also present.[35]

(3) Christian tradition offers evidence that the Christian movement in Rome was closely tied to the synagogue and maintained close ties to the Jewish roots of its faith into the second century. For example, Ambrosiaster, writing around 375, comments that the Roman Christians in the first century were characterized by a "Jewish bent."[36] Raymond Brown also argues that Roman Christianity maintained strong ties with the Jerusalem church until the destruction of Jerusalem in 70 C.E. Those links were maintained through Jewish circles, providing evidence of Jews among the Roman Christians.

In summary, the Christian communities in Rome consisted of believers from both Jewish and gentile backgrounds. Romans 16:3–16 offers concrete evidence of Jewish believers while Paul's direct address to gentile believers provides solid evidence for the presence of Christians from gentile backgrounds. The available evidence does not permit a definite decision as to which group was in the minority or majority,[37]

---

[34]The list does not, however, provide sufficient basis for a decision regarding the make-up of the entirety of Christians in Rome. Contra Lampe, "Roman Christians," 225.

[35]Daniel Fraikin states that "the audience is not the church of Rome in general but specifically Roman Gentile Christians." But how could Paul restrict the audience to only those listeners? See "The Rhetorical Function of the Jews in Romans," in *Anti-Judaism in Early Christianity*, vol. 1, *Paul and the Gospels*, eds. Peter Richardson with David Granskou, Studies in Christianity and Judaism, no. 2 (Waterloo, Ontario: Wilfrid Laurier University Press, 1986), 93.

[36]*Patrologia Latine* 17.46. Cited by Brown, *Antioch and Rome*, 110–11; Brown's translation.

[37]Cf. Cranfield, *Romans*, 1:21.

though Paul's statements to those of gentile birth indicate that they were likely the majority or at least exerted strong influence among the Christian groups. In light of the organization of Christians into house churches and the large number of Christians in the city, it can be assumed that the make-up of different house churches varied.

Expulsion of Jews Under Claudius. One additional matter regarding the Christians in Rome warrants mention. Evidence exists that the Roman Emperor Claudius expelled at least some Jews from Rome in 49 C.E.[38] Although the date and precise nature of this expulsion remain debated, this event is often employed in arguments regarding the ethnic profile of the Christians in Rome at the time of Paul's letter.[39] The argument runs as follows. The Roman Christians were mostly Jewish in origin and were associated with synagogues in Rome, giving Christianity in Rome a distinctive Jewish flavor. Suetonius reports an incident in Rome during Claudius' reign when "the Jews constantly made disturbance at the instigation of Chrestus" and were expelled from the city as a consequence.[40] "Chrestus" is regarded as a misspelling of "Christus," indicating the cause of the problem was Christian preaching among the Jews in Rome. On the basis of a statement by Suetonius (*The Deified Claudius*, 25.4) and the note that Prisca and Aquila left Rome "because Claudius had ordered all the Jews to leave" (Acts 18:2), this event is dated to 49 C.E. Once the Jewish Christians left the city, the gentile Christians who remained formed the core of the Christian communities. These groups were not associated with syna-

---

[38]Acts 18:2; Suetonius (*The Deified Claudius*, 25.4), and Orosius (*The Seven Books of History Against the Pagans*, 7.6.15).

[39]Though first proposed by Willi Marxsen (*Introduction to the New Testament*, trans. G. Buswell [Philadelphia: Fortress Press, 1968], 98–100), the article by Wolfgang Wiefel arguing the same point in greater detail has had lasting influence. See Wiefel, "Jewish Community in Ancient Rome," 85–101.

[40]This translation by J. C. Rolfe, *Seutonius*, vol. 2, *LCL* (Cambridge: Harvard University Press, 1979), 53.

gogues (since the Jews were no longer in Rome) nor did they continue the Jewish leanings and practices of the previous majority. In the absence of Jewish Christians, the gentile Christians began meetings in homes and their numbers multiplied. As a result, the Christian movement in Rome now developed a distinctively gentile character. After Claudius died in 54 C.E., the edict of 49 C.E. lapsed and Jewish Christians were free to return. When they did, they found the Christian communities in Rome were now largely gentile in their practices and they, the former majority, were now in the minority. The tensions created by this return serve as the basis for Paul's letter (particularly the instructions to the "strong" and "weak" in chs. 14–15), written only a few years after the Jews began returning to Rome.

This reconstruction has been challenged on several points, all of which are well-documented.[41] I suggest the evidence favors an expulsion of some Jews from Rome in the late 40's, since Acts 18:2 provides a corroborating witness for such an event around this time. It does not follow, though, that this event was the decisive factor shaping the Christian movement in Rome at the time Paul writes the letter.

Neither Suetonius nor Orosius states how many Jews were sent out of Rome, though Luke states it was "all the Jews of Rome." Since the Jewish population of Rome has been estimated as high as 40,000–50,000 in the mid-50's,[42] such a total expulsion would not have been feasible. More likely, the individuals at the heart of the dispute were sent away,

---

[41]See Dixon Slingerland, "Suetonius *Claudius* 25.4 and the Account of Cassius Dio," *JQR* 79 (1989): 305–22; idem, "Suetonius *Claudius* 25.4, Acts 18, and Paulus Orosius' *Historiarum Adversum Paganos Libri VII*: Dating the Claudian Expulsion(s) of Roman Jews," *JQR* 83 (1992): 127–44; Mason, "Ashamed of the Gospel," 263–66; Nanos, *Mystery of Romans*, 372–87; Paul J. Achtemeier, "Unsearchable Judgments and Inscrutable Ways: Reflections on the Discussion of Romans," in *Pauline Theology*, vol. 4, *Looking Back, Pressing On*, eds. E. Elizabeth Johnson and David M. Hay (Atlanta: Scholars Press, 1997), 5–7.

[42]Harry Leon, *The Jews of Ancient Rome*, updated ed. (Peabody, Mass.: Hendrickson, 1995), 15, 257; reprint, Jewish Publication Society of America, 1960 (page citations are to the reprint edition).

including Prisca and Aquila.[43] The expulsion under Claudius, therefore, was not the key event shaping the Christian communities at the time Paul writes Romans. A controversy large enough to attract the attention of the Roman authorities[44] would certainly become known among the other Christians at the time and be remembered by the Christians later, at the time of Paul's letter. Still, there were too many Christians and too many Christian groups for that one event to determine the outlook of them all years later. In summary, my claim that an expulsion did occur in 49 C.E. can be contested, but since I do not believe it had meaningful influence on the Christian communities in Rome at the time Paul writes, the entire issue becomes irrelevant for establishing a profile of Paul's audience.

The "Strong" and the "Weak"

In Rom. 14:1–15:6, Paul instructs two groups he labels "the strong" and "the weak." Most scholars consider these groups and the problems between them to offer a glimpse of the situation among the Roman Christians. The "strong" are gentile Christians whose "strong" faith enables to live apart from the strictures of the Mosaic Law. The "weak" are believers of Jewish origin whose faith is too "weak" to enable them to do the same. Not all scholars are persuaded that these terms refer to actual groups in Rome.[45] Their objections center

---

[43]Brown judges that it is "most reasonable to assume" only the "most vocal on either side of the Christ issue" were expelled (*Antioch and Rome*, 102).

[44]Leonard Victor Rutgers argues that the Romans were only concerned with preserving law and order, and that their responses to problems were limited to troublemakers rather than applied to entire groups. See "Roman Policy toward the Jews: Expulsions from the City of Rome during the First Century C.E.," in *Judaism and Christianity in First-Century Rome*, eds. Karl P. Donfried and Peter Richardson (Grand Rapids: William B. Eerdmans, 1998), 110, 114; and E. Mary Smallwood, *The Jews under Roman Rule*, SJLA, vol. 20 (Leiden: E. J. Brill, 1976), 210, 216.

[45]William Sanday and Arthur C. Headlam, *The Epistle to the Romans*, ICC (New York: Charles Scribner's Sons, n.d.), 399–403; Franz J. Leenhardt, *The Epistle to the Romans: A Commentary* (London: Lutter-

on the general nature of the paraenesis in this passage and its parallels to Paul's instructions to the Corinthians in 1 Cor. 8 and 10. Robert Karris writes, "Rom. 14:1–15:13 is a generalized adaptation of a position Paul had earlier worked out respecting actual known situations, especially in Corinth."[46]

A comparison of the arguments in 1 Cor. 8–10 and Rom. 14:1–15:6 suggests, however, that Paul addresses genuine differences among the Roman Christians.[47] First, leading issues in the passage in 1 Corinthians do not appear in Romans. In 1 Corinthians, Paul is concerned with eating meat offered to idols, a practice that involves Christians participating in pagan rituals. The issues of "conscience" and "knowledge" also play a vital role. In Romans, these issues are not mentioned. Furthermore, Paul's instructions to the Romans concern eating vegetables (14:2) and meat (14:21; without reference to idols), drinking wine (14:21), and observance of special days (14:5–6). None of these issues surface in 1 Corinthians. In other words, Paul gives detailed instructions about specific issues in both letters, but the issues differ at important points. Paul's instructions in Romans therefore echo aspects of 1 Corinthians but inexplicably leave out key issues from the earlier letter while introducing new

---

worth Press, 1961), 344–46; Günther Bornkamm, "The Letter to the Romans as Paul's Last Will and Testament," in *The Romans Debate*, 19–20; Robert J. Karris, "Romans 14:1–15:13 and the Occasion of Romans," in *The Romans Debate*, 65–84; Wayne A. Meeks, "Judgment and the Brother: Romans 14:1–15:13," in *Tradition and Interpretation in the New Testament: Essays in Honor of E. Earle Ellis for His 60th Birthday*, eds. Gerald F. Hawthorne with Otto Betz (Grand Rapids: William B. Eerdmans; Tübingen: J. C. B. Mohr [Paul Siebeck], 1987), 290–300.

[46]"Romans 14:1–15:13," 71. Wayne Meeks argues that ". . . there is no evidence, . . . of any present crisis around this issue in the Roman groups. Paul takes up the topic out of his experience, not theirs, because it is well suited to show in behavioral terms the outworking of the main themes of the letter" ("Judgment and the Brother," 292).

[47]The argument here closely follows A. J. M. Wedderburn, *The Reasons for Romans* (Minneapolis: Fortress Press, 1991), 30–35. See also Lampe, *Die stadtrömischen Christen*, 56–57; Douglas Moo, *The Epistle to the Romans*, NICNT (Grand Rapids: William B. Eerdmans, 1996), 827–28.

matters at the same time. A genuine problem in Rome best accounts for the differences between the passages.[48]

What, then, is the nature of the conflict between the "strong" and the "weak"?[49] The argument of this dissertation does not require a resolution to every detail of this knotty problem. Whatever the precise dynamics of the controversy addressed in 14:1–15:6, the text allows us to state with confidence that Roman Christians, whatever their ethnic origin, displayed varying degrees of loyalty toward Jewish traditions.[50] Such tensions were understandable and to be expected since early Christians were still trying to work out the practical implications of life in the new age.[51]

Paul provides additional insight into this problem in Rom. 15:7–9. In 15:7, Paul restates his opening exhortation of 14:1 for the "strong" to receive the weak, but in 15:7 he broadens the exhortations by calling for all to "receive one another." In

---

[48]Paul's past instructions to the Corinthians have shaped his admonitions to the Romans, but Paul's thought "is hardly intelligible unless a fresh situation has arisen to which Paul responds creatively in Romans" (Wedderburn, *Reasons for Romans*, 35 [cf. Wedderburn's conclusion on p. 62]).

[49]See the extensive lists of proposed options in Cranfield, *Romans*, 2:690–98; Moo, *Romans*, 828–31; Mark Reasoner, "The 'Strong' and the 'Weak' in Rome and in Paul's Theology" (Ph. D. diss., University of Chicago, 1990), 11–19.

[50]The categories of "clean" and "unclean" with regard to food (14:2–3, 6, 15, 17, 20–21, 23) and observance of special days (14:5–6) are distinctively Jewish concerns. Mark Reasoner argues that "the use of the term κοινός as impurity in 14:14 cannot be understood in a Hellenistic milieu." See "The 'Strong' and the 'Weak' in Rome," 16; citing Nelio Schneider, "Die 'Schwachen' in der christlichen Gemeinde Roms: Eine historisch-exegetische Untersuchung zu Röm 14,1–15,13" (D. Theol. diss., University of Wuppertal, 1989), 69–70. Schneider's dissertation was not available to me. See also Dunn, *Romans 9–16*, 800.

[51]". . . the conflict between those who practiced some form of Jewish custom and those who did not was the most significant issue within Christianity's first two generations" Alan F. Segal, *Paul the Convert: The Apostolate and Apostasy of Saul the Pharisee* [New Haven: Yale University Press, 1990], 150). See also Michael Thompson, *Clothed With Christ: The Example and Teaching of Jesus in Romans 12.1–15.13*, JSNTSup, vol. 59 (Sheffield: JSOT Press, 1991), 230.

chapter three I argued that the exhortation of 15:7 draws together the argument of the entire letter. Yet, the parallels between 14:1, 14:3, and 15:7, plus those between 15:1–6 and 15:7–13, make it clear that Paul has the problems between the "strong" and "weak" especially in view. Paul goes on to support his exhortation for mutual reception among all by citing Christ's work for both Jews and gentiles (15:8–9a). Paul does not mention the categories of Jew and gentile in 14:1– 15:6 (and has not mentioned them since ch. 11). Yet, the fact that Paul recalls these categories to support an exhortation so closely tied to the instructions of 14:1–15:7 suggests that the dividing line between "strong" and "weak" ran along ethnic lines.[52] The "weak" are therefore mostly Christians from a Jewish background who observe Jewish food laws and special days while the "strong" are largely gentile Christians who do not adhere to the Law on these matters.

Raymond E. Brown has warned against drawing the kind of distinctions between "Jewish" Christianity (meaning Law-observant) and "gentile" Christianity (meaning Law-free) that my analysis of the "strong" and the "weak" suggests. Jewish Christians such as Paul could take a lenient attitude toward Law-observance while gentile Christians could strongly adhere to it. Brown, therefore, proposed a spectrum of positions with regard to Law-observance, from full adherence to full non-observance, with Jews and gentiles found all along the spectrum.[53] Brown's interpretation rightly calls attention

[52]Ernst Käsemann, *Commentary on Romans*, trans. and ed. Geoffrey W. Bromiley (Grand Rapids: William B. Eerdmans, 1980), 384; David Kaylor, *Paul's Covenant Community: Jew and Gentile in Romans* (Atlanta: John Knox Press, 1988), 209; William S. Campbell, "Romans III as a Key to the Structure and Thought of the Letter," in *The Romans Debate*, 262; Moo, *Romans*, 874.

[53]Brown isolated four positions on this spectrum and identified examples from the NT for each group. See "Not Jewish Christianity and Gentile Christianity but Types of Jewish/Gentile Christianity," *CBQ* 45 (1983): 74–79; *Antioch and Rome*, 2–8; "Further Reflections," 98, 103– 04. He recognized that these are not rigid positions and that a spectrum of beliefs certainly existed within these groups. See "Further Reflections,"

to the oversimplification represented by the categorizing of "gentile" believers as necessarily less observant of the Law and "Jewish" believers as more observant. Nevertheless, Paul indicates that the problems between the "strong" and "weak" in Rome run largely along those lines.

Mutual Knowledge between Paul and Roman Christians

The fact that Paul has never been to Rome when he writes Romans is often used to argue that this letter serves as Paul's self-introduction to the Roman Christians.[54] This assumption must be reexamined. On the basis of both internal and external evidence, I suggest that Paul actually knew much about the Roman Christians and that they knew something of him as well.

Internal Evidence

At several points in the letter, Paul reveals that he is aware of circumstances among his auditors.

(1) The list of greetings in 16:3–16 demonstrates that Paul knows, or knows of, at least 27 people[55] in the city plus those who belong to families he names (vv. 10–11). As this list shows, Paul knows individuals in Rome, and is also aware that they meet together in homes and in whose homes they gather. This is the clearest evidence that Paul has knowledge of the situation in Rome in some detail.

(2) In 11:13–32, Paul directly addresses gentile believers and their arrogance regarding Jewish believers. Unless Paul is aware of such attitudes among his listeners, this directness would be out of order.

103–04. See also A. J. M. Wedderburn, "The Purpose and Occasion of Romans Again," in *The Romans Debate*, 201–02.

[54]Käsemann writes that Paul presents himself to a "congregation as yet unknown to him" (*Romans*, 404).

[55]Paul greets 26 people by name as well as Rufus' mother (v. 13), who is not named.

(3) In 13:1–5, Paul draws upon conventional Jewish wisdom and early Christian tradition in order to offer advice to the Roman Christians about appropriate relation to governing authorities.[56] His specific advice regarding taxes in vv. 6–7, however, finds no parallel in those traditions. This suggests that in 13:1–5 Paul prepares his audience with general guidance on relationships with governing authorities, drawn from familiar traditions, which he then applies in vv. 6–7 specifically to a matter he knows to be a point of controversy in Rome.[57]

(4) In both 6:17 and 16:17, Paul speaks of the "teaching" the Roman Christians have received. Paul can only do so if he is aware of the kind of instruction given to his hearers by others. I argued in chapter two that the fact that Paul can say he writes "as a way of reminding" (15:15) the Roman believers indicates he knows something about what they have been taught in the past.

(5) In 3:8, Paul asks, "And why not say (as some people slander us by saying that we say), 'Let us do evil so that good may come'?" (NRSV). Paul's parenthetical remark shows that he believes his hearers know of such criticism made against him. He could only do so on the basis of some knowledge of circumstances among the Roman Christians.

(6) Paul commends the faith (1:8), maturity (15:14), or obedience of the Roman Christians as "known to all" (16:19).

(7) Harry Gamble, Jr. believes the nature of Paul's argument in chs. 9–11 also presupposes knowledge of his audience. Gamble asks "how the tortuous effort in chs. 9–11 to comprehend and explicate the unbelief of Israel fits into the letter structurally and thematically; that problem is all the more intractable if it has no relevance to the Roman church."[58]

---

[56]Dunn lists Wis. 6:3–4 and 1 Pet. 2:13–17 as parallels (*Romans 9–16*, 759).

[57]This passage receives more detailed treatment in chapter six.

[58]*The Textual History of the Letter to the Romans*, SD, vol. 42 (Grand Rapids: William B. Eerdmans, 1977), 136.

In other words, there is no reason for this detailed argument unless it has relevance for known issues in Rome.

(8) Paul's argument betrays not only his knowledge of their situation, but also their knowledge of him. For example, Paul's brief comments about the collection (15:26) would hardly makes sense unless his audience knows something of his ministry in Macedonia and Achaia. He also indicates that he is aware the believers in Rome already know of his desire to visit them (1:9–11, 13; 15:18–23).[59]

These factors make it difficult to deny that Paul had at least some knowledge of the Christians and their circumstances in Rome. In particular, once ch. 16 is accepted as part of the original letter sent to Rome, some knowledge of the situation there becomes certain.

External Evidence

In addition to the evidence within Romans, several external factors make Paul's knowledge of the situation among the Christians in Rome likely. First, in order to facilitate the administration of the Empire, Rome developed a highly efficient system of travel and communication uniting the capital city with far-flung regions under its control.

> Within the bounds of the Empire, the principle of Roman Republican government had originally been to connect every subject, country, and district as closely as possible with Rome, and to keep them as much as possible disconnected from one another, so that each should look to Rome as the centre of all its interests, its trade, its finance, and its aspirations, and regard all other subjects as rivals and competitors for the favour of the governing city.[60]

---

[59]Sam K. Williams, "The 'Righteousness of God' in Romans," *JBL* 99 (1980): 250–51. Contra Fitzmyer, *Romans*, 246.

[60]William Ramsey, "Roads and Travel (in NT)," in *A Dictionary of the Bible*, vol. 5, ed. James Hastings (New York: Charles Scribner's Sons, 1904), 376. The fact that Rome was on a natural line across the northern Mediterranean between Palestine and Spain explains, at least in part, Paul's reason for stopping there on his way to Spain. Yet, since "all roads led to Rome," Paul scarcely had any choice but to pass through the city.

This policy made travel and communication between Rome and other parts of the Empire (as well as among communities along these travel routes) possible to an extent unknown before or after the *Pax Romana*.[61]

Movement along this network of road and sea routes was enjoyed not only by the Roman political establishment, but also by traders and adventurers—by anyone with the time and resources to take advantage of the opportunity. This included Jews and adherents of the Jewish sect known as Christians. The letters of the New Testament attest to communication among Christian groups, sometimes over a vast area (1 Pet. 1:1). The Book of Acts also testifies to the wide-ranging travel by and communication among both Jews and Christian groups. Best known among these are the accounts of Paul's missionary journeys and his voyage to Rome.[62] Luke also records the presence of Jewish pilgrims from around the empire at Pentecost (2:9–11).[63] Furthermore, upon Paul's arrival in Rome, the Roman Christians remark that, "We have received no letters from Judea about you" (NRSV; 18:21).

---

[61]Ramsey notes that the extensive travel plans expressed by classical or biblical writers of the period would scarcely be imaginable by someone living during medieval times (ibid., 396–97). Everett Ferguson quotes Epictetus (*Discourses* 3.13.9) regarding the freedom of travel: "Caesar has obtained for us a profound peace. There are neither wars nor battles, nor great robberies nor piracies, but we may travel at all hours, and sail from east to west" (*Backgrounds of Early Christianity*, 2d ed. [Grand Rapids: William B. Eerdmans, 1993], 78).

[62]The chronicles of Paul's travels are numerous. See, for example, William M. Ramsey, *St. Paul the Traveller and the Roman Citizen* (Grand Rapids: Baker Books, 1982; reprint, London: Hodder and Stoughton, 1925); Paul Trebilco, "Itineraries, Travel Plans, Journeys, Apostolic Parousia," in *DPL*, 446–56.

[63]S. Safrai, "Relations between the Diaspora and the Land of Israel," in *The Jewish People in the First Century*, vol. 1, eds. S. Safrai and M. Stern, CRINT, section 1 (Philadelphia: Fortress Press, 1974), 184–215. Safrai records at length the phenomenon of Jewish pilgrimages to Jerusalem from the Diaspora. See also George Foot Moore, *Judaism in the First Centuries of the Christian Era*, vol. 1 (Peabody, Mass.: Hendrickson, 1997), 106–09; reprint, Cambridge: Harvard University Press, 1927.

That remark demonstrates that such literary correspondence did in fact take place.

In summary, Paul knows at least some information about the situation among the Roman Christians. Writing from Corinth, Paul was in an excellent position to receive information about Christians in Rome from travelers and emissaries, for Corinth was on one of the primary routes of travel between Rome and the East.[64] Paul's friends and acquaintances in Rome, people who had met him during their travels in the East, served as Paul's points of contact with the Christian ἐκκλησίαι in Rome and as his sources of information about the situation there.

Yet, if Paul knows people in Rome and through them something of the Roman Christians, it follows that many among the Roman Christians know something about Paul as well. This information would come not only through those Paul greets in ch. 16, but also through others who had traveled in the East. In light of the controversies Paul sparked in Jerusalem and elsewhere, opinions of Paul among those who had heard of him could be mixed.

On the basis of this evidence, an approach to Romans which presupposes that Paul and the Roman Christians were total strangers, since Paul had never been to Rome, must be rejected. It is true that Paul did not have a formal relationship with the Roman Christians like he had with churches he had founded. Yet, Paul certainly knew of their circumstances and they knew something about him. How much they knew of one another is impossible to ascertain. Still, given the evidence in the letter, the means of communication available at that time,

---

[64]See Ferguson, *Backgrounds*, 79, for a list of the main routes between Rome and the eastern Mediterranean. Pliny the Elder (*Hist. Nat.* 19.1.3–4) estimated that mail could move from Rome to Corinth in 7–8 days (cited by Peter Stuhlmacher, "The Purpose of Romans," in *The Romans Debate*, 237–38). This, of course, assumes optimal travel conditions. See also Markku Kettunen, *Der Abfassungszweck des Römerbriefes*, Annales Academiae scientiarum Fennicai, dissertationes humanarum litterarum, bd. 18 (Helsinki: Suomalainen Tiedeakatemia, 1979), 61.

and Paul's location in Corinth, the burden of proof regarding the presence or absence of mutual knowledge lies with those who would deny it.

Conclusion

Paul is at a turning point in his ministry as he writes from Corinth to the Roman believers. He believes he has completed his ministry in the East and plans to travel to Spain to begin new evangelization there. Before he can do so, he first must deliver the collection to Jerusalem, a visit fraught with difficulties. Anticipating a successful outcome in Jerusalem, he plans to visit Rome on his way to Spain for refreshment and to gain the support he needs for the ministry in Spain.

The Roman Christians meet in several house churches scattered throughout the city. The groups Paul knows of are well-instructed in the faith and form a part of the large number of the Christians in the city. Paul intends his letter to circulate among these groups. Though the make-up of different groups varied, the Roman Christians included people who were both Jewish and gentile by birth. The general percentages of each are impossible to reconstruct, though Paul's direct address to gentile Christians indicates that they are in the majority or at least exert considerable influence among the Christian groups. Between and/or within these groups, tensions exist between those who believe that followers of Christ should adhere to Jewish laws regarding clean and unclean foods as well as observance of special days (the "weak"), and those who do not (the "strong"). Paul indicates these divisions basically fall along Jew/gentile lines.

Finally, although at the time Paul writes he has never been to Rome, Paul and the Roman Christians are not total strangers. The letter itself displays Paul's knowledge of Christians in Rome and numerous details of their life and spiritual maturity. On the basis of the realities of travel and communication in the world in the first century C.E. plus the presence in Rome of Paul's close associates, many in Rome also know of Paul and his preaching.

Chapter Five

ROMANS AND PAUL'S OPPONENTS

In light of the conclusions reached in the preceding chapters about Paul, his Roman auditors, and the argument of Romans, how can one explain why Paul wrote this letter to these people at this time in his life? Recent proposals that understand Romans as Paul's defense against opponents offer a promising way forward.[1] This chapter synthesizes the evidence of controversies that surrounded Paul's ministry in the East. It then compares that evidence with the content of the first eleven chapters of Romans. Finally, the chapter examines passages in Romans that mention opponents. I conclude that Paul believed opposition to his teaching was known in Rome and that he feared actual opponents would soon arrive in the city. As a result, Paul wrote to the Roman Christians in order to defend his message.

---

[1]These proposals will thus be referred to as the "apologetic" thesis or proposal.

Paul's Controversies in the East

Four leading proponents[2] of this "apologetic" understanding of Romans are Philipp Vielhauer,[3] Douglas A.
Campbell,[4] Peter Stuhlmacher,[5] and Markku Kettunen.[6] All
agree that Paul fears criticisms identical to those launched
against him in the East will be propagated in Rome before he
can get there to defend himself personally. If such opposition
takes root, he could lose the support he hopes to obtain from
the Roman Christians (15:24) for his mission to Spain, and
hence the entire mission would be threatened. Although these
scholars disagree over whether Paul's opponents are already
in Rome (Stuhlmacher; Kettunen) or likely to arrive soon
(Campbell; Vielhauer is non-committal), all agree this scenario
makes sense of the content of Paul's argument in Romans,
Paul's circumstances as he writes, and what is known of the
Roman believers (thereby meeting most of the criteria for a
resolution to the Romans Debate outlined in chapter one).

This "apologetic" proposal makes excellent sense of
Paul's extended argument in chs. 1–11 since those chapters
deal with issues that had generated the controversies which
dogged Paul's ministry for years. A brief summary of those

---

[2]Numerous scholars understand Paul's defense against opponents
to be one purpose, among others, for the letter. These four, however, have
argued that this constitutes Paul's overarching purpose, rather than one
motive among many.

[3]*Geschichte der urchristlichen Literatur* (New York: Walter de Gruyter, 1975), 183–84.

[4]"Determining the Gospel through Rhetorical Analysis in Paul's
Letter to the Roman Christians," in *Gospel in Paul: Studies on Corinthians, Galatians and Romans for Richard N. Longenecker*, JSNTSup, vol.
108, eds. L. Ann Jervis and Peter Richardson (Sheffield: Sheffield
Academic Press, 1994), 315–336.

[5]"The Purpose of Romans," in *The Romans Debate*, rev. and expanded ed. (Peabody, Mass.: Hendrickson, 1991), 231–242.

[6]*Der Abfassungszweck des Römerbriefes*, Annales Academiae scientiarum Fennicai, dissertationes humanarum litterarum, bd. 18 (Helsinki:
Suomalainen Tiedeakatemia), 1979.

issues and a comparison of those matters with the content of Romans 1–11 will make this apparent.

Controversial Issues

Paul believed that with the death and resurrection of Jesus the Messiah, the eschatological age had dawned. The death knell had been sounded over the age introduced by Adam, though its powers continued for the time being. With the arrival of the new age, the gentiles were joining the Jews in united praise of God as part of the eschatological people of God (15:8–12).

Within this historical framework, Paul locates the Mosaic Law under the reign of Adam (5:20; 7:1–24; 8:3a). The Law and the traditions that emerged from it had been crucial factors shaping the identity of the people of God for centuries. Now a new epoch had begun in salvation-history bearing continuities with the old order, but undeniable changes as well. Disagreements over where one drew the lines of continuity and discontinuity between old and new generated the sharp conflicts reflected in Paul's letters.[7]

Contentious issues emerged primarily in practical matters related to the incorporation of the nations into the people of God. At the core of Paul's proclamation stood the message that gentiles were now welcome *as gentiles*, meaning they did not have to submit to the Mosaic Law either to enter the people of God or to be considered faithful followers of the resurrected Jesus afterwards. This was a radical redefinition of the people of God.[8] Most of the controversies that surface in

---

[7]James D. G. Dunn helpfully provides a list of issues agreed upon by both Paul and his opponents in Galatians. He then observes, "much of the controversy of which the letter was part was the result of different interpretations of these shared convictions" (*The Theology of Paul's Letter to the Galatians*, New Testament Theology [Cambridge: Cambridge University Press, 1993], 35).

[8]With regard to the controversies in Galatians, Dunn comments, "The issues are not (yet) Jewish versus Christian issues. They are about what it means to be a practicing Jew, what it means to be an heir of Abraham, what differences the coming of Messiah Jesus has made for Israel's self-understanding and for Jewish relations with Gentiles"

Paul's letters reflect tensions generated by this one issue. Among the problems are:

(1) disputes over identity of the true children of Abraham (Gal. 3:6–29);[9]
(2) controversies regarding circumcision (Gal. 2:3; 5:2–6; 6:12–15; Phil. 3:2–4), calendrical observances (Gal. 4:10); and food laws (Gal. 2:11–14);
(3) conflicts over justification by faith and by works of law (Gal. 2:16–5:12; 6:12–15);
(4) questions of proper behavior (Gal. 5:13–6:10);[10]
(5) disputes over the source of the Spirit (Gal. 3:1–5; 2 Cor. 3),[11]

("Echoes of Intra-Jewish Polemic in Paul's Letter to the Galatians," *JBL* 112 [1993], 476). Borrowing the metaphor Paul employs in Rom. 11:17–24, one may say the details of grafting the gentile branches onto the Jewish root of the olive tree proved difficult at several critical junctures. Cf. W. D. Davies, "Paul and the People of Israel," in *Jewish and Pauline Studies* (Philadelphia: Fortress Press, 1984), 124.

[9]The statements regarding children of Abraham in Gal. 3:6–7 and 3:29 serve as an *inclusio* around the intervening material, demonstrating that this is precisely the point in question as Paul counters his opponents' arguments. Richard N. Longenecker comments that Paul's opponents in Galalatians focused on "being rightly related to Abraham and the Abrahamic covenant, and so on being legitimately Abraham's sons and experiencing fully the blessings of God's covenant with Abraham (and, by extension, the people of Israel)" (*Galatians*, WBC, vol. 41 [Dallas: Word Books, 1990], xcvii).

[10]This issue is also linked to the question of the identity of the people of God. Wayne Meeks recognizes that behavioral patterns serve to define group identity by establishing lines of demarcation between those within and those without. Meeks therefore frames the question in a more sociological perspective. He asks, "Would the abolition of the symbolic boundaries between Jew and Gentile *within* the Christian groups mean also lowering the boundaries between the Christian sect and the world?" In other words, lowering behavioral boundaries between Christians and those outside ran the risk of encouraging lifestyles typical of those outside the community as appropriate for those within (*The First Urban Christians: The Social World of the Apostle Paul* [New Haven: Yale University Press, 1983], 97 [emph. original]). Barclay likewise observes that "the questions of membership and behaviour are bound up together" in both the objections to Paul's teaching and in his response (*Obeying the Truth: Paul's Ethics in Galatians* [Minneapolis: Fortress Press, 1991], 216).

[11]In Galatians, this issue is related to points 1–3. Regarding the role of the Spirit, on Galatians. see J. Louis Martyn, *Galatians*, AB, vol.

(6) questions over Paul's interpretation of these matters which led to questions about the authenticity of his apostleship (Gal. 1:1, 11; Phil. 3:4b–11; possibly 2 Cor. 10–13).[12]

In summary, the troubles between Paul and his opponents came down to disagreements over the implications of the eschatological saving actions of God in Christ for the people of God. With the gentiles joining the people of God, disputes arose over which aspects of Jewish Law and traditions these gentile believers should observe or not observe. Determining which practices believers were to follow carried significant implications for defining the true children of Abraham, the people of God.[13]

33A (New York: Doubleday, 1997), 123; on 2 Corinthians see Scott J. Hafemann, *Paul, Moses, and the History of Israel: The Letter / Spirit Contrast and the Argument in 2 Corinthians 3* (Peabody, Mass.: Hendrickson, 1996), 444–49.

[12]The problems in 2 Corinthians 10–13 stem from other apostles claiming that spiritual experience and certain hellenistic rhetorical practices were the true marks of an apostle. The bone of contention does not seem to emerge from issues related to the Mosaic Law. Still, Paul does claim the "false apostles" proclaim a "another Jesus" and a "different gospel" (11:4), indicating matters of content and not just style and credentials were in dispute. See also Scott J. Hafemann, *Paul, Moses, and the History of Israel*, 444–49 on disagreements over the Mosaic Law and apostleship in 2 Corinthians 3.

[13]The evidence from Acts, while secondary, shows remarkable continuity with that found in Galatians and Philippians. Luke describes "certain people from Judea" (τινες κατελθόντες ἀπὸ τῆς Ἰουδαίας) coming to Antioch and teaching that gentiles must be circumcised in order to be saved, resulting in heated arguments (στάσεως καὶ ζητήσεως) with Paul and Barnabas (15:1–2). When Paul travels to Jerusalem in ch. 21, James and "all the elders" tell him the Jews in Jerusalem have been told Paul teaches "all the Jews among the gentiles to abandon Moses, telling them not to circumcise their children nor to observe the Jewish customs" (21:21). In 21:27–28, "Jews from Asia" stir up the crowd in opposition to Paul by shouting (v. 28), "This man teaches everyone everywhere against the people, the Law, and the place."

The Argument of Romans 1–11

The parallels between the content of Romans 1–11 and controversies reflected in Paul's other letters have often been noted.[14] The following paragraphs summarize each section of Romans 1–11 (roughly chs. 1–4, 5–8, and 9–11) and compare its contents to the controversial issues identified in Paul's other letters.

Beginning in 1:14, Paul states his theme for the letter. The good news Paul preaches is for all people: Greeks and barbarians, wise and foolish (1:14), Jew and Greek (1:16). God's righteousness is revealed to everyone who believes (1:16). This theme, a gospel equally available to all, sounds the key note for the argument of the letter.

Romans 1–4. Paul establishes the case for this universal gospel in chs. 1–4. All alike have sinned (1:18; 3:9, 23), eliminating any distinctions between human beings at judgment (2:11). This subverts, in particular, any Jewish presumption of favor in future judgment on the basis of one's Jewishness (2:1–29). God's saving faithfulness has been made known "apart from the Law" (3:20–21) through the atoning sacrifice of Jesus Christ to "all who believe" (1:17; 3:22). The example of Abraham provides the scriptural foundation (cf. 1:2; 3:21) for Paul's claim about faith. Scripture says (Gen. 15:6; Rom. 4:3, 22) Abraham was pronounced righteous by faith, the

---

[14]For example, Hendrikus Boers argues that the rhetorical questions which shape Paul's argument in chs. 3–11 all concern, in one way or another, "the problem of the Jews and the Law" ("The Problem of Jews and Gentiles in the Macro-Structure of Romans," *SEÅ* 47 [1982], 187). As we will see, this issue is at the heart of Paul's troubles with opponents. Ulrich Wilckens labels Romans, "eine apologetisch-reflektierte Wiederholung des Galaterbriefes" ("Über Afgassungszweck und Aufbau des Römerbriefes," in *Rechtfertigung als Freiheit: Paulusstudien* [Neukirchener-Vluyn: Neukirchener Verlag, 1974], 167; "a reflective, apologetic repetition of Galatians"). A full list of references in support of this point would be a lengthy one. See, for example, Günther Bornkamm, "The Letter to the Romans as Paul's Last Will and Testament," in *The Romans Debate*, rev. and expanded ed., ed. Karl P. Donfried (Peabody, Mass.: Hendrickson, 1991), 21, 23–25.

point that serves as the clincher for Paul's argument. Paul's exposition of Gen. 15:6 in Rom. 4 reveals that the issue underlying the discussion concerns the true identity of the children of Abraham. For Paul, the children of Abraham are those who, like Abraham, believe in God (4:22–24).

The issues that come into play in these four chapters of Romans reflect key disputes in Paul's other letters. For example, justification by Law versus justification by faith (3:21–5:1), circumcision (2:25–29), and the identity of the true children of Abraham (4:1–25) all play important roles in Galatians or Philippians. Furthermore, objections that Paul anticipates in response to his argument in chs. 1–2 appear in 3:1–8 in the form of a series of rhetorical questions and brief answers. Paul's response to these objections serves as the subject matter of chs. 5–11. In other words, the content of the first two chapters and the response Paul anticipates to it, forms the basis for Paul's argument at least through the end of ch. 11. That opening content and the Jewish, or at least "law-observant," nature of the objections to which Paul responds throughout chs. 5–11 are revealing. They reflect opposition to Paul in the East which came from those who more strictly observed the Mosaic Law and traditions based on it. Paul directs his argument in the first eleven against just such objections.

Romans 5–8. In chs. 5–8, Paul takes up unresolved tensions (regarding the Law) and anticipated objections from chs. 1–4. The end of ch. 4 and the first eleven verses of ch. 5 serve as the transition to this new section. The comparisons and contrasts between Adam and Christ in 5:12–21 establish the salvation-historical framework within which questions about Paul's understanding of the lifestyle of the people of God and the role of the Mosaic Law can be answered.[15] The

---

[15]Questions about lifestyle were not concerns secondary to more important matter of "doctrine." David E. Aune has argued that, "Jewish scholars are virtually unanimous in the opinion that uniformity of observance (orthopraxy) is a more fundamental constituent of historical

rhetorical questions of 6:1, 15; 7:1, 7, 13 guide Paul's discourse. Paul responds to an objection, first voiced in 3:8, that
his Law-free gospel promotes sin (6:1, 13). In the process, he
must also take up related objections to his views of the Law
(7:1, 7, 13), for he links sin and Law under the reign of Adam
(3:20; 5:20; 6:14). Paul summarizes this segment of his argument in 8:1–17 before returning to themes first sounded in
5:1–11 to conclude this portion of Romans.

Once again, Paul defends himself on issues that reflect
disputes in the East. The proper lifestyle for believers was at
the center of the uproar in Galatians. Although Paul does not
respond to these particular concerns regarding the Law in his
other letters, one can easily understand how they would
emerge from his views expressed in Galatians 3–4.

Romans 9–11. Chapters 9–11 raise the most crucial objections dealt with in the letter. If the Jew has no advantage
over the gentile on the basis of the Mosaic covenant (3:1), and
if God has now extended mercy to the gentiles through Christ
but the Jewish people have refused the same offer of mercy,
has God been either unwilling or unable to keep God's
covenant with the Jewish people (3:1–5; 9:6a; 11:1)?[16] As in
chs. 5–8, Paul's discussion follows rhetorical questions (9:14,
19, 30; 11:1, 11) that express genuine objections to Paul's
preaching. Paul's response can be broken down into three
points: (1) In extending mercy to the gentiles, God is not
acting in a manner inconsistent with God's actions in the past
(9:6b–29); (2) The current place of much of Israel, outside the
new covenant (9:3), is its own fault (9:30–10:21); (3) God has
not rejected the Jewish people, nor have they stumbled
beyond recovery (11:1–32).

Judaism than is theological orthodoxy" ("Orthodoxy in First Century
Judaism? A Response to N. J. McEleney," *JSJ* 7 [1978], 2).

[16]Paul's discussion in these chapters responds to questions first
posed in 3:1 as a consequence of Paul's contention that sin has placed the
Jews on the same plane before God as the gentiles (in chs. 1–2).

Charges that Paul's gospel called into question the covenant faithfulness of God do not appear in his other letters. Yet, such charges flow from Paul's equation of Jew and gentile under sin (as 3:1–4 demonstrates). In the process of defending God's righteousness, Paul recounts God's way in salvation-history by quoting Scripture in greater measure than in any other portion of his surviving letters.[17]

Additional Issues. Three aspects of this reading Romans require further comment. First, Paul's discussion of "Jewish" issues in a letter to what is apparently a largely gentile audience has often puzzled interpreters of Romans.[18] In chapter four, I argued that "Jewish" issues could also be of concern to gentiles. Still, the fact that issues of special interest to Jewish believers stand at the heart of these chapters cannot be overlooked.

Jacob Jervell argues that such content indicates Paul was "absorbed by what he is going to say in Jerusalem" where he would have to defend his gospel before Jewish and Jewish Christian critics (15:31).[19] Jervell was correct to realize that Paul would have to debate these issues in Jerusalem,[20] but he does not provide an adequate explanation for why Paul wrote about them to Rome.[21] In my judgment, the most sensible

---

[17]D. Moody Smith finds half of the OT quotations in the *Hauptbriefe* are in Romans, and half of those in Romans are in chs. 9–11. See "The Pauline Literature," in *It is Written: Scripture Citing Scripture. Essays in Honour of Barnabas Lindars*, eds. D. A. Carson and H. G. M. Williamson (Cambridge: Cambridge University Press, 1988), 274–75.

[18]See, for example, Dieter Zeller, *Juden und Heiden in der Mission des Paulus: Studien zum Römerbrief*, 2d aufl. (Stuttgart: Verlag Katholisches Bibelwerk, 1976), 38–39; and Kettunen, *Abfassungszweck*, 22. The "Jewish" issues that permeate the letter are listed on p. 11, n. 25 above.

[19]"The Letter to Jerusalem," in *The Romans Debate*, 60.

[20]Ibid., 61.

[21]Jervell suggests two reasons why Paul wrote this letter to the Roman Christians (his third reason [ibid., 64] is merely a combination of the first two). He claims (1) that Paul needed to explain himself thoroughly if the Roman Christians were to intercede for him (ibid., 62); and (2) that "this Roman congregation [sic] has taken on a central position on behalf of the entire church" (ibid., 63). Jervell fails, however, to provide

explanation[22] is that Paul needed to defend himself in Rome with regard to these matters but could not go there at the time to do it personally. The letter does not indicate that Paul believed opponents of his message were active in Rome at the time he wrote, though 3:8 shows that he did think criticisms of his teaching were known. Paul must have expected that such opposition would arrive soon (16:17–20a), before he could get there himself and answer his critics in person.[23]

Second, the reading offered above understands the rhetorical questions that give structure to much of chs. 3–11 as real questions that Paul felt he had to counter in Rome. These questions and their answers are in the form of diatribe, a dialogical method of instruction employing an interlocutor who voices objections and false conclusions. These allow the speaker to clarify his or her point and avoid possible mis-

---

adequate support for either of these arguments. In light of the parallels between Romans 1–11 and Paul's earlier controversies, E. P. Sanders believes "that the controversies in mind when Paul wrote Romans were those *behind* him, not *before* him in Rome" (*Paul and Palestinian Judaism* [Philadelphia: Fortress Press, 1977], 487; emph. original). Yet, one must ask why Paul should write about his past issues to Rome. Paul chose to write about particular issues to Christians in Rome. The search for his purpose in the letter must explain the connection between those two facts. Neither Jervell nor Sanders does so.

[22]"The view that Romans was written to pre-empt militant Jewish Christian opponents supplies just this motivation (while, as far as I can see, no other explanation really does)" (Campbell, "Determining the Gospel," 323).

[23]Daniel Fraikin writes of Rom. 1:18–4:25, "We are faced, then, with the interesting fact that Paul, in a discourse whose goal is to strengthen the Gentiles in the gospel, provides them with the arguments by which he would make his understanding of the gospel and its consequences credible to Jews" ("The Rhetorical Function of the Jews in Romans," in *Anti-Judaism in Early Christianity*, vol. 1, *Paul and the Gospels*, eds. Peter Richardson with David Granskou, Studies in Christianity and Judaism, no. 2 [Waterloo, Ontario: Wilfrid Laurier University Press, 1986], 98). Fraikin later adds, "Paul presents to the Gentiles the kind of argument he would have with another Jew when arguing for a gospel of justification by faith that would allow for the entry of the Gentiles" (ibid., 103). This is precisely the point that only the presence, or anticipated presence, of Pauline opponents in Rome can explain.

understandings.[24] Some scholars, however, argue that since the diatribe was a pedagogical device used in philosophical schools, Paul employs this form here in a similar manner in order to create a purely hypothetical situation for the purpose of educating his audience on his views.[25] It would, therefore, be a mistake to read the diatribal style in these passages as a polemical argument against genuine objections.

Responding to Stanley K. Stowers, one of the main proponents of this interpretation, Douglas A. Campbell[26] objects on four points. First, Campbell claims Stowers overlooks the differences between the letters of Paul and the formal, literary publications of Philo, Plutarch, Musonius Rufus, and Epictetus that Stowers uses to form his understanding of the diatribe. Campbell asks, "How could actual opponents emerge from this type of literature, which does not address practical situations as Paul's letters do . . . ?" ("Determining," 326). The

---

[24]See the introductory essays of Stanley K. Stowers, *ABD*, 2:190–93; D. F. Watson, *DPL*, 213–14.

[25]William S. Campbell states that rhetorical questions are intended for "someone whom Paul wishes to educate and strengthen in their faith" ("Paul's Strategy in Writing Romans: His Understanding and Use of Israel's Role in Eschatological Salvation," in *Paul's Gospel in an Intercultural Context: Jew and Gentile in the Letter to the Romans*, Studies in the Intercultural History of Christianity, vol. 69 (New York: Peter Lang, 1991), 152; cf. also 137–38. The origins of this interpretation go back largely to Rudolf Bultmann's dissertation, published as *Der Stil der paulinischen Predigt und die kynisch-stoische Diatribe*, FRLANT, bd. 13 (Göttingen: Vandenhoeck & Ruprecht, 1910). Though differing from Bultmann in several respects, this view has been furthered by Robert J. Karris ("Romans 14:1–15:13 and the Occasion of Romans," in *The Romans Debate*, 65–84) and several writings by Stanley K. Stowers. For Stowers' views, see (in addition to the article cited in n. 24) *The Diatribe and Paul's Letter to the Romans*, SBLDS, vol. 57 (Chico, Calif.: Scholars Press, 1981); "Paul's Dialogue with a Fellow Jew in Romans 3.1–9," *CBQ* 46 (1984): 707–22; "The Diatribe," in *Greco-Roman Literature and the New Testament*, ed. David E. Aune, SBLSBS, vol. 21, (Atlanta: Scholars Press, 1988), 71–83, esp. 81–82; *A Rereading of Romans: Justice, Jews, and Gentiles* (New Haven: Yale University Press, 1994).

[26]"Determining the Gospel," 325–27; hereafter cited in the text as "Determining." Campbell is also responding to Thomas Schmeller, *Paulus und die 'Diatribe'* (Münster: Aschendorff, 1987).

textual features shared by Paul and these philosophers do not mean the philosophical texts can determine the function of letters ("Determining," 326).[27] Second, Campbell examines other texts in Paul with diatribal features and concludes each responds to issues that are "acutely real" for Paul (Gal. 2:17–18; Rom. 11:13a; Rom. 3:8). In each case, Paul has real objectors and their protests in mind ("Determining," 326–27). Third, Campbell objects to Stowers' contention that "diatribes were discourses scripted entirely by teachers, over which they had complete control" ("Determining," 327). Instead of a quiet, orderly, teacher-directed address to pupils, Campbell claims the teacher-student relationship could also involve genuine give-and-take debate. Finally, Stowers' approach provides no reason for Paul to write Romans. Why, on the eve of his departure for Jerusalem, does Paul pause to write to a group of Christians, many of whom he does not know personally, in the style of a philosopher admonishing his disciples? ("Determining," 327).

Stowers' thesis is inadequate. Paul borrows common rhetorical conventions of his day to address real circumstances in Rome. The objections reflected in the questions are not hypothetical. They reflect the inflammatory issues known from Paul's other letters. Campbell concludes that the "main justification for this view of Romans is that no other explanation really fits the basic parameters of the situation: Paul must discuss *Jewish* issues extensively with the *Gentile* Christians at Rome" ("Determining," 323; emph. original).

A third aspect of the interpretation of the rhetorical questions offered in this dissertation claims that they express genuine Jewish objections to his Law-free gospel for the gentiles. This runs counter to the position of those who would

---

[27]A similar objection has been raised by Karl P. Donfried in response to Bultmann and Karris. Donfried concludes, "it has not been demonstrated that general theological discussions influenced by the rhetorical patterns of the Greco-Roman world could not be addressed to genuine and actual historical situations." See "False Presuppositions in the Study of Romans," in *The Romans Debate*, 112–19 (quotation is from 119).

read Paul's argument in the letter as directed primarily against gentile-Christian arrogance (culminating in the warning of 11:17–24).[28]

This latter interpretation is based on two mistaken assumptions. First, it assumes that the audience is largely gentile-Christian and, therefore, the criticisms mounted against presumption (in ch. 2, for example) must be directed to gentile-Christians.[29] Paul's argument, though, is not with gentile Christians in Rome, but with opponents to his gospel. Objections to his preaching stem from people more observant of the Law than Paul. In most cases, those people would be Jews. Second, this interpretation also assumes Paul must direct his criticisms against either Jewish or gentile presumption. In fact, Paul seeks to puncture both Jewish and gentile arrogance.[30] His claim in 1:18–3:20 is that all alike are united under sin (3:9). Paul's concluding statement in 15:7–12 highlights the same point. Presumption of superiority from any corner within the eschatological people of God runs directly counter to God's purpose (2:11; 3:22).[31] To claim that the letter is directed against only gentile superiority over Jews is to misread one of the central thrusts of Paul's argument.

---

[28]"Paul wrote Romans to oppose this gentile-Christian 'boasting' over Israel" (Neil Elliott, "Romans 13:1–7 in the Context of Imperial Propaganda," in *Paul and Empire: Religion and Power in Roman Imperial Society*, ed. Richard A. Horsley [Harrisburg, Penn.: Trinity Press International, 1997], 190). See also idem, *The Rhetoric of Romans: Argumentative Constraint and Strategy and Paul's Dialogue with Judaism*, JSNTSup, vol. 45 (Sheffield: JSOT Press, 1990), 270; William S. Campbell, "Romans III as a Key to the Structure and Thought of the Letter," in *Paul's Gospel*, 31–33; Mark D. Nanos, *The Mystery of Romans: The Jewish Context of Paul's Letter* (Minneapolis: Fortress Press, 1996), 10.

[29]This also stems from a misreading of 2:1–16 as an argument directed against gentile presumption only. In this context, Paul's argument can apply to both Jewish and gentile attitudes.

[30]See, for example, William S. Campbell, "Paul's Strategy in Writing Romans," 140.

[31]See chapter six in this dissertation on Romans 12–15.

Opponents in Romans

Although scholars have found allusions to opponents in Romans in numerous places in the letter,[32] this section will deal only with those passages that bear more direct evidence of Pauline opponents known to the Roman Christians. These passages include 3:8, 16:17–20a, and 15:31.

Romans 3:8

In 3:8, Paul states, "And why not say (as some people slander us by saying that we say), 'Let us do evil so that good may come'?" (NRSV). This remark comes at the end of a series of questions beginning in 3:1 and laid out as a diatribe. The precise logical connections between these questions as they progress remains debated.[33] What is not obscure is that Paul is aware of, and believes his Roman hearers also likely know of, critics who claim Paul's teaching opens the door to sin.[34]

---

[32]For example, Paul's claim that he is "not ashamed of the gospel" in 1:16 and the rhetorical questions in 8:31–35 regarding charges against the elect have both been understood as reflections of opponents known to Paul and the Roman Christians. On Rom. 1:16, see Bent Noack, "Current and Backwater in Romans," *ST* 19 (1965), 162. Ernst Käsemann sees Paul's defensiveness regarding suspicions of himself and his preaching in the tone of 1:8–15 (*Commentary on Romans*, trans. and ed. Geoffrey W. Bromiley [Grand Rapids: William B. Eerdmans, 1980], 18–19). On Rom. 8:31–39, see Fraikin. "Rhetorical Function of the Jews," 100. These are best classified as possible allusions to opponents that are extremely difficult to confirm due to the nature of the evidence.

[33]Matthew Black describes Paul's argument in 3:5–8 as "a little tortuous" (*Romans*, 2d ed., NCBC [Grand Rapids: William B. Eerdmans, 1989], 54. In addition to the critical commentaries, see David R. Hall, "Romans 3.1–8 Reconsidered," *NTS* 29 (1983), 183–197; Stowers, "Paul's Dialogue with a Fellow Jew," 707–22; and Charles H. Cosgrove, "What If Some Have Not Believed? The Occasion and Thrust of Romans 3.1–8," *ZNW* 78 (1987), 90–105; Paul J. Achtemeier, "Romans 3:1–8: Structure and Argument," in *Christ and His Communities: Essays in Honor of Reginald H. Fuller*, eds. Arland J. Hultgren and Barbara Hall (Cincinnati: Forward Movement Publications, 1990) 77–87.

[34]See also Douglas Moo, *The Epistle to the Romans*, NICNT (Grand Rapids: William B. Eerdmans, 1996), 195, and A. J. M. Wedderburn, *The Reasons for Romans* (Minneapolis: Fortress Press, 1991), 115.

This fact is significant for understanding Paul's argument in Romans. It is commonly recognized that Paul structures much of his discourse in chs. 1–11 around a series of rhetorical questions and answers. As noted, Rom. 3:8 provides unmistakable evidence that the questions reflect genuine objections to Paul's argument.[35] This becomes even more obvious when one recalls that Paul faced opposition elsewhere on the very issue mentioned in 3:8: the charge of promoting sin.[36]

Paul mentions the accusation raised by his opponents in 3:8, but does not respond to it at that point other than to pronounce judgment on the "some" (τινες)[37] who would accuse him. He returns to the issue later in 5:12, however, where he begins a series of contrasts and comparisons between Adam and Christ that establish the framework for his answer. The answer itself begins with the rhetorical question of 6:1 (and 6:15).[38] The discussion of the problem of sin, the implications

---

[35]Wedderburn (*Reasons,* 115) believes the objection in 3:8 "does not flow very obviously or naturally from the argument of 3.1–6." He adduces this as further evidence that this represented a real rather than fictitious charge leveled against Paul. In other words, the argument need not have arrived at this point unless Paul had concrete reasons to raise this particular objection.

[36]"Paul's gospel, we know, was charged with promoting moral indifferentism, if not with actively encouraging sin, and the form of his argument in this letter implies his awareness that this charge was not unknown in Rome" (F. F. Bruce, "The Romans Debate—Continued," in *The Romans Debate,* 183. John M. G. Barclay concludes that, "*a major ingredient in the Galatian dispute is the question of how the members of God's people should live*" (*Obeying the Truth,* 216; emph. original).

[37]Hall notes that "the use of the word τινες to refer to his opponents is characteristic of Paul's epistles (1 Cor. 15.12, 34; Gal. 1.7; 2:12)" ("Romans 3.1–8," 184). See also Käsemann, *Romans,* 417.

[38]Although the issues raised in 3:8, 6:1 and 6:15 are not identical (how one construes the basis for the objection in 3:8 depends on one how interprets the series of questions beginning in 3:1), the objection standing behind each question is the same—Paul's teaching promotes sin. Brendan Byrne considers the differing questions reformulations of the same objection (*Romans,* SacPag, vol. 6 [Collegeville, Minn.: Liturgical Press, 1996], 110). On grammatical grounds, David Hellholm argues the questions of 3:8 and 6:1 are one and the same ("Enthymemic Argumentation

of Paul's answer for the Law, and the response to sin by those "under grace" continues through 8:17. In fact, the issue raised in 3:8 occupies nearly all or part of four chapters later in Paul's argument. Judging by the tone (in 3:8) and length of his response, it is an objection he takes seriously.[39]

Romans 16:17–20a

This passage consists of a strongly worded call to watch out for people who cause dissension and scandals, and to keep away from them (v. 17). Paul gives three reasons for his warning: (1) he describes the nature and methods of such people (v. 18); (2) he commends his hearers' reputation for obedience and states his concern for their continued sensitivity to good and evil (v. 19); and (3) he proclaims God's future triumph over Satan, who stands behind the activity of these problematic people (v. 20).[40]

Paul does not appear to believe these people are active in Rome at the time he writes,[41] but the tone of the passage reveals he believes the threat is genuine. He apparently anticipates the presence of such people in Rome in the near future.[42] The use of the definite article τοὺς (ποιοῦντας) may

---

in Paul: The Case of Romans 6," in *Paul in His Hellenistic Context*, ed. Troels Engberg-Pedersen (Minneapolis: Fortress Press, 1995), 149.

[39]See also Peter Stuhlmacher, *Paul's Letter to the Romans: A Commentary*, trans. Scott J. Hafemann (Louisville: Westminster/John Knox Press, 1994), 53, on this point.

[40]On this final point, see Ulrich B. Müller, *Prophetie und Predigt im Neuen Testament: Formgeschichtliche Untersuchungen zur urchristlichen Prophetie*, Studien zum Neuen Testament, bd. 10 (Gütersloh: Gerd Mohn, 1975), 187.

[41]Contra Karl P. Donfried, "A Short Note on Romans 16," in *The Romans Debate*, 51–52. Donfried believes this passage refers to the controversy between the "strong" and the "weak" in 14:1–15:6. Nanos interprets these verses similarly (*Mystery of Romans*, 216, 333).

[42]So also John Murray, *The Epistle to the Romans*, NICNT (Grand Rapids: William B. Eerdmans, 1968), 2:235; Moo, *Romans*, 929; Thomas R. Schreiner, *Romans*, Baker Exegetical Commentary on the New Testament (Grand Rapids: Baker, 1998), 801; Hans Wilhelm Schmidt, *Der Brief des Paulus an die Römer*, THKNT, bd. 6 (Berlin: Evangelische Verlagsanstalt, 1962), 257; Käsemann, *Romans*, 418 (though Käsemann

indicate that Paul believes the Roman listeners know to whom he is referring.[43]

Several issues in this passage require separate treatment. These include its authenticity, the effects of the opponents, the place of this passage within the argument of the letter, and parallels between the description of the opponents in this passage and descriptions of opponents in other letters.

Authenticity. The authenticity of this passage has been called into question on the basis of its vocabulary[44] and especially its harsh tone. Its sharply expressed criticisms seem out of place within the friendly context of greetings to Roman Christians in 16:3–16, 21–23 (and some would say with the tenor of the letter as a whole). Ernst Käsemann summarizes as follows.

> The apostle is speaking here with an authority which he does sometimes indicate in relation to the Romans but which for the

---

later denies the authenticity of the passage); Peter Stuhlmacher, "Purpose of Romans" in *The Romans Debate*, 239; Hans-Werner Bartsch, "The Historical Situation of Romans," *Encounter* 33 (1972), 330. Raymond E. Brown, (*An Introduction to the New Testament* [New York: Doubleday, 1997], 563, n. 9) believes Paul thought them as "likely" to appear. Franz J. Leenhardt thinks they are present in Rome, but have not yet been allowed to influence the Christians there (*The Epistle to the Romans: A Commentary* [London: Lutterworth Press, 1961], 385).

[43]So Joseph A. Fitzmyer, *Romans*, AB, vol. 33 (New York: Doubleday, 1993), 745; Schmidt, *Romans*, 257; Moo, *Romans*, 930; Ulrich Wilckens, *Der Brief an die Römer* (Röm 12–16), 2d aufl., EKKNT, bd. 6.3 (Neukirchener-Vluyn: Neukirchener Verlag, 1989), 140. Contra James D. G. Dunn, *Romans 9–16*, WBC, vol. 38B (Milton Keynes, England: Word, 1991), 904. James Denney cites the presence of the definite article with (the) "dissensions" and (the) "scandals" as evidence that the Romans knew the identity of the opponents (*St. Paul's Epistle to the Romans*, Expositor's Greek Testament, vol. 2 [Grand Rapids: William B. Eerdmans, 1979; reprint], 722).

[44]Robert Jewett counts "six *hapax legomena* and at least eight expressions used in a non-Pauline way" ("Ecumenical Theology for the Sake of Mission: Romans 1:1–17 + 15:14–16:24," in *Pauline Theology*, vol. 3, *Romans* [Minneapolis: Fortress Press, 1995], 106).

most part he carefully avoids. He does it with a kind of fury which does not appear elsewhere in the epistle and in answer to opponents who cannot be identified from the letter. The situation and the reaction are completely different, and the interest of 15:14–32 is lost from view.[45]

These criticisms are not as convincing as they initially appear.[46] First, Paul finishes his greetings at v. 16. Those that follow beginning at v. 21 are not Paul's but Tertius'. The greetings that begin in 16:3, therefore, do not run continuously through v. 23, but break at the precise point where the warning of vv. 17–20a now stands. In other words, vv. 17–20a lies at a natural break in the flow of the closing section of the letter.[47] Furthermore, warnings that appear out of context are not unknown in Paul's letter closings (1 Cor. 16:22). So the presence of such a warning in Romans cannot be viewed as un-Pauline. Third, once one accepts ch. 16 as part of the original text of Romans, no textual evidence exists for omitting vv. 17–20a from the letter. Finally, as will become clear below, this passage fits well within the context of Paul's argument in the letter. Viewed in such a setting, the apparent abruptness of these verses at the end of Paul's greetings becomes less problematic.[48]

---

[45]*Romans*, 419. For a thorough critique which decides against authenticity, see Wolf-Henning Ollrog, "Die Abfassungsverhältnisse von Röm 16," in *Kirche: Festschrift für Günther Bornkamm zum 75. Geburtstag*, hrsg. Dieter Lührmann und Georg Strecker (Tübingen: J. C. B. Mohr [Paul Siebeck], 1980), 229–34.

[46]For detailed arguments in favor of authenticity, see Wilckens, *Römer*, 3:139–40; C. E. B. Cranfield, *The Epistle to the Romans*, vol. 2, ICC (Edinburgh: T & T Clark, 1979), 797–98; Kettunen, *Abfassungszweck*, 62–64.

[47]Although this can only be conjecture, it is likely that Paul added the warning in his own hand before returning the stylus to Tertius (cf. 1 Cor. 16:21; Gal. 6:11).

[48]Douglas Moo's judgment is sound. "But there is no textual basis for omitting the verses; and the problems are not nearly as great as some have made them" (*Romans*, 928).

Effects of the Opponents. In keeping with his usual practice, Paul does not identify these opponents by name. Instead, his concern lies with their potential effect on his auditors. Such people (οἱ τοιοῦτοι) provoke "dissensions" (τὰς διχοστασίας) and create "scandals" (τὰ σκάνδαλα) in opposition to the teaching they have learned. Both aspects of this impact are important.

Paul uses διχοστασία elsewhere in Gal. 5:20. In that context it stands between ἐριθεία ("selfish ambition;" *BAG(D)*, 309) and αἵρεσις ("dissension, a faction;" *BAG(D)*, 24) in Paul's list of the works of the flesh. It is apparent that διχοστασία is one of a host of terms Paul uses for factors that disrupt harmony in the community.[49] When one recalls the primary thrust of the "obedience of faith" Paul seeks to foster in Rome is that the community members "receive one another" (15:7), and that such mutual reception is the embodiment of the divine eschatological purposes for the people of God, the reason for Paul's severe tone becomes apparent.[50] These people stand opposed to the purpose of God which Paul has been commissioned to promote. Paul can therefore equate these people with Satan (v. 20) because they oppose God's good will (12:2) for Paul's hearers.[51]

These people also create σκάνδαλα ("scandals") against the teaching which the Romans have learned. Paul uses this term in two ways. The first refers to an "offense" involving the message about Jesus that cannot be avoided (Rom. 9:33; 11:9;

---

[49]Johannes P. Louw and Eugene A. Nida, eds. (*Greek-English Lexicon of the New Testament Based on Semantic Domains*, vol. 1, *Introduction & Domains* [New York: United Bible Societies, 1988]) classify διχοστασία as a synonym of σχίσμα, defining both as "division, discord" (39.13). They locate ἐριθεία within the same general semantic domain (39, "Hostility, Strife"). Αἵρεσις is placed within a separate domain (63 [specifically 63.27], "Whole, Unite, Part, Divide"), though they define the term as "a division of people into different and opposing sets" (63.27).

[50]See also Paul S. Minear, *The Obedience of Faith: The Purposes of Paul in the Epistle to the Romans*, SBT, 2d series, vol. 19 (London: SCM, 1971), 29.

[51]Denney, *Romans*, 722; Murray, *Romans*, 2:237.

1 Cor. 1:23; Gal. 5:11). The second concerns scandals that must be avoided at all costs (Rom. 14:13; 1 Cor. 8:13). In this second sense, both Rom. 14 and 1 Cor. 8 speak of scandals involving different convictions and practices regarding what is eaten, in other words, regarding the continued application of the Mosaic Law. In both situations, Paul commands his hearers not to offend a fellow member of God's people,[52] since to do so would disrupt the eschatological purposes of God. In summary, Paul warns the Roman Christians against people who cause divisions in the community of God's people.

One additional observation makes the connection between the σκάνδαλα in 16:17–20a and threats to unity among the Roman Christians even clearer. In v. 17, Paul warns that these people create scandals against the teaching (διδαχὴν) which the Romans have learned. This recalls Paul's statement in 6:17 where he gives thanks to God that his hearers obeyed from the heart (ὑπηκούσατε ἐκ καρδίας) the type of teaching (τύπον διδαχῆς) they had received.[53] This "teaching" is often interpreted as doctrine, as if it were purely conceptual theology that were at issue.[54] The problematic people of 16:17–20a are therefore typically labeled "teachers."[55] The διδαχή to which Paul refers in 6:17, however, concerns the Roman Christians' obedience (chapter three

---

[52]Gustav Stählin, "σκάνδαλον, σκανδαλίζω," *TDNT*, 7:352–56.

[53]Additional connections can be found between 16:17–20a and ch. 6. In both passages Paul commends the Roman Christians' obedience (6:17; 16:19). Paul also charges that these people do not serve our Lord Christ (τῷ κυρίῳ ἡμῶν Χριστῷ οὐ δουλεύουσιν; 16:18), a clear echo of the δουλεύω language of ch. 6.

[54]For catalog of interpretive problems and solutions regarding the phrase "τύπον διδαχῆς" in 6:17, see Robert A. J. Gagnon, "Heart of Wax and a Teaching that Stamps: ΤΥΠΟΣ ΔΙΔΑΧΗΣ (Rom 6:17b) Once More," *JBL* 112 (1993): 667–87.

[55]Among the many making this false identification, Gustav Stählin may be singled out. In his article in *TDNT* (7:356), he distinguishes the two senses of σκάνδαλον outlined above. He then identifies a third meaning of σκάνδαλον as heresy and gives Romans 16:17 as the sole example to justify his definition. Once one recognizes the nature of the "teaching" in 6:17, however, the meaning of the term in 16:17 fits precisely within σκάνδαλον as something to be avoided (meaning two above).

above). In Romans, that obedience is primarily rendered when Jews and gentiles, strong and weak, receive one another in the same manner Jesus Christ received them (15:7; cf. chapter three). When they do so, they will have embodied the eschatological will of God (12:2) to unite all peoples in the praise of God (15:8–12). The "teaching" they are to obey involves "doctrine,"[56] but that doctrine cannot be separated from the life that goes hand in hand with it. The context of 6:17 makes this clear.

Romans 16:17–20a within the Argument of the Letter. In addition to the connection with 6:17 cited above, two additional factors link Paul's argument earlier in the letter with 16:17–20a. These connections provide important contextual information within which this passage must be read.

Paul's claim in 16:18 that those who create scandals against this teaching do not serve (οὐ δουλεύουσιν) "our Lord Christ" also echoes his argument in ch. 6.[57] As outlined in chapter three above, in Rom. 5:12–21 Paul posits two reigns, one introduced by Adam and characterized by sin and death, while the other, introduced by Christ, is characterized by righteousness and life. In Romans 6, Paul explains that one must "offer" oneself as a slave (δοῦλος) to one realm or the other in order obey it. One then serves (δουλεύω) that master (6:16–22). In opposing the eschatological purposes of God, the people described in 16:17–20a do not serve the Lord Christ. Instead, they serve their own "belly" (16:18), a term linked to Paul's notion of "flesh."[58] They live under the reign introduced by Adam.

---

[56]One thinks of the passages in Romans where Paul speaks of important matters regarding the work of Christ in such succinct fashion, that Paul must have assumed his hearers knew and could fill in the details (1:3–4; 3:24–26).

[57]Serving "their belly" in v. 18 clearly stands in opposition to serving Christ. So, correctly, Wilckens, *Römer*, 3:142.

[58]"'Bauch', 'Fleisch' und 'Irdisches' gehören eng zusammen (Phil 3,19)." Otto Michel, *Der Brief an die Römer*, 10th aufl., KEK (Göttingen: Vandenhoeck & Ruprecht, 1955), 347 ('Belly,' 'flesh,' and 'earthly' belong

Paul also describes these people as using "smooth talk and flattery" (16:18; NRSV). As a result, the Roman believers must be "wise regarding what is good and innocent regarding what is evil" (16:19). Paul concludes by assuring his hearers that "God will soon crush Satan under our feet" (16:20a).[59] All three statements resound with echoes of the Garden of Eden narrative in Genesis. For example, when the Roman Christians live together in harmony Satan would soon be crushed under their feet in "an enactment of the redemption promised in Gen. 3.15."[60] As chapter three suggested above, that same narrative also informs Paul's description of human sin in Rom. 1:18–32; 5:12–6:23; 12:1–2; and 15:7–13.

In summary, these people live under the Adamic realm of sin and death. Since they oppose the eschatological purpose of God to create a unified people drawn from all nations, they must be watched carefully and must be avoided so that, by means of their wily ways, they do not lead the Roman Christians from the obedience for which they are known.

Parallels With Opponents Described Elsewhere in Paul. Paul's warning against troublemakers not only echoes themes from elsewhere in Romans, it also sounds much like his description of his opponents in other letters. These parallels are widely noted by commentators. An examination of two passages will suffice: Phil. 3 and 2 Cor. 11:13–15.

In Phil. 3:19, Paul speaks of enemies of the cross "whose end is destruction, whose god is their belly." In this context in Philippians, Paul also calls on his hearers to become imitators of him and "pay careful attention" (the same word, σκοπέω, is used negatively in Rom. 16:17) to those who walk "according to the example [τύπος; cf. Rom. 6:17] you have in us" (3:17; NRSV). Here again, the problem is not purely "doctrinal."

---

closely together). See also Moo, *Romans*, 931; Käsemann, *Romans*, 417; Heinrich Schlier, *Der Römerbrief*, HTKNT, bd. 6 (Freiburg: Herder, 1977), 448; James R. Edwards, *Romans*, New International Bible Commentary, vol. 6 (Peabody, Mass.: Hendrickson, 1992), 359.

[59]Minear, *Obedience of Faith*, 29

[60]See especially, Nanos, *Mystery of Romans*, 234.

Instead, Paul is concerned with a manner of life (how one "walks"). This does not mean theology is not a part of their problem. It does mean to assert that Paul is concerned with how any theology plays out in lifestyle. Theology and life cannot be separated.

In 2 Cor. 11:13–15 Paul describes his critics as false apostles, deceitful workers who disguise themselves as apostles of Christ just as Satan disguises himself as an angel of light. Ernst Käsemann remarks, "2 Cor 11:13ff. unmasks Jewish-Christian agitators as servants of Satan who use the deceitful methods of their master to lead the community astray."[61] As in Rom. 16:17–20a, these troublemakers are associated with Satan and their methods described as fostering deception.[62]

These parallels between Paul's warning to his Roman auditors in 16:17–20a and characterizations of his opponents in other letters are important for understanding the identity of the people about whom Paul warns the Romans. A more complete appraisal of that identity must await further analysis of the letter. For now it is sufficient to call attention to these connections.

Romans 15:31

In 15:30–32, Paul earnestly (see below) implores the Roman Christians to struggle together (συναγωνίσασθαι) with him in prayer for concerns that he expresses using two ἵνα

---

[61]*Romans*, 417.

[62]In general, it would not be inaccurate to describe the manifold problems Paul experienced with the Corinthian Christians as examples of διχοστασίαι and σκάνδαλα (cf. Adolf Schlatter, *Romans: The Righteousness of God*, trans. Siegrfried S. Schatzmann [Peabody, Mass.: Hendrickson, 1995], 275). Because of internal squabbles (1 Cor.) as well as the influence of problematic outsiders (2 Cor.), the unity of the Jesus community there became disrupted. For example, in 1 Cor. 8:13 Paul cautions against allowing food to cause a brother to stumble. Also, p[46] (and numerous miniscules and church fathers) reads ἔρις καὶ διχοστασίαι at 1 Cor. 3:3: "For you are fleshly. For where there are envy and strife <u>and dissensions</u>, are you not fleshly, walking according to human standards?"

clauses, one beginning in v. 31 and the other in v. 32. The first clause contains two requests: (1) that Paul may be rescued (ῥυσθῶ) from the unbelievers (ἀπὸ τῶν ἀπειθούντων) in Judea, and (2) that the collection may be well-received by the saints there. The second request, in v. 32, expresses the desired result of the first, namely that if the first turns out well Paul may then joyfully come to Rome by the will of God and be refreshed (συναναπαύσωμαι) there by his hearers.

Paul wants to ensure these requests are taken seriously in Rome. He emphasizes them by use of the verb παρακαλῶ ("I appeal"; cf. 12:1; 16:17)[63] and by his qualifying statement that it be made "through our Lord Jesus Christ and through the love of the Spirit" (v. 30). Furthermore, Paul's use of the verb ῥυσθῶ in this context indicates he believes his life is actually in danger.[64]

These verses make no mention of Pauline opponents in Rome, but they do make reference to anti-Pauline forces in Jerusalem. Since Jews in Rome and Jerusalem maintained frequent communication, it is reasonable to expect that the criticisms of Paul's opponents in Jerusalem would also be known in the Jewish communities in Rome. It is therefore worthwhile to ascertain what can be known regarding these "unbelievers" in Jerusalem.

Paul describes anyone who does not follow his understanding of the gospel as an "unbeliever."[65] Given that his description in 15:31 refers to the "unbelievers in Judea," it

---

[63]The argument by C. J. Bjerkelund (*Parakalô: Form, Funktion und Sinn der parakalô-Sätze in den paulinischen Briefen*, Bibliotheca theologica norvegica, bd. 1 [Oslo: Universitetsforlaget, 1967]) that the statements introduced by this word provide the key for understanding Paul's purpose in Romans overstates the significance of these phrases and overlooks other signal evidence. A. J. M. Wedderburn's otherwise fine monograph (*Reasons for Romans*) follows Bjerkelund on this point.

[64]Minear, *The Obedience of Faith*, 4; Käsemann, *Romans*, 406; James D. G. Dunn, *Romans 9–16*, 878 (citing Minear); Schreiner, *Romans*, 782.

[65]Romans 2:8; 10:21; 11:30–32. The verb ἀπειθέω and noun ἀπείθεια occur only in Romans in the undisputed Pauline letters.

is virtually certain that Paul speaks of people from a Jewish background who have rejected his message.

Additional information can be gleaned about Paul's Jerusalem opponents from Galatians. Two or three groups related to Jerusalem show up in Gal. 2:1–14. First, in 2:4 Paul speaks of "false believers" (NRSV; ψευδαδέλφους) who were secretly brought in to spy on the "freedom we have in Christ Jesus." In the context in Galatians, this means freedom from having to submit to the Mosaic law, especially circumcision (cf. 2:3). Paul's description of them as "false believers" (ψευδ-αδέλφοι) indicates that they at least thought of themselves as followers of Christ. The statement that these people were "brought in" (2:4) indicates that some group (not the "pillar apostles") stood opposed to Paul's view on the applicability of circumcision to the gentiles.

Second, in contrast to the "spies" and the people they represent, Paul speaks of James, Cephas and John who agreed with him that he should go to the gentiles while they (2:7) go to the Jews (2:9). According to Paul, his mission and the right of gentiles to be recognized as members of the people of God circumcision-free have the full recognition of the main leaders of the church in Jerusalem.

Paul then depicts a scene in Antioch, some time after the meeting in Jerusalem,[66] where Peter ate with gentiles in agreement with what had been discussed earlier in Jerusalem (2:6–10). Later, however, when "some people from James" (τινας ἀπὸ Ἰακώβου) arrived in Antioch, Peter withdrew from table fellowship with gentile believers "out of fear of those from the circumcision" (2:12).

The identity of these people "from James" is difficult to discern. Paul makes no disparaging remarks about James at this point, indicating Paul believed James remained faithful to their agreement. In fact, Paul makes no mention that any

---

[66]Paul gives no indication of the time lapse between the meeting described in 2:1–10 and the events in Antioch in 2:11–14.

of these apostles ever repudiates the agreement Paul describes in Gal. 2:7–10.[67]

Apparently, these people from James were influenced by a third group of more radical Jewish Christians[68] who demanded gentile loyalty to the Jewish Law: "those from the circumcision" (2:12; τοὺς ἐκ περιτομῆς). These people are likely the same group Paul designates as "false believers" who sent emissaries to "spy" on Paul (2:4) in Jerusalem. Paul, however, never makes an explicit link between them. J. Louis Martyn argues persuasively that the phrase "those of the circumcision" is used by Paul in one of two ways: (1) to refer to "congregations—or groups within congregations—made up of born Jews"; or (2) "as a technical term to refer to a party within that congregation intent on a mission to Gentiles that was at least partly Law-observant."[69] In Gal. 2, Paul uses the expression in the latter sense.

Paul's remarks provide clear-cut evidence that at least one group among the Christians in Jerusalem forcefully advocated for a more stringent adherence to the Law on the part of gentile converts. This included the demand for circumcision as well as strict fealty to food laws (Gal. 2:12) and likely Jewish calendrical observances (Gal. 4:10). As part of

---

[67]See Raymond E. Brown and John P. Meier, *Antioch and Rome: New Testament Cradles of Catholic Christianity* (New York: Paulist Press, 1983), 38.

[68]That they were Jewish Christians seems almost certain. In Rom. 4:11–12 Paul refers to Christians from gentile background simply as "the uncircumcision" and Christians from Jewish backgrounds as "the circumcision" (cf. Rom. 3:30; 4:9; contra Longenecker, *Galatians*, 73). The term can also be used to refer generically to the Jewish people as a whole irrespective of their faith or lack thereof (cf. Rom. 15:8; Gal. 2:7–9). In this context in Gal. 2, the genitive in the phrase "those of the circumcision" (τοὺς ἐκ περιτομῆς) is best understood as a genitive of source, indicating those "drawn from the Jewish nation" (Martyn, *Galatians*, 239).

[69]Ibid.

these efforts, these people openly opposed Paul and his position on these matters.[70]

Paul was also opposed by non-Christian Jews. Paul reports that, "Five times I have received from the Jews the forty lashes minus one. Three times I was beaten with rods" (2 Cor. 11:24–25; NRSV). These punishments indicate Paul had lost synagogue trials, been denounced as a sinner, and been punished according to Deut. 25:1–3 by his fellow Jews.[71] The Book of Acts also bears witness to Jewish unbelievers opposing Paul in Jerusalem and elsewhere (Acts 13:44–45; 14:2–5, 19; 17:1–7, 13; 18:5–6, 12–17; 20:3; 21:20–36). Given the controversial nature of Paul's message and Paul's own testimony regarding such opposition, there is no reason to question the historicity of Luke's record on this point.

Summary

Paul believes that objections to his preaching are known in Rome. Objections to Paul's message could easily become known in Rome through Jewish business travelers or normal communications between Jewish groups in Rome and the eastern Mediterranean. Paul would have received this knowledge through friends living there. Paul also anticipates the arrival of actual opponents in Rome in the near future. He

---

[70]See also 2 Cor. 11:26 and Gal. 5:11 where Paul speaks of being endangered or persecuted by false believers. These issues were as much a matter of lifestyle as they were "doctrine." The two cannot be bifurcated. How one interprets the continuities and discontinuities between the new salvation accomplished through Christ and the old dispensation of Moses carries implications that can be seen in everyday life. Once again, it must be restated that the "teaching" Paul mentions in 16:17 and 6:17, and commends his auditors for following, cannot be restricted simply to "doctrine." Paul's combination of "doctrinal" instruction ("I know and am persuaded in the Lord Jesus that nothing is unclean in itself," 14:14; NRSV) with practical implication ("If your brother or sister is being injured by what you eat, you are no longer walking in love," 14:15; NRSV) in his directions regarding the "weak" and the "strong" provides a sterling example of this inseparably.

[71]John M. G. Barclay, "Paul Among Diaspora Jews: Anomaly or Apostate?" *JSNT* 60 (1995): 115.

believes these people will stir up division among the Christians in opposition to God's purpose for a unified people drawn from all nations. Such factors account for the topics in Romans that reflect controversies found in Paul's other letters.[72]

Conclusions

This chapter makes three basic points. First, Paul's controversies in the East revolve around disagreements over the implications of what God had done in Christ for the people of God. The differing understandings of where the continuities and discontinuities lie between the pre-Christ dispensation and the one following the death and resurrection of the Messiah form the dividing lines between Paul and his opponents. Paul's language[73] as well as the threatening actions of his opponents indicate that this was no small matter.

Second, Paul defends his gospel in Romans 1–11 on points that had proved controversial in the East. The rhetorical questions that give structure to much of these chapters reflect real objections and are not mere teaching devices.

Finally, evidence in the letter indicates that Paul believes criticisms of his preaching are known in Rome and that he expects opponents to arrive in Rome soon. He also anticipates facing serious opposition during his upcoming visit to Jerusalem, a city where much of the opposition that has hounded his ministry has its roots.

---

[72]Contra Günther Bornkamm who finds no reason for the polemical arguments in Rome. See "Paul's Last Will and Testament," in *The Romans Debate*, 25.

[73]"Their condemnation (τὸ κρίμα) is deserved!" (Rom. 3:8); "As regards the gospel they are enemies of God . . ." (Rom. 11:28; cf. 16:18–20; Gal. 5:12).

Chapter Six

ROMANS 12:1–15:6 AND PAUL'S CONCERN FOR COMMUNITY

Thus far I have argued for two major theses about the letter to Romans. First, Romans is Paul's attempt to shape a "community of the new age" by fostering the "obedience of faith" among the Christians in Rome. Specifically, that entails persuading the believers of various degrees of loyalty to the Mosaic Law and Jewish traditions to "receive one another just as Christ received you to the glory of God" (15:7). Second, Romans is also Paul's defense against charges made against him in the East. Paul believes these objections are already known in Rome and will soon be made in person by actual opponents from the East.

Two key issues remain to be resolved. First, the "apologetic" understanding of Romans accounts for chs. 1–11 and parts of ch. 15. Yet, the criteria set forth for a resolution to the Romans Debate in chapter one require that the entire letter be explained. Second, how can the two conclusions outlined above be combined in such a manner that the criteria for a resolution to the Romans Debate can be satisfied? In other words, why did Paul write to these people in order to shape a community of the new age and to defend himself at this time in his life?

In response to this second issue, I argue that forming a true community of the eschatological people of God is Paul's best defense against the encroachment of his opponents. If the

151

"weak" and "strong," Jew and gentile truly receive one another just as Christ received them to the glory of God, God's eschatological purposes for believers in Rome will be realized. The Roman Christians will have thus actualized the "obedience of faith" that is the purpose of Paul's call. If that happens, the believers will be "strengthened" (1:11) and the natural tensions between Christians adhering to the Law and those living apart from the Law's requirements cannot be exploited to create division and turn people against Paul (as so often had been the case in the East). For it was precisely at such points of tension that Paul had been attacked in Antioch and among the Galatians.

This proposal makes sense of Paul's circumstances, what is known of the Christians in Rome, and the contents of the letter examined thus far. It has not, however, accounted for the instructions of 12:1–15:6. In this chapter I argue that Romans 12:1–15:6 consistently focuses on relationships among community members. The instructions beginning in 12:1 flow from the argument of chs. 1–11 and move the listeners from general instructions (basically chs. 12–13) to application of those same instructions to a specific matter of controversy among the Roman Christians (14:1–15:6). The admonitions find their focal point, finally, with the exhortation of 15:7. With this final piece of the puzzle in place, a reconstruction of the purpose of Romans can be offered that meets the criteria outlined in chapter one.

Communal Focus of Romans 12:1–8; 13:8–15:6

Romans 12:1–15:13 has often been viewed as (1) a mostly unstructured[1] collection of moral instructions which are (2) appended, but largely unrelated, to the argument of chs. 1–11.[2] I have already contended (chapter three) that this section displays strong ties to the argument of chs. 1–11. Additional links will be highlighted below.

Difficulties discerning structure focus particularly on chs. 12–13.[3] For example, Gordon M. Zerbe isolates the following segments: 12:1–2; 12:3–8; 12:9–21; 13:1–7; 13:8–10 and 13:11–14. Yet, he sees chs. 12–13 as "comprised of a series of independent thematic units" with no "overall logical structure or thematic development."[4]

---

[1]Although certain sections (e.g. 13:1–7; 14:1–15:6) clearly focus on a single issue, most passages within 12:1–15:6 are usually understood as random collections of sayings on a particular theme. Peter Stuhlmacher describes these chapters as a "loose succession of themes and statements" (*Paul's Letter to the Romans: A Commentary*, trans. Scott J. Hafemann [Louisville: Westminster/John Knox Press, 1994], 186. This is especially true of 12:9–21. Similarly, Otto Merk observes that in this passage, "werden in loser Reihenfolge . . . Mahnungen aneinandergereiht" ("exhortations are strung together in a loose succession") (*Handeln aus Glauben: Die Motivierungen der paulinischen Ethik*, Marburger Theologische Studien, bd. 5 [Marburg: N. G. Elwert Verlag, 1968], 161).

[2]Robert J. Karris declares that Romans 14:1–15:13, "should be analyzed for what it is: general, Pauline paraenesis and not so many pieces of polemic from which a scholar may reconstruct the positions of the parties in Rome who occasioned this letter" ("Romans 14:1–15:13 and the Occasion of Romans," in *The Romans Debate*, rev. and expanded ed., ed. Karl P. Donfried [Peabody, Mass.: Hendrickson, 1991], 66).

[3]Typically, chs. 12–13 are viewed as general paraenesis (unrelated to circumstances in Rome) while 14:1–15:13 contains specific instructions addressing realities in Rome. See, for example, Ernst Käsemann, *Commentary on Romans*, trans. and ed. Geoffrey W. Bromiley (Grand Rapids: William B. Eerdmans, 1980), 323; Stuhlmacher, *Romans*, 186; and William Sanday and Arthur C. Headlam, *The Epistle to the Romans*, ICC (New York: Charles Scribner's Sons, n.d.), 351.

[4]*Non-Retaliation in Early Jewish and New Testament Texts: Ethical Themes in Social Contexts*, JSPSup, vol. 13 (Sheffield: JSOT Press, 1993), 220–21.

I contend that Romans 12:1–15:13 reveals both a discernible structure and thematic emphasis. The structure involves a progression from general admonitions to more specific application of those instructions.[5] Thematically, those instructions focus consistently on relationships among believers.[6]

Structure

Romans 12:1–2 consists of a general exhortation that is illustrated in particular attitudes and behaviors in the chapters that follow. This movement from general to particular takes places in stages as the chapters progress. The broad imperatives of 12:1–2 gain greater specificity in the attitudes and actions depicted in 12:3–13:13. Those instructions form the ideological backdrop for Paul's explicit directions to the "strong" and "weak" in 14:1–15:6.[7] All of this leads to the focal

---

[5]"One cannot fully appreciate Paul's intention in Rom. 12–15 without seeing the movement and the heightening specificity, beginning with Rom. 12:1 and moving through Rom. 15:13" (Karl P. Donfried, "False Presuppositions in the Study of Romans," in *The Romans Debate*, 108). Wilhelm Wuellner believes 13:1–7 and 14:1–15:13 "concretize" the more general admonitions of ch. 12 ("Paul's Rhetoric of Argumentation in Romans: An Alternative to the Donfried-Karris Debate Over Romans," in *The Romans Debate*, 144).

[6]It is widely recognized that Paul's general instructions in chs. 12–13 reflect paraenesis employed in the Greco-Roman and early Christian moral instruction. It does not follow, however, that Paul's exhortations in these chapters must have no specific reference to the situation in Rome. The claim made here is that Paul selected particular elements from common early Christian paraenesis in order to further his intentions for the letter's recipients.

[7]"In addition, the many links between 12:1–21 and 14:1–15:13 suggest strongly that the somewhat more general chap. 12 functions as the theoretical foundation for the more specific exhortations in chaps. 14–15" (Kent L. Yinger, "Romans 12:14–21 and Nonretaliation in Second Temple Judaism: Addressing Persecution within the Community," *CBQ* 60 [1998]: 74–96); Walter T. Wilson contends that ch. 12 forms the basis for chs. 13–15 (*Love without Pretense: Romans 12.9–21 and Hellenistic-Jewish Wisdom Literature*, WUNT, series 2, vol. 24 [Tübingen: J. C. B. Mohr {Paul Siebeck}, 1991], 128). Wilson, however, misses (1) the continuation of 12:9–21 in 13:8–10 and (2) the framing effect of 12:1–2 and 13:11–14 which unites chs. 12–13 (see below).

point of Paul's argument in the letter, the call for mutual acceptance in 15:7.

Several examples can be used to illustrate this movement. One can trace the progression from the broad exhortation "do not be conformed to this age" (12:2) to a general principle embodying that exhortation: "do not think more highly of yourself than you ought" (12:3; cf. 12:16). That principle is then applied specifically to the situation among Paul's hearers, "Do not let what you eat cause the ruin of one for whom Christ died" (14:15; NRSV). All of this is then concretized in the final exhortation to "Receive one another, therefore, just as Christ received you, to the glory of God" (15:7). In addition, Paul announces the general principle in 12:18, "As far as it is possible with you, seek peace with everyone." He then applies this principle specifically to the Roman situation in 14:19, "Therefore, let us pursue the things of peace and the things that build up one another." Furthermore, in 13:8, Paul instructs his hearers to "Owe no one anything, except to love one another." In 14:15 he specifies the implications of this principle when he says, "If your brother is injured by what you eat, you are no longer walking in love." In each of these instances, this movement from general principle to specific application of that same principle is apparent.

Theme

If Paul's exhortations and instructions in these chapters move toward a specific end, then these chapters are not a collection of general paraenesis, but form a unified argument. The claim made here is that Paul's instructions exhibit a consistent emphasis on the theme of relationships among believers designed to support that argument. This does not mean other topics are not touched on briefly. It does mean that the persistent emphasis falls upon how believers relate to one another.

Since the contention about thematic consistency in Romans 12–15 is more controversial than the thesis regarding its structure, the former receives more extensive treatment below. I will first examine passages about which there is no controversy regarding the community-related focus of their content, highlighting the emphasis there on relationships among believers in Rome. Second, I analyze two passages, 12:9–21 and 13:1–7, where an internal focus throughout is not as evident.

The Community Focus of 12:1–15:13

The examination of the following passages gives close attention to the focus on relationships among Christians in Rome. No attempt is made to address every interpretive issue that arises.

Romans 12:1–2. Paul's opening thematic[8] exhortation in 12:1 calls on the Christians in Rome to "offer your bodies" (τὰ σώματα ὑμῶν; plural) as a living sacrifice (θυσίαν ζῶσαν; singular), not as living sacrifices. The many members make one communal offering of themselves.

Paul makes several explanatory statements about this exhortation in 12:2. First, Paul defines this sacrifice in both a negative and a positive manner. Paul exhorts the Roman Christians, "do not be conformed to this age" (12:2a; μὴ συσχηματίζεσθε τῷ αἰῶνι τούτῳ) but "be transformed by the renewing of the mind" (12:2b; μεταμορφοῦσθε τῇ ἀνακαινώσει τοῦ νοὸς). The purpose of such renewal of the mind is that Paul's hearers may approve (εἰς τὸ δοκιμάζειν) the good, pleasing (εὐάρεστον), and perfect will of God (12:2c). Given that the will of God is now to create a unified people drawn from all nations (chapter three above), it is not unreasonable to read the exhortation as Paul's call for a replacement of the measures his hearers would employ to categorize and relate to one another under the standards of this present age (being

---

[8]Ulrich Wilckens judges that 12:1–2 "hat die Funktion einer Überschrift über die folgende Vielfalt von Mahnungen" ("has the function of a heading over the following variety of exhortations"), (*Der Brief an die Römer, [Röm 12–16]*, 2d. aufl., EKKNT, 6.3 [Neukirchener-Vluyn: Neukirchener Verlag, 1989], 1). Cf. Merk, *Handeln aus Glauben*, 157.

conformed to this age; cf. on 12:3 below).[9] Instead, with a renewed and transformed mind, Paul's auditors will collectively recognize God's will in the present eschatological moment and adopt the divine standards (2:11; 3:22) for relating to others in the community of the new age. Such a communal sacrifice, therefore, is one pleasing (εὐάρεστον) to God because it embodies the eschatological purpose of God for a unified people drawn from all nations (1:14–17; 15:8–12).[10] Further support for this reading emerges when one looks at how Paul follows up his opening exhortation.

Romans 12:3–8. When Paul begins to elaborate his general exhortation in greater detail, he immediately addresses a matter at the heart of community harmony.[11] Each member (12:3) is not to think too highly (ὑπερφρονεῖν παρ᾽ ὃ δεῖ φρονεῖν) of himself or herself, but think of the self according to a proper measure (φρονεῖν εἰς τὸ σωφρονεῖν).[12]

Following this admonition in 12:3, Paul illustrates (γάρ) this call to proper self-estimation with regard to spiritual gifts (12:4–8). The driving theme of these verses is that there are many members but one body (12:4–5), recalling the many individuals but one sacrifice of 12:1. As Paul employs the gift given to him (12:3), so the Roman Christians are to use the differing gifts given to each of them (12:6) with proper judgment (12:3). Walter T. Wilson summarizes Paul's instructions here as follows:

---

[9]This is not a claim that Paul intends only this point in 12:2. It does claim that this interpretation of the phrase makes sense as Paul's primary emphasis given its context in Romans.

[10]Such a link between 12:1–2 and 15:8–12 provides additional evidence that these passages frame the discussion in these chapters.

[11]With regard to 12:3, Franz-Josef Ortkemper states, "Jetzt wird die in den Versen 1–2 gegebene allgemeine Mahnung konkretisiert" ("Now the general exhortation given in vv. 1–2 is concretized" (*Leben aus dem Glauben: Christliche Grundhaltungen nach Römer 12–13*, NTAbh., neue folge, bd. 14 [Münster: Aschendorff, 1980], 6).

[12]Ulrich Luck, "σώφρων, σωφρονέω, σωφροσύνη," *TDNT*, 7:1102.

In mutual relationships within the church there is no place for presumptuous or self-serving attitudes; all of the various practical functions exercised by individual Christians are to be directed towards the edification of the entire group.[13]

Yet, as James D. G. Dunn notes, this instruction applies to issues in the letter beyond the use of spiritual gifts.

> The emphatic warning against inflated thinking (v 3) recalls the similar warning against Gentile presumption in 11:17–24 (particularly 11:20), but also the similar theme of the earlier diatribes against Jewish presumption (chaps. 2–4): the 'us' over 'them' attitude which Paul saw as the heart of Jewish failure and as a potential danger for Gentile Christians must not be allowed to characterize the eschatological people of God.[14]

It is precisely this point that chapter three of this dissertation demonstrated to be at the heart of Paul's call for the "obedience of faith" in 15:7. The arrogant attitudes Paul counters in chs. 2–4 and 11:17–24 reflect ways of categorizing and relating to one another under the standards of this present age (12:2). Paul will apply this broad mindset to such divisive attitudes in 14:1–15:6.

An emphasis on mutual relationships pervades not only Paul's opening thematic exhortations in 12:1–3, but also the concluding statement of this section in 15:7–12. In other words, Paul frames the entire paraenetic section with this theme. He reinforces both 12:1 and 12:3 with solemn statements reminding his hearers that what he is about to say is

---

[13]*Love without Pretense*, 130.

[14]*Romans 9–16*, WBC, vol. 38B (Milton Keynes, England: Word, 1991), 720. With regard to this statement in 12:3, Ernst Käsemann adds, "It could be said that everything which follows stands under the watchword 'Do not be conceited'" ("Worship and Everyday Life: A Note on Romans 12," in *New Testament Questions of Today* [London: SCM Press, 1969], 192). Jews and gentiles have now been united in the praise of God as members of God's people just as scripture foretold (15:8–12). Here again, one sees a connection between the paraenesis of ch. 12 and earlier parts of the letter.

rooted in his divine call.[15] In 15:7, Paul places the weight of his argument in Romans in support of his call for mutual reception (15:8–12). Since this issue is so central to Paul's argument in the rest of the letter (chapter three above), this emphasis should not be surprising.

Additional factors reinforce this reading of 12:1–3 and its relation to 15:7–12. In Romans 12:3, Paul uses the verb "to think" (φρονέω; or a compound form ὑπερφρονέω or σωφρονέω) four times. After emphasizing the word in this general exhortation, Paul returns to the term in other strategic locations in chs. 12–15. For example, he employs the participle and adjectival form of the word in 12:16 in an admonition that obviously echoes 12:3.[16] Paul uses the word again in 15:5 where, in summarizing his instructions to the "strong" and "weak," he prays that by the gift of God the Roman Christians may "think the same thing [τὸ αὐτὸ φρονεῖν] among one another according to Christ Jesus."[17] The purpose of such united thought is that they may in one voice glorify God (v. 6). As Paul's statements in 15:7–12 make clear, this "thinking the same thing" takes place among those with differing degrees of adherence to the Mosaic Law and Jewish traditions. Having the same mind "according to Christ Jesus," therefore, indicates thinking along the lines of what Jesus Christ accomplished (15:8–9a) for these differing people. Once again, an emphasis on community harmony becomes apparent.

---

[15]12:1: Παρακαλῶ οὖν ὑμᾶς, ἀδελφοί, διὰ τῶν οἰκτιρμῶν τοῦ θεοῦ. 12:3: Λέγω γὰρ διὰ τῆς χάριτος τῆς δοθείσης μοι. These phrases should be read in parallel, both referring to Paul's merciful, graceful call. See Victor Paul Furnish, *Theology and Ethics in Paul* (Nashville: Abingdon, 1968), 102.

[16]Romans 12:16 reads "Thinking (φρονοῦντες) the same thing among yourselves, not being too high-minded (φρονοῦντες), but associated with the humble. Do not claim to be wiser than you are (φρόνιμοι παρ' ἑαυτοῖς)." Walter T. Wilson argues that 12:16 stands at the center of a chiasm that structures 12:9–21, meaning that this specific point is Paul's chief concern in these verses (*Love without Pretense*, 176–77).

[17]The NRSV translates this phrase as "to live in harmony with one another, in accordance with Christ Jesus."

One further point about Paul's use of the verb φρονέω in chs. 12–15 deserves mention. Prior to 12:3, Paul last used the term (and the noun φρόνημα) in 8:5–7 to describe the contrast between living under the reign of Adam and living under the reign introduced by Christ. Those living according to the flesh let their mind dwell (φρονοῦσιν) on fleshly matters (8:5a). The opposite is true of those living according to the Spirit (8:5b). Paul goes on to contrast the mindset (τὸ φρόνημα) of the flesh and of those led by the Spirit. In chapter three, I argued that the positive depictions in this passage portray those walking in the new obedience made possible by Christ's death and resurrection (8:3–4). The general descriptions of this new obedience, begun in ch. 6 and continued in ch. 8, are then spelled out in greater detail in chs. 12–15, culminating in Paul's call for mutual acceptance in 15:7. Paul's return to the terminology of 8:5–7 at key points in chs. 12–15 provides a terminological linkage running through these passages. When Paul portrays the mindset of the those who walk in this new obedience (8:5–7) in chs. 12–15, he does so by describing a mindset that produces a lifestyle contributing to the unity of the people of God.

Romans 13:8–10. In 13:8–10, Paul calls his auditors to love one another, for "the one who loves has fulfilled the Law" (13:8; repeated in different form twice more in vv. 9–10).[18] Though linked to 13:1–7 by the theme of "obligation" (13:7–8), these verses serve as a fitting conclusion to the instructions on love begun at 12:9.[19] The theme of love, therefore, serves as the common motif uniting a notable portion of chs. 12–13.

---

[18]The theme of love recalls the heading in 12:9a over Paul's instructions in 12:9–21, "Let love be genuine."

[19]The awkwardness of 13:1–7 within this context presents several difficulties (see below). For example, the connection of 13:8 with 12:9–21 is clear. The words that begin 13:8, Μηδενὶ μηδὲν ὀφείλετε ("Owe no one anything"), take up the five negations using μή or μηδενί in 12:16–21 (cf. Ortkemper, *Leben aus dem Glauben*, 5). Following so closely on the heels of Paul's instructions regarding governing authorities and taxes in 13:7, some commentators want to continue to read 13:8–10 with reference to

Several scholars note the connection between fulfilling the Law (13:8) and Paul's unexplained remark in 8:4 that "the righteous requirements [τὸ δικαίωμα] of the Law may be fulfilled in us" who "walk according to the Spirit."[20] Joseph A. Fitzmyer comments, "Paul is simply repeating in other words what he already said in 8:4."[21] We noted in chapter three that the expression in 8:4 was one of Paul's general ways of describing the eschatological "obedience of faith" which he was called to foster. When Paul's auditors love one another, they carry out the eschatological obedience that fulfills the Law. Here is another piece of evidence placing the "obedience of faith" within the realm of relationships among believers.

Paul has already specified the model of love by citing Christ's death for Paul and his hearers as an example of God's love (5:6–10). Christ died for them when they were unworthy of that love.[22] In the climactic statement of the entire letter, Paul will call upon the Roman Christians to receive one another "just as Christ received you" (15:7), a clear call to imitate Christ's manner of love in their relationships other believers.

Romans 13:11–14. With a sweeping reminder of the eschatological moment in which they live (vv. 11–12a) and broad exhortations resembling those of 12:1–2 (13:12b–14),

---

outsiders. The confusion that surfaces in these attempts to connect vv. 8–10 with outsiders only provides further evidence that internal relationships are Paul's concern here. For examples of awkward attempts to include outsiders, see Douglas Moo, *The Epistle to the Romans*, NICNT (Grand Rapids: William B. Eerdmans, 1996), 813; and Dunn, *Romans 9–16*, 776.

[20]For example, William S. Campbell, "The Rule of Faith in Romans 12:1–15:13: The Obligation of Humble Obedience to Christ as the Only Adequate Response to the Mercies of God," in *Pauline Theology*, vol. 3, *Romans*, eds. David M. Hay and E. Elizabeth Johnson (Minneapolis: Fortress Press, 1995), 282 (with additional sources cited there).

[21]*Romans*, AB, vol. 33 (New York: Doubleday, 1993), 677.

[22]Paul makes this point unmistakable. In these four verses, the recipients of God's love are characterized as "weak" (v. 6; ἀσθενῶν), "ungodly" (v. 6; ἀσεβῶν; cf. 1:18; 4:5), "sinners" (v. 8; ἁμαρτωλῶν), and "enemies" (v. 10; ἐχθροὶ).

Paul rounds off the general instructions begun in 12:1.
Several factors link these closing statements to the exhortations of 12:1–2. The contrasting exhortations to "put off"
and "put on" in vv. 12b–14 recall the contrasting imperatives
of 12:1–2. By ending this section with a call to take on the
character of Christ (v. 14), Paul also echoes a similar call to
take on the "newness of life" like the new life of Christ's (6:4),
a call first sounded in ch. 6 and taken up again in the opening
thematic exhortations of 12:1–2.[23] Finally, the eschatological
emphasis of 13:11–14 echoes a theme first mentioned in these
chapters (and assumed throughout) in 12:2. These verses,
along with 12:1–2, serve as a frame for the intervening
content.[24] Placed at this point, they draw together and bring
to a conclusion the general admonitions before Paul turns in
14:1 to apply these exhortations to specific issues disrupting
community harmony in Rome.

Romans 14:1–15:6. In the treatment of 12:1–3 and 15:7–
12 above, a contrast was identified between the attitude Paul
advocates in 12:3 ("do not think more highly of yourself than
is proper") and the Jewish (chs. 1–2) and gentile (11:17–24)
presumption of superiority Paul countered earlier in the letter.
In 14:1–15:6, Paul returns to these issues and applies his
advice by calling on his auditors to stop "judging one another"
(14:4, 10, 13; cf. 2:1). Rather than judging, Paul's auditors are
to "resolve instead never to put a stumbling block or hindrance in the way of another" (14:13; NRSV). To place such
impediments in the way of a brother or sister means "you are
no longer walking in love" (14:15). In the context identified in
this study, that means such a person is no longer walking in
the obedience of faith (13:8), because she or he is causing
division among those for whom Christ died (14:15). Paul can,
therefore, summarize the behavior he advocates in 14:19, "Let

---

[23]Paul will return to the theme of imitating Christ when he closes
off his instructions in 15:3, 7.

[24]Ortkemper, *Leben aus dem Glauben*, 10; Zerbe, *Non-Retaliation*,
221.

us pursue the things of peace and the things which build up one another."

He further instructs the strong to bear the weaknesses of the weak and not please themselves (15:1). Like Christ (15:3), they are to please their neighbor "for the good purpose of building up" (NRSV) the community (15:2).[25] William S. Campbell succinctly summarizes Paul's focus in this passage: "It is not in fact the differences in life-style that concern Paul . . . . Righteousness and the unity of the church are his concern."[26]

In summary, Paul's interest throughout this section is with the unity of the eschatological people of God. Any attitude or action that violates that unity constitutes walking according the standard of an age other than one introduced by Christ. Paul calls for behavior that builds up the community "in accordance with Christ Jesus" (15:5; κατὰ Χριστὸν ᾿Ιησοῦν).

Relationships with Outsiders?
Romans 12:9–21; 13:1–7.

The two remaining sections of 12:1–15:6 are typically understood to concern, all or in part, relationships of the believers with outsiders. I contend that general instructions in 12:14, 17–21 can apply both to relationships among believers and to relationships of believers with outsiders. Yet, the context in Romans 12–13, especially the instructions on love begun in 12:9, interrupted at 12:21, and continued in 13:8, indicates that Paul's emphasis lies on internal relations.

25The NRSV translation completes this verse "for the good purpose of building up *the neighbor*" (emph. added). This final phrase can be a reference to the neighbor. Paul's larger concern, however, is community harmony (cf. 15:5).

26"Rule of Faith," 278. Later in his essay, Campbell adds, "They tended to boast in their *distinctions* rather that in their *common faith*" (emph. original). This attitude and associated behavior stems from "an inflated self-estimate" (making the connection with 12:3 clear; ibid., 283).

Romans 13:1–7 is Paul's response to a controversy current in Rome in which Christians have become involved. His remarks on this issue are inserted rather awkwardly, as the asyndeton that begins the passage shows. Paul wanted to mention this issue before he turned to more extended comments that applied his general moral instructions to the controversial issue of the relevance of Jewish Law and traditions. In this sense, 13:1–7 constitutes a brief digression. Paul returns to his main line of thought in 13:8, rounding off in 13:8–14 his general instructions begun in 12:1–2.

Given the state of the evidence, such a reconstruction cannot be conclusive. Nevertheless, even if one remains unpersuaded that these verses are directed to internal relations, the fact remains that the predominant concern of chs. 12–15 is relationships within the community of believers. If 12:14, 17–21 and 13:1–7 do focus on outsiders, the amount of material Paul devotes to the topic within these chapters makes the subject of both passages a digression from his main topic. For this reason, I argue Paul focuses "consistently," not "exclusively," on relationships among believers in these chapters.

The treatment of Rom. 12:9–21 and 13:1–7 which follows attempts to establish the plausibility of reading these verses as instructions regarding relationships within the Christian community. Once again, in light of the general nature of this teaching such a reading cannot be final.

Romans 12:9–21

Most scholars divide this section between instructions for relationships within the community (vv. 9–13) and relationships with those outside (vv. 14–21). Whereas the instructions of vv. 9–13 clearly apply to internal matters, the introduction of "those who persecute" (τοὺς διώκοντας) in v. 14 seems to indicate Paul changes his focus to outsiders who are troubling the Christians in Rome. Kent L. Yinger has recently argued, however, that the entire section applies to differences between groups within the community.[27] Because his interpretation runs contrary to the usual reading of this passage and because it carries importance for the argument of this dissertation, an extensive summary and evaluation of Yinger's work appears below.

Yinger's argument can be condensed into four stages. First, he faults the traditional division between internal and external relations in 12:9–21 on three grounds: (1) If 12:14 begins the section of instructions on relations with outsiders, Paul immediately interrupts those instructions in vv. 15–16 by returning to internal matters.[28] Romans 12:14 cannot serve as a turning point from a focus on internal to external relationships. (2) Romans offers no evidence of external persecution of the believers in Rome.[29] (3) This view places vv. 15–16 out of context not only within vv. 14–21, but also within the "larger argument aimed at fostering genuine love,

---

[27]"Romans 12:14–21 and Nonretaliation in Second Temple Judaism: Addressing Persecution within the Community," *CBQ* 60 (1998): 74–96; hereafter cited in the text as "Nonretaliation." David Alan Black argues in this direction also, but sees "those who persecute" referring to outsiders as well as insiders ("The Pauline Love Command: Structure, Style, and Ethics in Romans 12.9–21," *Filologia Neotestamentaria* 2 [1989]: 3–22).

[28]David Alan Black comments, "The words εὐλογεῖτε τοὺς διώκοντας [ὑμᾶς] in v 14 remain, therefore, somewhat enigmatic, as scholars freely admit. Had Paul had persecution *Christi causa* in mind in vv 14–16, one is hard-pressed to explain why he apparently defers his discussion of the topic to vv 17–21" ("Love Command," 10).

[29]Gordon M. Zerbe believes Paul "is apparently preoccupied with the problem of suffering and persecution when writing Romans. This is indicated by the centrality of the themes of persecution, suffering, endurance and the eschatological victory over evil earlier in the letter" (*Non-Retaliation*, 228). Paul is hardly 'preoccupied' with these issues. Zerbe reads external persecution into every reference to suffering earlier in the letter even though no specific mention is made of such external problems. Paul's statements about suffering in 5:1–11 and 8:17–39 are very broad and are more likely general references to eschatological sufferings ("birth pangs"; 8:22) that precede the return of Christ. Zerbe later admits the evidence for external persecution of the Roman Christians "is largely circumstantial and inconclusive" (ibid., 231).

harmony, and mutual acceptance among believers who are disdaining one another" ("Nonretaliation," 76).

Second, Yinger examines several Jewish texts from the Second Temple period in order to "identify the thematic elements common to the emerging tradition of non-retaliation, and compare these elements to those found in Paul's argument" ("Nonretaliation," 76). The themes identified in Rom. 12:14–21 are:

1. Bless or do good to those who wrong you (vv. 14a, 20, 21b).
2. Do not curse them or repay evil for evil (vv. 14b, 17a).
3. Maintain solidarity, harmony, peace (vv. 15, 16, 18).
4. Consider what is 'noble in the sight of all' (v. 17b).
5. Do not avenge yourselves (v. 19a).
6. Vengeance belongs to God (v. 19bc).[30]

Although these items have been identified individually in biblical, Jewish and hellenistic literature, Yinger claims the combination of these elements in a few Jewish inter-testamental texts has been overlooked.

Yinger examines the following texts to buttress his point: CD 9:2–5; 1QS 10:17–18; 2 Enoch 50:3–4; T. Gad. 6–7; Ps.-Phoc. 76–78; and Jos. Asen. 28: 10, 14. In none of these texts do all of the thematic elements found in Rom. 12:14–21 appear. In fact, element 4 appears in none. Still, Yinger is able to demonstrate an emerging tradition of these themes occurring in clusters that first appears during the 200 years before Paul's time.[31]

Third, Yinger claims each of these passages occurs in a context where internal problems in the community are the concern. He contends that Romans 12 should be read in this context as well. He offers three arguments in support of this interpretation: (1) He uses the work of Walter T. Wilson to

---

[30]"Nonretaliation," 77.

[31]Although the tradition is rooted in Lev. 19:17–18 (an admonition echoed in Prov. 20:9c [LXX]) where members of Israel are instructed not to avenge a wrong done by a neighbor, it was not until the inter-testamental era that prohibitions against personal vengeance were specifically grounded in God's right to avenge ("Nonretaliation," 78).

argue that Romans 12 presents one unified argument. Since Romans 12 clearly deals with internal relations through v. 13, one expects that focus to continue. (2) Yinger argues that the term "persecutors" (διώκοντας) in 12:14, which is typically assumed to refer to outsiders, designates not outsiders but other Jews. He cites the use of this term in the Gospels and in Paul's other letters as evidence.[32] Consequently, "διώκειν alone cannot identify these 'persecutors' as outsiders. At most, it alerts us to a situation of enmity producing hostile actions by one person or group toward another" ("Nonretaliation," 91).[33] (3) Yinger suggests that Paul uses "language of enmity" in chapter 12 to prepare the Roman Christians for his treatment of the problems between the "strong" and the "weak" in chs. 14–15 ("Nonretaliation," 92). Although the term "persecutors" is not used of the parties in those chapters, Yinger suggests the language fits the context of the Jewish tradition where "people *within* the community could be spoken of as 'adversaries' and 'enemies'" ("Nonretaliation," 92; emph. original). (4) Yinger suggests that the instructions found in vv. 17–21 do not require a reference to persons outside the community. For example, Paul employs the admonition to not "repay evil with evil" (12:17a) elsewhere (1 Thess. 5:15) in a context that clearly refers to fellow Christians. Furthermore, in v. 18 he instructs his auditors, "If you are able, live peacefully with all people." Although used in Jewish and Greco-Roman moral instruction to refer to relations with insiders as well as outsiders,[34] Yinger contends the phrase is used by Paul here "in order to make a point against the hindrances to peace now evident in the Roman

---

[32]Gospels: Matt. 5:10–12; 10:16–23; 23:24; Luke 11:49; 21:12–19. Paul: Gal. 4:29; 5:22; 1 Thess. 2:15 (ibid., 90, nn. 72–74.).

[33]Regarding the διώκοντας , Jeremy Moiser likewise argues "there is nothing in this usage which prevents us from seeing in the persecutors of Rom 12:14 members of the Christian communities whose attitudes are excoriated in 12.1–13" ("Rethinking Romans 12–15," *NTS* 36 [1990], 576, n. 22).

[34]Yinger cites Sir. 6:6; Ps. 34:14; Arrian, *Epict. Diss.* 4.5.24 ("Nonretaliation," 92, nn. 82, 83).

congregation, especially the members' haughty attitudes toward one another" (12:16; "Nonretaliation," 93). Thus, when Paul specifically returns to the subject of "pursuing peace" (τὰ τῆς εἰρήνης διώκωμεν) and the "things that build one another up" (14:19), he does so in the context of relationships with other members of the Christian communities.

In summary, according to Yinger, neither the participle διώκοντας nor the universal sounding language of vv. 17–21 demands a reference to people outside the community. Instead, Paul draws upon Jewish traditions for dealing with enmity within the community to address problems among believers in Rome. Paul's general admonitions of ch. 12, therefore, lay the groundwork for the specific instructions to the "strong" and "weak" in chs. 14–15.

Yinger successfully demonstrates that the kind of language found in vv. 14–21 is applied to internal community relations in Jewish hellenistic texts from near Paul's time. This evidence does not demand that Paul's statements in 12:14, 17–21 refer to insiders, nor does it require a reference to outside "persecutors." What Yinger establishes, however, is the genuine plausibility of reading these verses, in Paul's historical and cultural context, as references to internal problems among the Roman Christians.

Two factors weigh heavily in Yinger's favor. First, he correctly emphasizes the problem that 12:15–16 (esp. v. 16) presents for any reconstruction of 12:9–21 that posits a transition from relationships with insiders to outsiders beginning at v. 14. He draws upon Walter T. Wilson's contention that Rom. 12 is a unified argument to support his assertion that one can reasonably expect the topic that dominates 12:1–13 (internal relations) to continue throughout.[35] Second, the emphasis given to relationships among the eschatological people of God in the letter as a whole (chapter three above) and at key points in ch. 12–15 in particular

---

[35]Yinger, "Nonretaliation," 88–89; citing Wilson, *Love without Pretense*, 93–94, 130, 132.

provides a context within Romans that lends considerable credibility to Yinger's interpretation.

Given the general nature of Paul's statements in 12:14, 17–21, both sides of this dispute can mount good arguments for their case. For example, the fact that Paul discusses submission to governing authorities and payment of taxes in 13:1–7 lends credence to the view that Paul's remarks in 12:14–21 concern relations with outsiders.[36] Still, the context established by Paul's statements that frame these chapters (12:1–2/15:7–12 as well as 12:1–2/13:8–13), the basis of those framing statements in the argument of chs. 1–11, the line of thought he pursues from 12:3–13, plus Yinger's marshaling of evidence from Jewish texts on the themes found in 12:9–21, all argue in favor of reading Paul's instructions in these verses as directed toward relationships within the community. Further evaluation must await analysis of 13:1–7.

Romans 13:1–7

This clearly defined pericope constitutes one of the most difficult texts in Romans for several reasons. First, Paul introduces the topic of governing authorities abruptly, using no conjunction to connect 13:1 with what precedes. In addition, he does so to introduce a subject that receives no mention elsewhere in the letter. Furthermore, the passage interrupts the discussion of love found in 12:9–21 and continued in 13:8–10. If these seven verses are excised, Paul's thought flows smoothly from 12:21 to 13:8. Finally, the instructions offered here seem to contradict the eschatological emphasis that frames these chapters (12:2; 13:11–14). If the hour of salvation is near (13:11), why submit to authority structures of this present age?

For these reasons,[37] the passage has been regarded as an non-Pauline interpolation.[38] Yet, although the topic

---

[36]In 13:1–7, however, Paul gives no indication that the "governing authorities" are "persecuting" the Roman believers in any way.

[37]The unique vocabulary of this section has also been used to call its authenticity into question. Yet, given the unique nature of the subject

170   *The Obedience of Faith*

appears abruptly, the passage has verbal and thematic connections with its context. Friedrich, Pöhlmann, and Stuhlmacher cite, among other links, the key words τὸ ἀγαθόν and τὸ κακόν (12:2, 9, 17, 21; 13:3, 4); the close relationship of ἐκδίκησις (12:19) and ἔκδικος (13:4); the use of τιμή (12:10; 13:7); the mention of divine wrath (12:19; 13:4–5); and the smooth transition from τὰς ὀφειλάς (13:7) to ὀφείλετε (13:8).[39] These factors, in addition to its undisputed place in the textual tradition, argue decisively in favor of its authenticity.

Affirming the passage as genuine, the problem becomes one of making sense of it in this context in Romans. In chapter four, vv. 6–7 were cited as evidence that Paul knows something of the situation of the Christians in Rome.[40] Paul's awareness of a matter among his audience regarding payment of Roman taxes therefore serves as a starting point for the following reconstruction of the situation in Rome and Paul's response.[41]

matter and Paul's use of common early Christian tradition in this passage, such vocabulary is not surprising. See Johannes Friedrich, Wolfgang Pöhlmann, and Peter Stuhlmacher, "Zur historischen Situation und Intention von Röm 13,1–7," *ZTK* 73 [1976]: 147–48; and Ulrich Wilckens, "Römer 13,1–7," in *Rechtfertigung als Freiheit: Paulusstudien* (Neukirchen-Vluyn: Neukirchener Verlag, 1974), 214–15.

[38]"Kurzum: der Abschnitt 13,1–7 ist, literarisch betrachtet, eine Interpolation" ("In short, the section 13:1–7, literarily observed, is an interpolation"; Walther Schmithals, *Der Römerbrief als historisches Problem*, SNT, bd. 9 [Gütersloh: Gerd Mohn, 1975], 187).

[39]"Röm 13,1–7," 149. They conclude, "Röm 13,1–7 sind demnach *fest in den Zusammenhang der paulinischen Paränese eingebettet*" (ibid.; emph. original; "Rom. 13:1–7 is therefore firmly embedded in the context of the Pauline paraenesis").

[40]In vv. 1–5, Paul offers advice that echoes Jewish wisdom and early Christian traditions about relating to governing authorities. His specific instructions regarding taxes in vv. 6–7, however, find no parallels.

[41]The reconstruction offered here closely follows aspects of Marcus Borg, "A New Context for Romans XIII," *NTS* 19 (1972–73): 209–13; Ernst Bammel, "Romans 13," in *Jesus and the Politics of His Day*, eds. Ernst Bammel and C. F. D. Moule (Cambridge: Cambridge University Press, 1984), 367–70; and especially Friedrich, et al, "Röm 13,1–7," 156–59; and James D. G. Dunn, "Romans 13.1–7—A Charter for Political Quietism?" *Ex Auditu* 2 (1986): 58–59.

The Jewish population of Rome was considerable and influential during Paul's time. Evidence exists of difficulties between Jews in Rome and Roman authorities during the first century.[42] These tensions led to expulsions of Jews from Rome in 19 C.E. and 49 C.E.[43] The latter expulsion would, of course, be fresh in the memory of Paul's audience.

Tacitus (*Annals* 13.50-51) tells of public complaints regarding indirect taxes (collected by non-government revenue collectors) brought to Nero in 58 C.E., shortly after Romans was written. Since Tacitus speaks of "repeated demands from the public"[44] about this matter, it is reasonable to suppose that the problems with taxes had been going on for some time. Leonard Victor Rutgers argues that Roman authorities usually intervened in the affairs of religious groups in the city during times of "general unrest."[45] It is likely this dissatisfaction with tax policy that was found in Rome generally had also taken root among Roman Christians. Aware of this situation, Paul seeks to squelch radical tendencies in order to keep the Jewish and Jewish-Christian communities from potential harm (cf. 13:4). Rutgers concludes his study of Roman policy towards the Jews by stating that it was guided by the desire for law and order. "When law and order were maintained (in the eyes of the Roman authorities), Jews had nothing to fear."[46] To have nothing to fear is precisely Paul's wish for the Roman Christians (13:3).[47]

---

[42]For catalogs of problems, see Borg, "Romans XIII," 209–13; Friedrich, et al, "Röm 13,1–7," 156–59; Bammel, "Romans 13," 367–70; and Dunn, "Romans 13.1–7," 58–59.

[43]See Leonard Victor Rutgers, "Roman Policy toward the Jews: Expulsions from the City of Rome during the First Century C.E.," in *Judaism and Christianity in First-Century Rome*, eds. Karl P. Donfried and Peter Richardson (Grand Rapids: William B. Eerdmans, 1998), 93–116.

[44]*Annals*, 13.50. *LCL*, trans. John Jackson (Cambridge, Mass.: Harvard University Press, 1937), 89.

[45]"Roman Policy," 115.

[46]Ibid.

[47]Marcus Borg ("New Context," 212–13) and Ernst Bammel ("Romans 13," 369) also point out the close ties between the Jewish

Jeremy Moiser has suggested that the issue of taxation was a cause of division among the Roman Christians.[48] Paul, however, makes no mention of this problem as a cause of a division. It could be that Paul does not speak specifically of tax controversies because he has no need to do so; if they existed, both he and his hearers already knew it. Yet, if controversy over taxes was dividing believers, one would expect him to be as forthright about this problem as he is about problems between the "strong" and "weak" in 14:1–15:6. Nevertheless, positing such a problem among the Roman Christians provides a plausible rationale for Paul's advice here.

In summary, Paul may be aware of opposition among the Christians in Rome to Nero's current tax policies. Drawing upon Jewish and early Christian tradition, Paul attempts to muffle any such opposition among the Roman Christians. It is possible that this issue was a divisive one among Paul's auditors and therefore Paul addresses it within the context of instructions regarding relationships within the community. Although this would make sense within this context, Paul nowhere states this is the case. Insufficient evidence exists to enable a decisive conclusion. Most likely, Paul knew of problems in Rome regarding this specific issue and interrupted his directions on internal relationships in order to interject instructions on this one particular matter.

Summary

The analysis of 12:9–21 and 13:1–7 has offered possibilities for reading them in such a way that they address relationships among Christians throughout. This reading is possible, but can neither be conclusively demonstrated nor refuted. As with many other passages in Paul, the modern

---

communities in Rome and in Palestine, where opposition to Rome was fomenting. They point out that such militant Palestinian influence among the Christians in Rome could be a reason (for Borg, *the* reason) for Paul's attempt to promote submission to Roman government. This is possible, but Paul gives no indications that this is the target of his instruction in 13:1–7.

[48]"Rethinking Romans," 576–77.

interpreter is left with tantalizing possibilities, but insufficient evidence to support a certain resolution. Nevertheless, such a reading is plausible given the overall context within chs. 12–15 and the letter as a whole.

Conclusions

I have argued that Paul's instructions in Rom. 12:1–15:6 progress in stages from general exhortations to specific applications of those instructions to disagreements among the Christians in Rome. With the exception of a short digression concerning unrest in Rome over Nero's tax policy, Paul's instructions focus consistently on relationships among community members.

These instructions flow from Paul's argument in chs. 1–11 (an argument summarized in 15:8–12) and culminate in the exhortation of 15:7 for mutual reception. Through Jesus' death and resurrection, God has fulfilled the promises to the fathers involving the welcoming of the nations into the eschatological people of God. The diverse believers in Rome should, therefore, make one offering of themselves to God (12:1). Such an offering involves not being conformed to the standards of this present age for relating to one another, but being transformed by the renewing of their minds so that they can know the will of God for God's eschatological people and relate to one another accordingly (12:2).

Relationships among members of the community of the new age are to be patterned after Christ (6:4–10; 15:7). God's standard for relationships within the eschatological people of God, therefore, is mutual love (5:6–10; 13:8, 10). Love[49] will achieve concrete expression among believers in Rome when they do not judge one another over their differences (14:13–15), but receive one another after the model of Christ (15:7).

---

[49]"In short, the crucial issue which alienated the Roman congregations was not the choice of food or days, but the unloving attitude toward those who made a contrary choice" (Black, "Love Command," 13).

When they do so, God's will becomes enfleshed and God is glorified (15:7; contra 1:21).

Communities of believers faithful to the will of God for the eschatological people of God offer Paul his best defense against opponents in Rome. Tensions between Christians marked by different degrees of adherence to the Mosaic Law and Jewish traditions provided issues for opponents to divide Christians in Rome and arouse opposition against Paul and his Law-free gospel for the gentiles. Romans is Paul's attempt to "strengthen" (1:11) his audience at this point of potential weakness. If Paul successfully inoculates the Roman Christians against the overtures from his opponents (whom he expects will soon arrive in Rome), he will prevent the loss of the support he needs from the Roman Christians for his mission to Spain.

Chapter Seven

CONCLUSIONS AND CONTRIBUTIONS

I began this study by defining the "Romans Debate" as the quest for the purpose(s) of Paul's letter to the Romans. Any resolution to this debate must answer the following question:

> How does one unite the information found in the frame of the letter with the particular contents of the body in such a way that it provides a rationale for why Paul wrote about these specific issues (and not others) to these particular Christians at this time in his ministry? Any attempt to answer this question will take seriously Paul's own signals of key themes and his purpose(s) in the frame of the letter, while aligning that information with the argument of the entire body.

Conclusions

In light of these standards, I began this study by examining Paul's statements of intent and emphases in the frame of the letter. Paul writes to "strengthen" (1:11) the Roman Christians by speaking "rather boldly" as a "way of reminding" (15:15) them of matters that are mostly already known to them. "Reminding" was no insignificant activity, but served as an important part of Paul's apostolic task. Paul also emphasizes that his call is to bring about the "obedience of faith" (1:5; 15:18; 16:26), a call carried out through the letter. Tracing the theme of obedience through Romans, I concluded that this obedience refers to an act of eschatological worship whereby one offers the entire self to God. In Romans, that

175

obedience takes concrete form when Christians from Jewish
and gentile backgrounds receive one another in the same
manner Christ received them to the glory of God (15:7). Such
mutual reception embodies the will of God for God's eschatological people (15:8–12). Paul's purpose, therefore, involves
forming a "community of the new age."

Having examined the frame of the letter and linked its
emphases to the letter-body, I then turned to what can be
known about Paul's circumstances, the Roman Christians,
and what the author and recipients know about one another.
Paul has completed his ministry in the East and plans to
begin new work in Spain. First, he must deliver the collection
to Jerusalem, where he expects heated opposition.
Anticipating a successful outcome in Jerusalem, he will pass
through Rome on his way to Spain, stopping for refreshment
and to obtain the support required from the Roman Christians
for his Spanish mission (15:19–32).

Paul intends his letter to circulate among several house-
churches in Rome. The Roman Christians include believers
from both Jewish and gentile birth, some of whom have been
well-instructed in the faith. Writing from Corinth, Paul is in
good position to receive news of the Roman Christians from
friends and associates in Rome. Paul is aware tensions exist
among the Christians there over what aspects of the Mosaic
Law believers should or should not follow. Paul indicates these
tensions run along Jew/gentile lines (15:8–9a).

In an effort to ascertain why Paul would write this letter
to these people at this time, I argued that Paul defends
himself against the types of criticisms he faced in the East.
Paul's difficulties revolved around differing understandings of
God's saving actions through Christ. In particular, controversy centered on the role of Mosaic Law now that the
gentiles were joining the people of God. Paul's defense of his
views on these issues accounts for the content of chs. 1–11. In
chs. 1–4, Paul explains the inclusion of the gentiles as gentiles
into the people of God. Paul anticipates two objections to his
argument: that placing the Jews on the same level as the
gentiles at judgment calls into question God's faithfulness to
the Jews (3:1–4) and that such a law-free gospel encourages

sin (3:8). Paul deals with the second objection in chs. 5–8 and the first in chs. 9–11. These arguments become important in the letter to Rome because Paul believes criticisms of his preaching are already known there (3:8). He also anticipates the arrival in Rome of opponents who would create divisions among the Christians (16:17–20a).

So Paul writes not only to shape a community of the eschatological people of God, but also to defend his understanding of the gospel. Two questions remain: Can these two purposes be integrated? And how do chs. 12–15 fit into the argument of the letter? I contend that shaping a community of the new age serves as Paul's best defense against the overtures of Paul's opponents. It would be precisely at the points of tension over observance of the Law that Paul's opponents could create division (16:17) among the Roman Christians. If Paul's opponents succeed in exacerbating problems among the Roman Christians over controversial issues in Paul's gospel or even turn the Roman Christians against him, Paul will lose the support he needs from Rome for his Spanish mission. The community-forming intent of the letter, therefore, not only carries out Paul's apostolic call but serves an apologetic purpose as well.

In order to help shape the obedient people of God in Rome, Paul instructs his auditors concerning their relationships with one another in 12:1–15:6. These instructions flow from Paul's arguments concerning the people of God in chs. 1–11. Following Paul's broad exhortation in 12:1–2, Paul lays down general guidelines (chs. 12–13) that he then applies specifically to the tensions among his hearers over adherence to the Law (14:1–15:6). Paul's admonitions culminate in the exhortation for mutual reception in 15:7.

Paul's letter to the Romans is, therefore, a preemptive strike[1] against opposition that Paul expects will arrive in

---

[1]Douglas A. Campbell, "Determining the Gospel Through Rhetorical Analysis in Paul's Letter to the Roman Christians," in *Gospel in Paul: Studies on Corinthians, Galatians and Romans for Richard N. Longenecker*, JSNTSup, 108, eds. L. Ann Jervis and Peter Richardson (Sheffield: Sheffield Academic Press, 1994), 323.

Rome before he does. He also writes to shape a certain kind of Christian community among the believers in Rome. In doing so he not only carries out his apostolic call (1:5), he also attempts to form his best defense against his opponents and thereby preserve his Spanish mission.

Meeting the criteria required for a resolution to the Romans Debate, this reconstruction builds from Paul's own signals of key themes and intent in the letter-frame. Furthermore, it unites that information with the entire body of the letter in a manner that offers an explanation for why Paul wrote this letter to these people at this time in his ministry.

Contributions

This dissertation makes several contributions to the study of Romans. Most significant is my argument that Paul's purpose throughout is to shape an eschatological community of the people of God in order to increase resistance to criticism against his preaching. This extends previous findings about Romans in two ways: (1) Although others have argued that Paul seeks to promote unity between Jewish and gentile Christians in Rome, I contend that such community-building serves an additional purpose essential for Paul's goal to preach in Spain: shaping a community resistant to his critics. (2) Although others have argued that Paul wanted to preempt expected criticism in Rome, those reconstructions did not account for the exhortations of chapters 12–15. I provide a reconstruction that makes sense of Paul's total argument throughout the letter. In other words, it offers a satisfactory solution to the key problem in the Romans Debate.

Second, I argue for a new understanding of the phrase "obedience of faith" in Romans and its relationship to Paul's exhortation in 15:7 for the Roman Christians to "welcome one another" to the glory of God. Paul emphasizes the importance of "obedience of faith" by his repetition of the phrase in the letter's framework and the centrality of both "faith" and "obedience" in the argument of the letter body. Yet, it has seldom been accorded the central role it deserves in determining Paul's purpose in writing the letter. Furthermore, the phrase has typically been read within the context of Paul's theology and mission in general rather than as part of his specific instructions to the Roman Christians in particular. I maintain that the phrase must be accorded a central place in reconstructing Paul's purpose in writing the letter and propose an interpretation of it as part of specific instructions for the Roman Christians. Those directions find their focal point at 15:7 where Paul exhorts his hearers to accept one another after the model of Christ to the glory of God.

Third, the dissertation argues for a "practical" reading of chs. 1–11. Paul's argument there responds to anticipated criticism of his preaching, but it also serves as the salvation-historical basis for the kind of unity the Roman believers should enjoy as part of the eschatological people of God. Far from abstract theological reflections, these chapters concern matters vital to the lives of Roman Christian communities and Paul's plans to evangelize in Spain.

Finally, contrary to those who find ecclesiology absent from Romans,[2] I suggest that Paul's understanding of the church is actually central to the argument of the letter. Paul does not express this in discussion of the Eucharist or polity. Rather, he contends throughout for a particular vision of the people of God in the eschatological age. He first sounds this distinctive note in the opening thematic section beginning in 1:14. This people is made up of Greeks and barbarians, wise and foolish, and Jews and gentiles. This emphasis continues on through the body of the letter. Sin obliterates all differences between peoples at judgment. The righteousness of God, therefore, extends to all alike who believe, there is no difference (3:22). God's people are to be a holy people. A life lived dead to sin but alive to God stands at the core of what it means to be baptized as a follower of Christ (ch. 6). God's people are to make one joint offering of themselves to God (12:1), making every effort to overcome differences in light of their common calling and destiny (15:7–12). Far from being a

---

[2]"One would also be hard pressed to derive Paul's thinking about the church from Romans" (Thomas R. Schreiner, *Romans*, Baker Exegetical Commentary on the New Testament [Grand Rapids: Baker, 1998], 16).

peripheral or neglected issue in Romans, Paul's understanding of the church stands at the heart of his argument in
the letter.

APPENDIX

Concluding Doxology: 16:25–27

Among the numerous difficulties encountered in the interpretation of Romans, the textual problems involving chapter 16 rank among the most difficult to resolve. Evidence exists for both fourteen and sixteen chapter versions of the letter (with numerous smaller variations at the end of chapter sixteen), resulting in doubts about the authenticity of chapters 15–16. First expressed in the eighteenth century, these questions eventually developed into a hypothesis that chapter 16 was originally part of a separate letter to Ephesus that was later appended to the text of Romans.[1] Since the publication of Harry Gamble, Jr.'s *The Textual History of the Letter to the Romans*,[2] the authenticity of 16:1–23 is seldom challenged. Yet, questions about the authenticity of the closing doxology in 16:25–27, a passage echoing several key themes in Romans, remain unresolved.[3]

---

[1]Jerome Murphy-O'Connor, *Paul: A Critical Life* (New York: Oxford University Press, 1997), 325. In an influential essay, T. W. Manson posited that chapter 16 originated as Paul's addition to a fifteen chapter copy of Romans sent to Ephesus ("St. Paul's Letter to the Romans—and Others," in Karl P. Donfried, ed., *The Romans Debate*, rev. and expanded ed. [Peabody, Mass.: Hendrickson, 1991], 3–15).

[2]SD, vol. 42. Grand Rapids: William B. Eerdmans, 1977.

[3]Gamble accepts 16:24 as authentic. This aspect of his argument, however, has not found acceptance in the critical commentaries published after Gamble's book was released. See, for example, Ulrich Wilckens, *Der Brief an die Römer (Röm. 12–16)*, 2d aufl., EKKNT, bd. 6.3 (Neukirchener-Vluyn: Neukirchener Verlag, 1989), 143; James D. G. Dunn, *Romans 9–16*, WBC 38B (Milton Keynes, England: Word, 1991),

It must be noted here that even if one is convinced the text is not original, its presence throughout the textual tradition indicates that it must have been added to the text of Romans early in the letter's history.[4] Certainly where it echoes Paul's argument in Romans, it does so reliably. James D. G. Dunn, who denies its authenticity, nevertheless notes

> Even if the idiom is not quite Paul's, the doxology succeeds quite well in summing up the central themes of the letter—God's power (1:16), Paul's gospel (2:16), the message of Christ (cf. 1:9), the mystery revealed (11:25), the 'now' revelation (3:21), the prophetic scriptures (1:2; 3:21), and not least 'the obedience of faith' 'to all nations' (1:5).[5]

Argument against Authenticity

Scholars cite three problems with the concluding doxology. First, it appears not only at the end the letter in the sixteen-chapter versions of the text, but also after 14:23 in the shorter fourteen-chapter form.[6] Although the verses are

---

901; and Joseph A. Fitzmyer, *Romans*, AB 33 (New York: Doubleday, 1993), 751. Douglas Moo (*Romans*, NICNT [Grand Rapids: William B. Eerdmans, 1996]) omits 16:24 but provides no reasons for its exclusion other than to note that the prayer wish of 16:20b is omitted in some manuscripts and found after v. 23 in others (928, n. 2). Both NA[27] and UBS[4] omit the verse.

[4]Gamble, *Textual History*, 100–14, demonstrates that 16:25–27 did not arise as a second-century Marcionite addition to a fourteen-chapter version of Romans.

[5]James D. G. Dunn, *Romans 9–16*, 913. For similar judgments by those who do not accept the passage as genuine, see C. E. B. Cranfield, *The Epistle to the Romans*, vol. 2, ICC (Edinburgh: T & T Clark, 1979), 809 and Fitzmyer, *Romans*, 753.

[6]For a detailed presentation of the witnesses, see Kurt Aland, "Der Schluss und die ursprüngliche Gestalt des Römerbriefes," in *Neutestamentliche Entwürfe*, Theologische Bücherei, bd. 63 (Munich: Chr. Kaiser Verlag, 1979), 287–290. See also W. G. Kümmel, *Introduction to the New Testament*, 2d ed. (trans. Howard Clark Kee; London: SCM Press, 1975), 314–320 and Donald Guthrie, *New Testament Introduction*, 4th ed. (Leicester, England: Apollos, 1990), 412–427 for detailed, yet succinct summaries of the evidence and arguments on this issue.

entirely missing from only two major uncials,[7] this variation in the textual tradition leads many to suspect that they were not part of the original letter. Second, 16:25–27 contains expressions that resemble statements in Ephesians, the Pastoral Epistles, and other writings widely regarded as post-Pauline. They are therefore thought to reflect concepts current at a time after Paul's death. Finally, Paul concludes no other letter with a doxology. Hence, based on stylistic grounds, 16:25–27 is judged to have been added at a later date. Each of these objections requires closer examination.

Textual Tradition. The evidence for the genuineness of 16:25–27 is actually strong. The important uncials A, B, C, and ℵ all show it in this place,[8] as do p[61], 81, 256, 1962, 2127, 1739 and 2464.[9] In addition, it appears in nearly all major manuscripts. Scholars give different reasons for its presence in various locations in the tradition, but the evidence for its absence is slim.

Vocabulary. The more difficult problems involve the language of the passage. Phrases such as μόνῳ σοφῷ θεῷ in v. 27 and in κατὰ ἀποκάλυψιν μυστηρίου χρόνοις αἰωνίοις σεσιγημένου in v. 25 sound unlike the language found in the Pauline letters usually regarded as genuine. In 1 Corinthians, however, Paul refers to the gospel using the term μυστήριον

---

[7]Neither F nor G contains these verses, though G has a blank space after 14:23 indicating the scribe knew something was meant to go there. p[46] alone places the verses after chapter 15.

[8]Codex A shows these verses after 14:23. But they appear after 16:23 as well. The latter fact must not be overlooked.

[9]These texts are all classified as either Category I ("Manuscripts of a very special quality which should always be considered in establishing the original text.") or Category II ("Manuscripts of a special quality, but distinguished from manuscripts of category I by the presence of alien influences . . . , and yet of importance for establishing the original text."). Kurt Aland and Barbara Aland, *The Text of the New Testament*, 2d ed., trans. Erroll F. Rhodes (Grand Rapids: William B. Eerdmans; Leiden: E. J. Brill, 1989), 106.

("mystery"; 2:1; 4:1). In addition, wisdom language is used of Jesus Christ in 1 Cor. 1:24.[10]

Romans 16:25–27 may contain unusual language for Paul because the passage is a highly stylized doxology. As such, it may reflect confessional language drawn from traditions known to Paul and his Roman hearers.[11] For example, scholars suspect the peculiar vocabulary in 1:3–4 indicates the presence of traditional confessional material known to the Roman Christians. Paul uses these traditions in his letter-opening, so the argument goes, in order to show he is on common ground with his hearers from the outset and thereby gain credibility with them. The same may be true of 16:25–27. In this case, Paul draws upon known confessional language to close off his letter in a final bid to increase the adherence of the recipients to his argument. The concluding doxology would therefore form with 1:3–4 an *inclusio* of confessional language around the entire letter.[12]

In conclusion, the language of the passage presents greater difficulties than the textual problems. Yet, I do not

---

[10]"In the Pauline corpus the term μυστήριον is firmly connected with the *kerygma* of Christ." Günther Bornkamm, "μυστήριον," in *TDNT*, vol. 4 (Grand Rapids: William B. Eerdmans, 1967), 819. This statement is followed by four paragraphs analyzing 1 Corinthians in these terms. At the end of this analysis, Bornkamm adds,

> Thus Paul could simply say μυστήριον for θεοῦ σοφίαν ἐν μυστηρίῳ, τὴν ἀποκεκρυμμένην. The μυστήριον is God's pre-temporal counsel which is hidden from the world but revealed to the spiritual. This has been eschatologically fulfilled in the cross of the κύριος τῆς δόξης, . . . (ibid., 820)

Bornkamm's summary of the themes of mystery and wisdom in 1 Corinthians displays numerous parallels with the content of Romans 16:25–27.

[11]James D. G. Dunn observes that the "structure is clearly liturgical in character" (*Romans 9–16*, 913). Cranfield judges that the fact "that it has a liturgical flavour is, of course, clear" (*Romans*, 2:809).

[12]In addition, one may note along this line that Paul makes references to τῶν προφητῶν αὐτοῦ ἐν γραφαῖς ἁγίαις in 1:2 and to the γραφῶν προφητικῶν in 16:26 as well.

find that language warrants a decision against Paul's authorship of Rom. 16:25–27.[13]

Pauline Letter Style. Although he recognizes that Paul does not usually end his letters with a benediction, Larry Hurtado nevertheless offers a convincing response to those who claim the presence of this benediction demands that Romans 16:25–27 be ruled non-authentic.[14] First, 1 Cor. 16:24 provides evidence of a doxology at the end of a Pauline letter. Hurtado rightly notes that in light of the 1 Cor. passage, "it seems unwarranted to insist that Paul was incapable of writing a letter that did not conform with his usual practice."[15] Citing Galatians as a letter that does not contain Paul's usual 'thanksgiving' section, he wryly comments, "It is plain that there is a customary Pauline letter form, but neither the evidence nor logic demands the idea that Paul was a slave to this form."[16] Second, Romans constitutes an exception the customary Pauline letter form no matter how one reconstructs the ending. Stylistic grounds, therefore, make a poor argument for judging 16:25–27 as non-Pauline.

Conclusion

On the strength of textual evidence and close parallels with the argument of Romans, this dissertation accepts 16:25–27 as part of the original text following 16:23. As noted above,

---

[13]J. B. Lightfoot judged the language of 16:25–27 to be Pauline, but suggested that it was written by Paul on a different occasion and appended to Romans at a later date. See *Biblical Essays* (London: MacMillan and Co., 1893), 318. If the words are Paul's and the passage contains clear parallels with themes in the letter, why Lightfoot would need to posit that it was written at another time is unclear.

[14]"The Doxology at the End of Romans," in *New Testament Textual Criticism: Its Significance for Exegesis. Essays in Honour of Bruce M. Metzger*, eds. Eldon Jay Epp and Gordon D. Fee (Oxford: Clarendon Press, 1981), 185–99. Hurtado's argument on this point, summarized below, appears in its entirety on p. 190. His three point argument is condensed into two points here.

[15]Ibid.

[16]Ibid.

the textual evidence for these verses in this position is strong.[17] In addition, the vocabulary of the passage reflects numerous themes found throughout the letter. Four can be singled out as most significant. (1) Paul addresses the doxology τῷ δυναμένῳ ὑμᾶς στηρίξαι. Paul stated the purpose of his letter in 1:11 as enabling the Romans believers to be strengthened (στηριχθῆναι). (2) God is able to strengthen Paul's hearers κατὰ τὸ εὐαγγέλιόν, the gospel which serves as the subject of the letter (1:16). (3) Paul's statement in 1:5 εἰς ὑπακοὴν πίστεως ἐν πᾶσιν τοῖς ἔθνεσιν, a phrase signaling a key theme in the letter, is repeated almost word for word in 16:26. This theme occurs in the letter-closing at 15:18 as well. (4) The concluding note of the doxology exclaims, ἡ δόξα εἰς τοὺς αἰῶνας. The important role δόξα plays in Paul's argument has also been highlighted.

It is impossible to avoid the difficulties raised by the complicated textual tradition and somewhat unusual expressions found in the passage. The arguments for authenticity, however, are more persuasive.

In summary, the passage is treated as authentic within the argument of this dissertation. The overall argument is in no way dependent on that judgment; these verses merely add weight to arguments rooted elsewhere in the text.

---

[17]". . . the quality of the ancient witnesses supporting the positioning of it at 16:25–27, the geographical spread of their testimony, and the diversity of the textual traditions represented are decisive for reading it after 16:23." Fitzmyer, *Romans*, 50.

BIBLIOGRAPHY

Achtemeier, Paul J. "Apropos the Faith of/in Christ: A Response to Hays and Dunn." In *Pauline Theology*. Vol. 4, *Looking Back, Pressing On*, eds. E. Elizabeth Johnson and David M. Hay, 82–92. Atlanta: Scholars Press, 1997.

———. *The Quest for Unity in the New Testament Church*. Philadelphia: Fortress Press, 1987.

———. *Romans*. IBC. Louisville: John Knox Press, 1985.

———. "Romans 3:1–8: Structure and Argument." In *Christ and His Communities: Essays in Honor of Reginald H. Fuller*, eds. Arland J. Hultgren and Barbara Hall, 77–87. Cincinnati: Forward Movement Publications, 1990.

———. "Unsearchable Judgments and Inscrutable Ways: Reflections on the Discussion of Romans." In *Pauline Theology*. Vol. 4, *Looking Back, Pressing On*, eds. E. Elizabeth Johnson and David M. Hay, 3–21. Atlanta: Scholars Press, 1997.

———. *1 Peter*. Hermeneia. Minneapolis: Fortress Press, 1996.

Aland, Barbara, et al, eds. *Novum Testamentum Graece*, 27th ed. Stuttgart: Deutsche Bibelgesellschaft, 1995.

Aland, Kurt. "Der Schluss und die ursprüngliche Gestalt des Römerbriefes." In *Neutestamentliche Entwürfe*, TBü, bd. 63, 284–301. Munich: Chr. Kaiser Verlag, 1979.

Aland, Kurt, and Barbara Aland. *The Text of the New Testament: An Introduction to the Critical Editions and to the Theory and Practice of Modern Textual Criticism*, 2d ed. Translated by Erroll F. Rhodes. Grand Rapids: William B. Eerdmans, 1989.

Althaus, Paul. *Der Brief an der Römer übersetzt und erklärt.* NTD. Göttingen: Vandenhoeck & Ruprecht, 1978.

Anchor Bible Dictionary. Edited by David Noel Freedman. 6 vols. New York: Doubleday, 1992.
S.v. "Diatribe," by Stanley K. Stowers. 2:190–93.
S.v. "Erastus," by Florence Morgan Gillman. 2:571.
S.v. "Resurrection (Early Judaism and Christianity)," by George W. E. Nickelsburg. 5:684–91.
S.v. "Romans, Epistle to the," by Charles D. Myers, Jr. 5:816–30.
S.v. "Travel and Communication (NT World)," by F. F. Bruce. 6:648–53.

Aune, David E. *The New Testament in Its Literary Environment.* Cambridge: James Clarke, 1988.

———. "Orthodoxy in First Century Judaism? A Response to N. J. McEleney." *JSJ* 7 (1978): 1–10.

———. "Romans as a *Logos Protreptikos.*" In *The Romans Debate,* revised and expanded ed., ed. Karl P. Donfried, 278–96. Peabody, Mass.: Hendrickson, 1991.

Aus, Roger D. "Paul's Travel Plans and the 'Full Number of Gentiles' of Rom. xi. 25." *NovT* 21 (1979): 232–62.

Austin, J. L. "Performative Utterances." In *Philosophical Papers,* eds. J. O. Urmson and G. J. Warnock, 220–39. Oxford: Clarendon Press, 1961.

Austin, J. L. *Philosophical Papers,* eds. J. O. Urmson and G. J. Warnock. Oxford: Clarendon Press, 1961.

Bacon, Benjamin W. "The Doxology at the End of Romans." *JBL* 18 (1899): 167–76.

Bailey, James L., and Lyle D. Vander Broek. *Literary Forms in the New Testament: A Handbook.* Louisville: Westminster/John Knox Press, 1992.

Bammel, Ernst. "Romans 13." In *Jesus and the Politics of His Day,* eds. Ernst Bammel and C. F. D. Moule, 365–83. Cambridge: Cambridge University Press, 1984.

Bammel, Ernst, and C. F. D. Moule, eds. *Jesus and the Politics of His Day.* Cambridge: Cambridge University Press, 1984.

Barclay, John M. G. "Mirror-Reading a Polemical Letter: Galatians as a Test Case." In *The Pauline Writings*, eds. Stanley E. Porter and Craig A. Evans, The Biblical Seminar, vol. 34, 247–67. Sheffield: Sheffield Academic Press, 1995.

———. *Obeying the Truth: Paul's Ethics in Galatians*. Minneapolis: Fortress Press, 1991.

———. "Paul among Diaspora Jews: Anomaly or Apostate?" *JSNT* 60 (1995): 89–120.

Barnett, Paul W. "Opposition in Corinth." *JSNT* 22 (1984): 3–17.

Barrett, C. K. *The Epistle to the Romans*. HNTC. Peabody, Mass.: Hendrickson, 1957.

———. *Essays on Paul*. Philadelphia: Westminster Press, 1982.

———. "The Gentile Mission as an Eschatological Phenomenon." In *Jesus and the Word*. Allison Park, Pa.: Pickwick Publications, 1995.

———. "Paul's Opponents in 2 Corinthians." In *Essays on Paul*, 60–86. Philadelphia: Westminster Press, 1982.

———. "ΨΕΥΔΑΠΟΣΤΟΛΟΣ." In *Essays on Paul*, 87–107. Philadelphia: Westminster Press, 1982.

Barth, Karl. *The Epistle to the Romans*. Translated by Edwyn C. Hoskyns. New York: Oxford University Press, 1933.

Bartsch, Hans-Werner. "Die antisemitischen Gegner des Paulus im Römerbrief." In *Antijudaismus im Neuen Testament? Exegetische und systematische Beiträge*, hrsg. Willehad Paul Eckert, Nathan Peter Levinson und Martin Stöhr. Abhandlungen zum christlich-jüdischen Dialog, bd. 2, ed. Helmut Gollwitzer, 27–43. Munich: Chr. Kaiser Verlag, 1967.

———. "Die Empfänger des Römerbriefes." *ST* 25 (1971): 81–89.

———. "The Concept of Faith in Paul's Letter to the Romans." *BR* 13 (1968): 41–53.

———. "The Historical Situation of Romans." *Encounter* 33 (1972): 329–39.

———. ". . . . wenn ich ihnen diese Frucht versiegelt habe. Röm 15.28. Ein Beitrag zum Verständnis der paulinischen Mission." *ZNT* 63 (1972): 95–107.

Bassler, Jouette M. "Centering the Argument: A Response to Andrew T. Lincoln." In *Pauline Theology*. Vol. 3, *Romans*, eds. David M. Hay and E. Elizabeth Johnson, 160–68. Minneapolis: Fortress Press, 1995.

Bauer, Walter, William F. Arndt, F. Wilbur Gingrich, and Frederick W. Danker, eds. *A Greek-English Lexicon of the New Testament and Other Early Christian Literature*, 2d ed. Chicago: University of Chicago Press, 1979.

Beker, J. Christiaan. "Conversations with a Friend about Romans." In *Faith and History: Essays in Honor of Paul W. Meyer*, eds. John T. Carroll, Charles H. Cosgrove, and E. Elizabeth Johnson, 90–98. Atlanta: Scholars Press, 1990.

———. *Paul the Apostle: The Triumph of God in Life and Thought*. Philadelphia: Fortress Press, 1980.

Betz, Hans Dieter. *Galatians*. Hermeneia. Philadelphia: Fortress Press, 1979.

Bjerkelund, C. J. *Parakalô: Form, Funktion und Sinn der parakalô-Sätze in den paulinischen Briefen*. Bibliotheca theologica norvegica, bd.1. Oslo: Universitetsforlaget, 1967.

Black, David Alan. "The Pauline Love Command: Structure, Style, and Ethics in Romans 12:9–21." *Filologia Neotestamentaria* 2 (1989): 3–22.

Black, Matthew. *Romans*, 2d ed. NCB. Grand Rapids: William B. Eerdmans, 1989.

Blass, F., and A. DeBrunner. *A Greek Grammar of the New Testament and Other Early Christian Literature*. Translated and revised by Robert W. Funk. Chicago: University of Chicago Press, 1961.

Boers, Hendrikus. "The Problem of Jews and Gentiles in the Macro-Structure of Romans." *SEÅ* 47 (1982): 184–96.

Borg, Marcus. "A New Context for Romans XIII." *NTS* 19 (1972–73): 205–18.

Bornkamm, Günther. "The Letter to the Romans as Paul's Last Will and Testament." In *The Romans Debate*, revised and expanded ed., ed. Karl P. Donfried, 16–28. Peabody, Mass.: Hendrickson, 1991.

Borse, Udo. "Die geschichtliche und theologische Einordnung des Römerbriefes." *BZ* 16 (1972): 70–83.

Bowers, Paul. "Fulfilling the Gospel: The Scope of the Pauline Mission." *JETS* 30 (1987): 185–98.

Brändle, Rudolf, and Ekkehard W. Stegemann. "The Formation of the First 'Christian Congregations' in Rome in the Context of the Jewish Congregations." In *Judaism and Christianity in First-Century Rome*, eds. Karl P. Donfried and Peter Richardson, 117–27. Grand Rapids: William B. Eerdmans, 1998.

Brown, Raymond E. "Further Reflections on the Origins of the Church of Rome." In *The Conversation Continues: Studies in Paul and John in Honor of J. Louis Martyn*, eds. Robert T. Fortna and Beverly R. Gaventa, 98–115. Nashville: Abingdon Press, 1990.

———. *An Introduction to the New Testament*. The Anchor Bible Reference Library. New York: Doubleday, 1997.

———. "Not Jewish Christianity and Gentile Christianity but Types of Jewish/Gentile Christianity." *CBQ* 45 (1983): 74–79.

Brown, Raymond, and John P. Meier. *Antioch and Rome: New Testament Cradles of Catholic Christianity*. New York: Paulist Press, 1983.

Bruce, F. F. *Romans*, 2d ed. TynNTC. Grand Rapids: William B. Eerdmans, 1985.

———. "The Romans Debate—Continued." In *The Romans Debate*, revised and expanded ed., ed. Karl P. Donfried, 175–94. Peabody, Mass.: Hendrickson, 1991.

Bultmann, Rudolf. *Der Stil der paulinischen Predigt und die kynisch-stoische Diatribe*. FRLANT, bd. 13. Göttingen: Vandenhoeck and Ruprecht, 1910.

Byrne, Brendan. "'Rather Boldly' (Rom 15,15): Paul's Prophetic Bid to Win Allegiance of the Christians in Rome." *Bib* 74 (1993): 83–96.

————. *Romans*. SacPag, vol. 6. Collegeville, Minn.: The Liturgical Press, 1996.

Calvin, John. *Commentary on the Epistle of Paul the Apostle to the Romans*. Translated and ed. by John Owen. Grand Rapids: William B. Eerdmans, 1947.

Campbell, Douglas A. "Determining the Gospel through Rhetorical Analysis in Paul's Letter to the Roman Christians." In *Gospel in Paul: Studies on Corinthians, Galatians and Romans for Richard N. Longenecker*, eds. L. Ann Jervis and Peter Richardson. JSNTSup, vol. 108, 315–36. Sheffield: Sheffield Academic Press, 1994.

————. *The Rhetoric of Righteousness in Romans 3.21–26*. JSNTSup, vol. 65. Sheffield: JSOT Press, 1992.

Campbell, William S. "The Freedom and Faithfulness of God in Relation to Israel: Romans 9–11." In *Paul's Gospel in an Intercultural Context: Jew and Gentile in the Letter to the Romans*. Studies in the Intercultural History of Christianity, vol. 69, 43–59. New York: Peter Lang, 1991.

————. *Paul's Gospel in an Intercultural Context: Jew and Gentile in the Letter to the Romans*. Studies in the Intercultural History of Christianity, vol. 69. New York: Peter Lang, 1991.

————. "Paul's Strategy in Writing Romans." In *Paul's Gospel in an Intercultural Context: Jew and Gentile in the Letter to the Romans*. Studies in the Intercultural History of Christianity, vol. 69, 132–60. New York: Peter Lang, 1991.

————. "Romans III as a Key to the Structure and Thought of Romans." In *The Romans Debate*, revised and expanded ed., ed. Karl P. Donfried, 251–64. Peabody, Mass.: Hendrickson, 1991.

————. "The Rule of Faith in Romans 12:1–15:13: The Obligation of Humble Obedience to Christ as the Only Adequate Response to the Mercies of God." In *Pauline Theology*. Vol. 3, *Romans*, eds. David M. Hay and E. Elizabeth Johnson, 259–86. Minneapolis: Fortress Press, 1995.

————. "A Theme for Romans?" In *Paul's Gospel in an Intercultural Context: Jew and Gentile in the Letter to the Romans*. Studies in the Intercultural History of Christianity, vol. 69, 161–99. New York: Peter Lang, 1991.

———. "Why did Paul write Romans?" In *Paul's Gospel in an Intercultural Context: Jew and Gentile in the Letter to the Romans.* Studies in the Intercultural History of Christianity, vol. 69, 14–24. New York: Peter Lang, 1991.

Canales, Isaac J. "Paul's Accusers in Romans 3:8 and 6:1." *EvQ* 57 (1985): 237–45.

Caragounis, Chrys C. "From Obscurity to Prominence: The Development of the Roman Church between Romans and *1 Clement.*" In *Judaism and Christianity in First-Century Rome*, eds. Karl P. Donfried and Peter Richardson, 245–79. Grand Rapids: William B. Eerdmans, 1998.

Carroll, John T., Charles H. Cosgrove, and E. Elizabeth Johnson, eds. *Faith and History: Essays in Honor of Paul W. Meyer.* Atlanta: Scholars Press, 1990.

Carson, Donald A., and H. G. M. Williamson, eds. *It Is Written. Scripture Citing Scripture: Essays in Honour of Barnabas Lindars.* Cambridge: Cambridge University Press, 1993.

Casson, Lionel. *Ships and Seamanship in the Ancient World.* Princeton: Princeton University Press, 1971.

———. "Speed Under Sail of Ancient Ships." In *TAPA* 82 (1951): 136–48.

———. *Travel in the Ancient World.* Baltimore: John Hopkins University Press, 1994.

Chae, Daniel Jong-Sang. *Paul as Apostle to the Gentiles: His Apostolic Self-Awareness and its Influence on the Soteriological Argument in Romans.* Paternoster Biblical and Theological Monographs. Carlisle, England: Paternoster Press, 1997.

Charlesworth, James H., ed. *The Old Testament Pseudepigrapha.* Vol. 1, *Apocalyptic Literature & Testaments.* New York: Doubleday, 1983.

Clement of Rome. *The Apostolic Fathers*, vol. 1. *LCL.* Translated by Kirsopp Lake. Cambridge: Harvard University Press, 1935.

Collins, John J. *The Apocalyptic Imagination: An Introduction to Jewish Apocalyptic Literature*, 2d ed. Grand Rapids: William B. Eerdmans, 1998.

Cosgrove, Charles H. "What If Some Have Not Believed? The Occasion and Thrust of Romans 3.1–8." *ZNW* 78 (1987): 90–105.

Cousar, Charles B. "Continuity and Discoutinuity: Reflections on Romans 5–8 (In Conversation with Frank Thielman)." In *Pauline Theology*. Vol. 3, *Romans*, eds. David M. Hay and E. Elizabeth Johnson, 196–210. Minneapolis: Fortress Press, 1995.

Crafton, Jeffrey A. "Paul's Rhetorical Vision and the Purpose of Romans." *NovT* 32 (1990): 317–39.

Cranfield, C. E. B. *The Epistle to the Romans*. Vol. 1, *Introduction and Commentary on Romans 1–8*. ICC. Edinburgh: T & T Clark, 1975.

———. *The Epistle to the Romans*. Vol. 2, *Commentary on Romans 9–16 and Essays*. ICC. Edinburgh: T & T Clark, 1979.

Dahl, Nils A. "Anamnesis: Memory and Commemoration in Early Christianity." In *Jesus in the Memory of the Early Church*, 11–29. Minneapolis: Augsburg, 1976.

———. *Jesus in the Memory of the Early Church*. Minneapolis: Augsburg, 1976.

———. *Jesus the Christ: The Historical Origins of Christological Doctrine*, ed. Donald H. Juel. Minneapolis: Fortress Press, 1991.

———. "The Messiahship of Jesus in Paul." In *Jesus the Christ: The Historical Origins of Christological Doctrine*, ed. Donald H. Juel, 15–26. Minneapolis: Fortress Press, 1991.

———. "The Missionary Theology in the Epistle to the Romans." In *Studies in Paul*, 70–88. Minneapolis: Augsburg, 1977.

———. *Studies in Paul*. Minneapolis: Augsburg, 1977.

Davies, Glenn N. *Faith and Obedience in Romans: A Study in Romans 1–4*. JSNTSup, vol. 39. Sheffield: JSOT Press, 1990.

Davies, W. D. *Jewish and Pauline Studies*. Philadelphia: Fortress Press, 1984.

———. "Paul and the People of Israel." In *Jewish and Pauline Studies*, 123–52. Philadelphia: Fortress Press, 1984.

Denney, James. *St. Paul's Epistle to the Romans.* The Expositor's Greek Testament, vol. 2, ed. W. Robertson Nicholl, 555–725. Grand Rapids: William B. Eerdmans, 1979.

Dibelius, Martin. *From Tradition to Gospel.* New York: Charles Scribner's Sons, n. d..

Dictionary of Paul and His Letters. Edited by Gerald R. Hawthorne and Ralph P. Martin. Downers Grove, Ill.: InterVarsity Press, 1993.
S.v. "Diatribe," by D. F. Watson. 213–14.
S.v. "Eschatology," by Larry J. Kreitzer. 253–69.
S.v. "Holy Spirit," by Terence Paige. 404–13.
S.v. "Itineraries, Travel Plans, Journeys, Apostolic Parousia," by Paul Trebilco. 446–56.
S.v. "Mission," by W. P. Bowers. 608–19.
S.v. "Opponents of Paul," by Paul W. Barnett. 644–53.
S.v. "Romans, Letter to the," by James D. G. Dunn. 838–50.
S.v. "Travel in the Roman World," by Larry J. Kreitzer. 945–46.

Dodd, C. H. *The Epistle of Paul to the Romans.* MNTC, ed. James Moffatt. London: Hodder and Stoughton, 1932.

Donaldson, Terence L. *Paul and the Gentiles: Remapping the Apostle's Convictional World.* Minneapolis: Fortress Press, 1997.

Donfried, Karl P. "False Presuppositions in the Study of Romans." In *The Romans Debate*, revised and expanded ed., ed. Karl P. Donfried, 102–24. Peabody, Mass.: Hendrickson, 1991.

———. "A Short Note on Romans 16." In *The Romans Debate*, revised and expanded ed., ed. Karl P. Donfried, 44–52. Peabody, Mass.: Hendrickson, 1991.

———., ed. *The Romans Debate*, revised and expanded ed. Peabody, Mass.: Hendrickson, 1991.

Donfried, Karl P., and Peter Richardson, eds. *Judaism and Christianity in First-Century Rome.* Grand Rapids: William B. Eerdmans, 1998.

Doty, William G. *Letters in Primitive Christianity.* GBS, New Testament Series, ed. Dan O. Via, Jr. Philadelphia: Fortress Press, 1973.

Drane, John W. "Why Did Paul Write Romans?" In *Pauline Studies*, eds. Donald A. Hagner and Murray J. Harris, 208–27. Exeter, England: Paternoster Press, 1980.

Drummond, James. "Occasion and Object of the Epistle to the Romans." *HibJ* 11 (1912–1913): 787–804.

Dunn, James D. G. "Echoes of Intra-Jewish Polemic in Paul's Letter to the Galatians." *JBL* 112 (1993): 459–77.

———. *Jesus and the Spirit*. Grand Rapids: William B. Eerdmans, 1997. Reprint, London: SCM Press, 1975.

———. "Paul's Epistle to the Romans: An Analysis of Structure and Argument." In *ANRW*, part II, vol. 25, no. 4, eds. Wolfgang Haase and Hildegard Temporini, 2845–90. New York: Walter de Gruyter, 1987.

———. *Romans 1–8*. WBC, vol. 38A. Milton Keynes, England: Word, 1991.

———. *Romans 9–16*. WBC, vol. 38B. Milton Keynes, England: Word, 1991.

———. "Romans 13:1–7—A Charter for Political Quietism?" *Ex Auditu* 2 (1986): 55–68.

———. *The Theology of Paul the Apostle*. Grand Rapids: William B. Eerdmans, 1998.

———. *The Theology of Paul's Letter to the Galatians*. New Testament Theology. Cambridge: Cambridge University Press, 1993.

du Toit, A. B. "Faith and Obedience in Paul." *Neot* 25 (1991): 65–74.

———. "Die Kirche als doxologische Gemeinschaft im Römerbrief." *Neot* 27 (1993): 69–77.

Edwards, James R. *Romans*. New International Biblical Commentary. Peabody, Mass.: Hendrickson, 1992.

Ehrman, Bart D. *The New Testament: A Historical Introduction to the Early Christian Writings*. New York: Oxford University Press, 1997.

Elliott, J. K. "The Language and Style of the Concluding Doxology to the Epistle to the Romans." *ZNW* 72 (1981): 124–30.

Elliott, Neil. *The Rhetoric of Romans: Argumentative Constraint and Strategy and Paul's Dialogue with Judaism.* JSNTSup, vol. 45. Sheffield: JSOT Press, 1990.

————. "Romans 13:1–7 in the Context of Imperial Propaganda." In *Paul and Empire: Religion and Power in Roman Imperial Society*, ed. Richard A. Horsley, 184–204. Harrisburg, Pa.: Trinity International Press, 1997.

Ellis, E. Earle. "'Those of the Circumcision' and the Early Christian Mission." In *SE*. Vol. 4, *Part 1: The New Testament Scriptures*, ed. F. L. Cross. TU, bd. 102, 390–99. Berlin: Akademie-Verlag, 1968.

————. "Paul and his Opponents: Trends in Research." In *Christianity, Judaism and other Greco-Roman Cults: Studies for Morton Smith at Sixty*, vol. 1, ed. Jacob Neusner. SJLA, vol. 12.1, 264–98. Leiden: E. J. Brill, 1975.

Engberg-Pedersen, Troels, ed. *Paul in His Hellenistic Context.* Minneapolis: Fortress, 1995.

Fahy, T. "Epistle to the Romans 16:25–27." *ITQ* 28 (1961): 238–41.

————. "St. Paul's Roman were Jewish Converts." *ITQ* 26 (1959): 182–91.

Fee, Gordon D. *God's Empowering Presence: The Holy Spirit in the Letters of Paul.* Peabody, Mass.: Hendrickson, 1994.

————. *Paul's Letter to the Philippians*, NICNT. Grand Rapids: William B. Eerdmans, 1995.

Ferguson, Everett. *Backgrounds of Early Christianity*, 2d ed. Grand Rapids: William B. Eerdmans, 1993.

Fitzmyer, Joseph A. *According to Paul: Studies in the Theology of the Apostle.* New York: Paulist Press, 1993.

————. *Romans.* AB, vol. 33. New York: Doubleday & Co., Inc., 1993.

Fraikin, Daniel. "The Rhetorical Function of the Jews in Romans." In *Anti-Judaism in Early Christianity.* Vol. 1, *Paul and the Gospels,* eds. Peter Richardson and David M. Granskou, 91–105. Waterloo, Ont: Wilfrid Laurier University Press, 1986.

Friedrich, Gerhard. "Muß ὑπακοὴ πίστεως Röm 1:5 'Glaubengehorsam' übersetz werden?" *ZNW* 72 (1981): 118–23.

Friedrich, Johannes, Wolfgang Pöhlmann, and Peter Stuhlmacher. "Zur historischen Situation und Intention von Röm 13,1–7." *ZTK* 73 (1976): 131–66.

Funk, Robert W. "The Apostolic *Parousia*: Form and Significance." In *Christian History and Interpretation: Studies Presented to John Knox*, eds. W. R. Farmer, C. F. D. Moule, and R. R. Niebuhr, 249–68. Cambridge: Cambridge University Press, 1967.

———. *Language, Hermeneutic, and Word of God: The Problem of Language in the New Testament and Contemporary Theology.* New York: Harper & Row, 1966.

Furnish, Victor Paul. *Theology and Ethics in Paul.* Nashville: Abingdon Press, 1968.

Gagnon, Robert A. J. "Heart of Wax and a Teaching that Stamps: ΤΥΠΟΣ ΔΙΔΑΧΗΣ (Rom 6:17b) Once More." *JBL* 112 (1993): 667–87.

Gamble, Harry, Jr. *The Textual History of the Letter to the Romans.* SD, vol. 42. Grand Rapids: William B. Eerdmans, 1977.

Garlington, Don B. *Faith, Obedience and Perseverance: Aspects of Paul's Letter to the Romans.* WUNT, reihe 2, bd. 79. Tübingen: J. C. B. Mohr (Paul Siebeck), 1994.

———. *"The Obedience of Faith": A Pauline Phrase in Historical Context*, WUNT, reihe 2, bd. 8. Tübingen: J. C. B. Mohr (Paul Siebeck), 1991.

Georgi, Dieter. "Der Kampf um die reine Lehre im Urchristentum als Auseinandersetzung um das rechte Verständnis der an Israel ergangenen Offenbarung Gottes." In *Antijudaismus im Neuen Testament?* Abhandlungen zum christlich-jüdischen Dialog, bd. 2, 82–94. Munich: Chr. Kaiser Verlag, 1967.

———. *The Opponents of Paul in Second Corinthians.* Edinburgh: T & T Clark, 1987.

————. *Remembering the Poor: The History of Paul's Collection for Jerusalem*. Nashville: Abingdon Press, 1992.

Godet, F. *Commentary on St. Paul's Epistle to the Romans*. Vol. 1, translated by A. Cusin. Edinburgh: T & T Clark, 1886.

————. *Commentary on St. Paul's Epistle to the Romans*. Vol. 2, translated by A. Cusin. Edinburgh: T & T Clark, 1889.

Gowan, Donald E. *Eschatology in the Old Testament*. Philadelphia: Fortress Press, 1986.

Guerra, Anthony J. *Romans and the Apologetic Tradition: The Purpose, Genre and Audience of Paul's Letter*. SNTSMS, vol. 81. Cambridge: Cambridge University Press, 1995.

————. "Romans: Paul's Purpose and Audience with Special Attention to Romans 9–11." *RB* 97 (1990): 219–37.

Gunther, John J. *St. Paul's Opponents and Their Background. A Study of Apocalyptic and Jewish Sectarian Teachings*. NovTSup, vol. 35. Leiden: E. J. Brill, 1973.

Guthrie, Donald. *New Testament Introduction*, 4th ed. Leicester, England: Apollos, 1990.

Gyllenberg, R. "Glaube und Gehorsam." *ZST* 14 (1937): 547–66.

Haacker, Klaus. "Der Römerbrief als Friedensmemorandum." *NTS* 36 (1990): 25–41.

Hafemann, Scott J. *Paul, Moses, and the History of Israel: The Letter / Spirit Contrast and the Argument from Scripture in 2 Corinthians 3*. Peabody, Mass.: Hendrickson, 1996.

Hahn, Ferdinand. *Mission in the New Testament*. SBT, vol. 47. London: SCM Press, 1965.

Hall, David R. "Romans 3.1–8 Reconsidered." *NTS* 29 (1983): 183–97.

Harder, G. "Der Konkrete Anlass des Römerbriefes." *Theologia Viatorum* 6 (1954): 13–24.

Harvey, A. E. "The Opposition to Paul." In *SE*. Vol. 4, *Part 1: The New Testament Scriptures*, ed. F. L. Cross. TU, bd. 102, 319–32. Berlin: Akademie-Verlag, 1968.

Hawthorne, Gerald F. *Philippians*. WBC, vol. 43. Waco, Tex.: Word, 1983.

Hawthorne, Gerald, with Otto Betz, eds. *Tradition and Interpretation in the New Testament: Essays in Honor of E. Earle Ellis for His 60th Birthday*. Grand Rapids: William B. Eerdmans, 1987.

Hay, David M., and E. Elizabeth Johnson, eds. *Pauline Theology*. Vol. 3, *Romans*. Minneapolis: Fortress Press, 1995.

Hays, Richard B. "Adam, Israel, Christ—The Question of Covenant in the Theology of Romans: A Response to Leander E. Keck and N. T. Wright." In *Pauline Theology*. Vol. 3, *Romans*, eds. David M. Hay and E. Elizabeth Johnson, 68–86. Minneapolis: Fortress Press, 1995.

———. "Christ Prays the Psalms: Paul's Use of an Early Christian Exegetical Convention." In *The Future of Christology: Essays in Honor of Leander E. Keck*, eds. Abraham J. Malherbe and Wayne A. Meeks, 122–36. Minneapolis: Fortress Press, 1993.

———. *Echoes of Scripture in the Letters of Paul*. New Haven: Yale University Press, 1989.

———. "ΠΙΣΤΙΣ and the Pauline Christology: What is at Stake?" In *Pauline Theology*. Vol. 4, *Looking Back, Pressing On*, eds. E. Elizabeth Johnson and David Hay, 35–60. Atlanta: Scholars Press, 1997.

———. "Psalm 143 and the Logic of Romans 3." *JBL* 99 (1980): 107–15.

———. "The Role of Scripture in Paul's Ethics." In *Theology & Ethics in Paul and His Interpreters: Essays in Honor of Victor Paul Furnish*, eds. Eugene H. Lovering, Jr. and Jerry L. Sumney, 30–47. Nashville: Abingdon, 1996.

Heil, John Paul. *Romans—Paul's Letter of Hope*. AnBib, vol. 112. Rome: Biblical Institute Press, 1987.

Hellholm, David. "Enthymemic Argumentation in Paul: The Case of Romans 6." In *Paul in His Hellenistic Context*, ed. Troels Engberg-Pedersen, 119–79. Minneapolis: Fortress, 1995.

Hock, Ronald F. *The Social Context of Paul's Ministry: Tentmaking and Apostleship*. Philadelphia: Fortress Press, 1980.

Holmberg, Bengt. *Paul and Power: The Structure of Authority in the Primitive Church as Reflected in the Pauline Epistles.* Philadelphia: Fortress Press, 1978.

Hooker, M. D. *From Adam to Christ: Essays on Paul.* Cambridge: Cambridge University Press, 1990.

Hooker, M. D., and S. G. Wilson, eds. *Paul and Paulinism: Essays in Honour of C. K. Barrett.* London: SPCK, 1982.

Horsley, Richard A., ed. *Paul and Empire: Religion and Power in Roman Imperial Society.* Harrisburg, Pa.: Trinity International Press, 1997.

Hurtado, Larry W. "The Doxology at the End of Romans." In *New Testament Textual Criticism: Its Significance for Exegesis. Essays in Honour of Bruce M. Metzger,* eds. Eldon Jay Epp and Gordon D. Fee, 185–200. Oxford: Clarendon Press, 1981.

Jeremias, Joachim. *Jesus' Promise to the Nations,* Translated by S. H. Hooke. Philadelphia: Fortress Press, 1982.

Jervell, Jacob. "The Letter to Jerusalem." In *The Romans Debate,* revised and expanded ed., ed. Karl P. Donfried, 53–64. Peabody, Mass.: Hendrickson, 1991.

Jervis, L. Ann. *The Purpose of Romans. A Comparative Letter Structure Investigation.* JSNTSup, vol. 55. Sheffield: JSOT Press, 1991.

Jervis, L. Ann, and Peter Richardson, eds. *Gospel in Paul: Studies on Corinthians, Galatians and Romans for Richard N. Longenecker.* JSNTSup, vol. 108. Sheffield: Sheffield Academic Press., 1994.

Jewett, Robert. "The Agitators and the Galatian Congregation." *NTS* 17 (1970–71): 198–212.

———. *A Chronology of Paul's Life.* Philadelphia: Fortress Press, 1979.

———. "Ecumenical Theology for the Sake of Mission: Romans 1:1–7 + 15:14–16:24." In *Pauline Theology.* Vol. 3, *Romans,* eds. David M. Hay and E. Elizabeth Johnson, 89–108. Minneapolis: Fortress Press, 1995.

———. "Following the Argument of Romans." In *The Romans Debate,* revised and expanded ed., ed. Karl P. Donfried, 265–77. Peabody, Mass.: Hendrickson, 1991.

———. "The Form and Function of the Homiletic Benediction." *ATR* 51 (1969): 18–34.

———. *Paul's Anthropological Terms: A Study of Their Use in Conflict Settings*. AGJU, bd. 10. Leiden: E. J. Brill, 1971.

———. "Romans as an Ambassadorial Letter." *Int* 36 (1982): 5–20.

Johnson, E. Elizabeth. "Romans 9–11: The Faithfulness and Impartiality of God." In *Pauline Theology*. Vol. 3, *Romans*, eds. David M. Hay and E. Elizabeth Johnson, 211–39. Minneapolis: Fortress Press, 1995.

Johnson, E. Elizabeth, and David M. Hay, eds. *Pauline Theology*. Vol. 4, *Looking Back, Pressing On*. Atlanta: Scholars Press, 1997.

Johnson, Luke T. *Reading Romans: A Literary and Theological Commentary*. Reading the New Testament Series. New York: Crossroad, 1997.

———. *The Writings of the New Testament: An Interpretation*. Philadelphia: Fortress Press, 1986.

Judge, E. A., and G. S. R. Thomas. "The Origin of the Church at Rome: A New Solution?" *RTR* 25 (1966), 81–94.

Karris, Robert J. "The Occasion of Romans: A Response to Prof. Donfried." In *The Romans Debate*, revised and expanded ed., ed. Karl P. Donfried, 125–27. Peabody, Mass.: Hendrickson, 1991.

———. "Romans 14:1–15:13 and the Occasion of Romans." In *The Romans Debate*, revised and expanded ed., ed. Karl P. Donfried, 65–84. Peabody, Mass.: Hendrickson, 1991.

Käsemann, Ernst. *Commentary on Romans*. Translated and ed. by Geoffrey W. Bromiley. Grand Rapids: William. B. Eerdmans, 1980.

———. *New Testament Questions of Today*. London: SCM Press, 1969.

———. "Principles of the Interpretation of Romans 13." In *New Testament Questions of Today*, 196–216. London: SCM Press, 1969.

———. "Worship in Everyday Life: a note on Romans 12." In *New Testament Questions of Today*, 188–95. London: SCM Press, 1969.

Kaye, B. N. "To the Romans and Others' Revisited." *NovT* 19 (1976): 37–77.

Kaylor, R. David. *Paul's Covenant Community: Jew & Gentile in Romans*. Atlanta: John Knox Press, 1988.

Keck, Leander E. "Christology, Soteriology, and the Praise of God (Romans 15:7–13)." In *The Conversation Continues: Studies in Paul & John In Honor of J. Louis Martyn*, eds. Robert T. Fortna and Beverly R. Gaventa, 85–97. Nashville: Abingdon Press, 1990.

———. "Searchable Judgments and Scrutable Ways: A Response to Paul J. Achtemeier." In *Pauline Theology*. Vol. 4, *Looking Back, Pressing On*, eds. E. Elizabeth Johnson and David M. Hay, 22–32. Atlanta: Scholars Press, 1997.

———. "What Makes Romans Tick?" In *Pauline Theology*. Vol. 3, *Romans*, eds. David M. Hay and E. Elizabeth Johnson, 3–29. Minneapolis: Fortress Press, 1995.

Kettunen, Marku. *Der Abfassungszweck des Römerbriefes*. Annales Acadmiae scientarum Fennicae: dissertationes humanarum litterarum 18. Helsinki: Soumalainen Tiedeakatemia, 1979.

Klein, Günther. "Paul's Purpose in Writing the Epistle to the Romans." In *The Romans Debate*, revised and expanded ed., ed. Karl P. Donfried, 29–43. Peabody, Mass.: Hendrickson, 1991.

Knox, John. "A Note on the Text of Romans." *NTS* 2 (1955–1956): 191–93.

Koch, Dietrich-Alex. *Die Schrift als Zeuge des Evangeliums: Untersuchungen zur Verwendung und zum Verständnis der Schrift bei Paulus*. BHT, bd. 69. Tübingen: J. C. B. Mohr (Paul Siebeck), 1986.

Koester, Helmut. "The Purpose of the Polemic of A Pauline Fragment (Philippians III)." *NTS* 8 (1961–62): 317–32.

Kreitzer, Larry J. *2 Corinthians*. NTG. Sheffield: Sheffield Academic Press, 1996.

Kruger, M. A. "*TINA KARPON*, 'Some Fruit' in Romans 1:13." *WJT* 49 (1987): 167–73

Kümmel, W. G. *Introduction to the New Testament*, 2d ed. Translated by Howard Clark Kee. London: SCM Press, 1975.

Kuss, Otto. *Der Römerbrief (Rom. 1,1–6,11)*. Regensburg: Verlag Friedrich Pustet, 1957.

———. *Der Römerbrief (Rom. 6,12–8,19)*. Regensburg: Verlag Friedrich Pustet, 1959.

———. *Der Römerbrief (Rom. 8:20–11:36)*. Regensburg: Verlag Friedrich Pustet, 1978.

LaGrange, M.-J. *Saint Paul: Epître aux Romains*, 6th ed. Etudes Bibliques. Paris: Gabalds, 1950.

Lampe, Peter. *Die stadtrömischen Christen in den ersten beide Jahrhunderten*. WUNT, reihe 2, bd. 18. Tübingen: J. C. B. Mohr (Paul Siebeck), 1987.

———. "The Roman Christians of Romans 16." In *The Romans Debate*, revised and expanded ed., ed. Karl P. Donfried, 216–30. Peabody, Mass.: Hendrickson, 1991.

Lane, William. *Hebrews 1–8*. WBC, vol. 47A.. Dallas: Word, 1991.

———. "Social Perspectives on Roman Christianity during the Formative Years from Nero to Nerva: Romans, Hebrews, *1 Clement*." In *Judaism and Christianity in First-Century Rome*, eds. Karl P. Donfried and Peter Richardson, 196–244. Grand Rapids: William B. Eerdmans, 1998.

Leenhardt, Franz J. *The Epistle to the Romans. A Commentary*. Translated by Harold Knight. London: Lutterworth Press, 1961.

Lenski, R. C. H. *The Interpretation of St. Paul's Epistle to the Romans*. Minneapolis: Augsburg, 1961.

Leon, Harry J. *The Jews of Ancient Rome*, updated ed. Peabody, Mass.: Hendrickson, 1995.

Lichtenberger, Hermann. "Jews and Christians in Rome in the Time of Nero: Josephus and Paul in Rome." In *ANRW*, part 2, vol. 26.3, eds. Wolfgang Haase and Hildegard Temporini, 2142–76. New York: Walter de Gruyter, 1996.

Liddell, Henry George, and Robert Scott, eds. *A Greek-English Lexicon*, 9th ed. Oxford: Clarendon Press, 1968.

Liddon, H. P. *Explanatory Analysis of St. Paul's Epistle to the Romans*. London: Longmans, Green, and Co., 1893.

Lietzmann, D. Hans. *An die Römer*, 2d aufl. HNT, bd. 3. Tübingen: J. C. B. Mohr (Paul Siebeck), 1919.

Lightfoot, J. B. *Biblical Essays*. London: MacMillan and Co., 1893.

———. *Notes on Epistles of St. Paul*, ed. J. R. Harmer. Grand Rapids: Baker Books, 1980.

Lincoln, Andrew T. "From Wrath to Justification: Tradition, Gospel, and Audience in the Theology of Romans 1:18–4:25." In *Pauline Theology*. Vol. 3, *Romans*, eds. David M. Hay and E. Elizabeth Johnson, 130–59. Minneapolis: Fortress Press, 1995.

Lohse, Eduard. *The Formation of the New Testament*. Translated by M. Eugene Boring. Nashville: Abingdon Press, 1981.

Longenecker, Richard N. *Galatians*. WBC, vol. 41. Dallas: Word, 1990.

Louw, Johannes P., and Eugene A. Nida, eds. *Greek-English Lexicon of the New Testament Based on Semantic Domains*. Vol. 1, *Introduction and Domains*. New York: United Bible Societies, 1988.

Luedemann, Gerd. *Opposition to Paul in Jewish Christianity*. Translated by M. Eugene Boring. Minneapolis: Fortress Press, 1989.

Lütgert, D. W. *Der Römerbrief als historisches Problem*. BFCT, bd. 17, no 2, hrsg. D. A. Schlatter and D. W. Lütgert. Gütersloh: C. Bertelsmann, 1913.

Luther, Martin. *Lectures on Romans*. Translated and ed. by Wilhelm Pauck. LCC, vol. 15. Philadelphia: Westminster Press, 1961.

MacRory, J. "The Occasion and Object of the Epistle to the Romans." *ITQ* 9 (1914): 21–32.

Malherbe, Abraham J. "Exhortation in 1 Thessalonians." In *Paul and the Popular Philosophers,* 49–66. Minneapolis: Fortress Press, 1989.

————. *Paul and the Popular Philosophers*. Minneapolis: Fortress Press, 1989.

Manson, T. W. "St. Paul's Letter to the Romans—and Others." In *The Romans Debate*, revised and expanded ed., ed. Karl P. Donfried, 3–16. Peabody, Mass.: Hendrickson, 1991.

Martin, James P. "The Kerygma of Romans." *Int* 25 (1971): 303–28.

Martin, Ralph P. "The Opponents of Paul in 2 Corinthians: An Old Issue Revisited." In *Tradition and Interpretation in the New Testament: Essays in Honor of E. Earle Ellis for His 60th Birthday*, eds. Gerald F. Hawthorne and Otto Betz, 279–89. Grand Rapids: William B. Eerdmans, 1987.

Martyn, J. Louis. *Galatians*. AB, vol. 33A. New York: Doubleday, 1997.

————. "A Law-Observant Mission to the Gentiles." In *Theological Issues in the Letters of Paul*, 7–24. Nashville: Abingdon Press, 1997.

————. "Romans as One of the Earliest Interpretations of Galatians." In *Theological Issues in the Letters of Paul*, 37–46. Nashville: Abingdon Press, 1997.

————. *Theological Issues in the Letters of Paul*. Nashville: Abingdon Press, 1997.

Marxsen, Willi. *Introduction to the New Testament: An Approach to its Problems*. Translated by G. Buswell. Philadelphia: Fortress Press, 1968.

Mason, Steve. "'For I am not Ashamed of the Gospel' (Rom. 1.16): The Gospel and the First Readers of Romans." In *Gospel in Paul: Studies on Corinthians, Galatians and Romans for Richard N. Longenecker*, eds. L. Ann Jervis and Peter Richardson. JSNTSup, vol. 108, 254–87. Sheffield: Sheffield Academic Press, 1994.

McClelland, Scott E. "'Super-Apostles, Servants of Christ, Servants of Satan': A Response." *JSNT* 14 (1982): 82–87.

Meeks, Wayne A. "Judgment and the Brother: Romans 14:1–15:13." In *Tradition and Interpretation in the New Testament: Essays in Honor of E. Earle Ellis for His 60th Birthday*, eds. Gerald F. Hawthorne with Otto Betz, 290–300. Grand Rapids: William B. Eerdmans, 1987.

Merk, Otto. *Handeln aus Glauben: Die Motivierungen der paulinischen Ethik*. Marburger Theologische Studien, bd. 5. Marburg: N. G. Elwert Verlag, 1968.

Michel, Otto. *Der Brief an die Römer*, 10th aufl., KEK. Göttingen: Vandenhoeck & Ruprecht, 1955.

Mills, Watson E. *Bibliographies for Biblical Research, New Testament Series*. Vol. 6, *Romans*. Lewiston, NY: Mellen Biblical Press, 1996.

Minear, Paul S. *The Obedience of Faith: The Purposes of Paul in the Epistle to the Romans*. SBT, second series, vol. 19. London: SCM Press, 1971.

Moiser, Jeremy. "Rethinking Romans 12–15." *NTS* 36 (1990): 571–82.

Moo, Douglas. "The Theology of Romans 9–11: A Response to E. Elizabeth Johnson." In *Pauline Theology*. Vol. 3, *Romans*, eds. David M. Hay and E. Elizabeth Johnson, 240–258. Minneapolis: Fortress Press, 1995.

———. *The Epistle to the Romans*. NICNT. Grand Rapids: William B. Eerdmans, 1996.

Moore, George Foot. *Judaism in the First Centuries of the Christian Era*. 3 vols. Peabody, Mass.: Hendrickson, 1997. Reprint, Cambridge: Harvard University Press, 1927.

Morgan, Robert. *Romans*. NTG, ed. A. T. Lincoln. Sheffield: JSOT Press, 1995.

Morris, Leon. *The Epistle to the Romans*. Grand Rapids: William B. Eerdmans, 1988.

———. "The Theme of Romans." In *Apostolic History and the Gospel: Biblical and Historical Essays presented to F. F. Bruce on his 60th Birthday*, eds. W. Ward Gasque and Ralph P. Martin, 249–263. Exeter, England: Paternoster Press, 1970.

Moule, C. F. D. *An Idiom Book of New Testament Greek*, 2d ed. Cambridge: Cambridge University Press, 1959.

Moulton, James Hope, and George Milligan. *The Vocabulary of the Greek New Testament illustrated from the Papyti and other nonliterary Sources*. London: Hodder, 1930.

Moulton, James Hope, and Wilbert Francis Howard. *A Grammar of New Testament Greek*. Vol. 2, *Accidence and Word-Formation*. Edinburgh: T & T Clark, 1929.

Mowry, Lucetta. "The Early Circulation of Paul's Letters." *JBL* 63 (1944): 73–86.

Moxnes, Halvor. "The Quest for Honor and the Unity of the Community in Romans 12 and in the Orations of Dio Chrysostom." In *Paul in His Hellenistic Context*, ed. Troels Engberg-Pedersen, 203–230. Minneapolis: Fortress Press, 1995.

Müller, Ulrich B. *Prophetie und Predigt im Neuen Testament: Formgeschichtliche Untersuchungen zur urchristlichen Prophetie*. Studien zum Neuen Testament, bd. 10. Gütersloh: Gerd Mohn, 1975.

Munck, Johannes. *Paul and the Salvation of Mankind*. London: SCM Press, 1959.

Murphy-O'Connor, Jerome. *Paul: A Critical Life*. New York: Oxford University Press, 1997.

————. *Paul the Letter-Writer: His World, His Options, His Skills*. GNS, vol. 41. Collegeville, Minn.: The Liturgical Press, 1995.

Murray, John. *The Epistle to the Romans*. NICNT. Grand Rapids: William B. Eerdmans, 1968.

Nanos, Mark D. *The Mystery of Romans: The Jewish Context of Paul's Letter*. Minneapolis: Fortress Press, 1996.

Neusner, Jacob, Peder Borgen, Ernest S. Frerichs, and Richard Horsley, eds. *The Social World of Formative Christianity and Judaism: Essays in Tribute to Howard Clark Kee*. Philadelphia: Fortress Press, 1988.

Nickle, Keith F. *The Collection: A Study in Paul's Strategy*. SBT, vol. 48. London: SCM Press, 1966.

Noack, Bent. "Current and Backwater in the Epistle to the Romans." *ST* 19 (1965): 155–66.

Nygren, Anders. *Commentary on Romans*. Translated by Carl C. Rasmussen. Philadelphia: Muhlenberg Press, 1949.

O'Brien, P. T. *The Epistle to the Philippians: A Commentary on the Greek Text*. NIGTC. Grand Rapids: William B. Eerdmans, 1991.

―――. *Introductory Thanksgivings in the Letters of Paul*. NovTSup, vol. 49. Leiden: E. J. Brill, 1977.

―――. "Thanksgiving and the Gospel in Paul," *NTS* 21 (1974): 144–55.

Ollrog, Wolf-Henning. "Die Abfassungsverhältnisse von Röm 16." In *Kirche: Festschrift für Günther Bornkamm zum 75. Geburtstag*, hrsg. Dieter Lührmann und Georg Strecker, 221–44. Tübingen: J. C. B. Mohr (Paul Siebeck), 1980.

Olson, Stanley N. "Epistolary Uses of Expression of Self-Confidence." *JBL* 103 (1984): 585–97.

―――. "Pauline Expressions of Confidence in His Addressees." *CBQ* 47 (1985): 282–95.

Ortkemper, Franz-Josef. *Leben aus dem Glauben: Christliche Grundhaltungen nach Römer 12–13*. NTAbh, reihe 2, bd. 14. Münster: Aschendorff, 1980.

Osten-Sacken, Peter von der. "Erwägungen zur Abfassungsgeschichte und zum literarisch-theologischen Charakter des Römerbriefes." In *Evangelium und Tora: Aufsätze zu Paulus*. TBü, bd. 77, 119–30. Munich: Chr. Kaiser Verlag, 1987.

Parke-Taylor, G. H. "A Note on 'εἰς ὑπακοὴν πίστεως' in Romans i. 5 and xvi. 26," *ExpTim* 55 (1943–44): 305–06.

Penna, Romano. "Paul's Detractors in Romans 3:8." In *Paul the Apostle*. Vol. 1, *Jew and Greek Alike*. Translated by Thomas P. Wahl, 111–23. Collegeville, Minn.: The Liturgical Press, 1996.

―――. *Paul the Apostle*. Vol. 1, *Jew and Greek Alike*. Translated by Thomas P. Wahl. Collegeville, Minn.: The Liturgical Press, 1996.

―――. "The Structural Function of 3:1–8 in the Letter to the Romans." In *Paul the Apostle*. Vol. 1, *Jew and Greek Alike*. Translated by Thomas P. Wahl, 60–89. Collegeville, Minn.: The Liturgical Press, 1996.

Pesch, Rudolph. *Römerbrief*, 2 aufl., NEchtB. Würzburg: Echter Verlag, 1987.

Petersen, Norman R. *Rediscovering Paul: Philemon and the Sociology of Paul's Narrative World*. Philadelphia: Fortress Press, 1985.

Piper, John. *'Love Your Enemies': Jesus' Love Command in the Synoptic Gospels and in the Early Christian Paraenesis*. SNTSMS, vol. 38. Cambridge: Cambridge University Press, 1979.

―――. "The Righteousness of God in Romans 3,1–8." *TZ* 36 (1980): 3–16.

Pliny. *Natural History*, vol. 1. *LCL*. Translated by H. Rackham. Cambridge: Harvard University Press, 1938.

Porter, Stanley E. *Idioms of the Greek New Testament*, 2d ed. Biblical Languages: Greek, vol. 2. Sheffield: JSOT Press, 1994.

Preisker, H. "Das historische Problem des Römerbriefes." *Wissenschaftliche Zeitschrift der Friedrich-Schiller*, hft. 1, 25–30. Jena: Universität Jena, 1952/53.

Puskas, Charles B., Jr. *The Letters of Paul: An Introduction*. GNS, vol. 25. Collegeville, Minn.: The Liturgical Press, 1993.

Ramsey, William M. *Pauline and Other Studies in Early Christian History*. London: Hodder and Stoughton, 1906.

―――. "Roads and Travel (in NT)." In *A Dictionary of the Bible*, vol. 5, ed. James Hastings, 375–402. New York: Charles Scribner's Sons, 1904.

―――. *St. Paul the Traveller and the Roman Citizen*. Grand Rapids: Baker, 1982. Reprint, 15th ed., London: Hodder and Stoughton, 1925.

Reasoner, Mark. "The 'Strong' and the 'Weak' in Rome and in Paul's Theology." Ph. D. diss., University of Chicago, 1990.

―――. "The Theology of Romans 12:1–15:13." In *Pauline Theology*. Vol. 3, *Romans*, eds. David M. Hay and E. Elizabeth Johnson, 287–99. Minneapolis: Fortress Press, 1995.

Rengstorf, K. H. "Paulus und die älteste römische Christenheit." In *SE*. Vol. 2, *Part 1: The New Testament Scriptures*, ed. F. L. Cross. TU, bd. 87, 447–64. Berlin: Akademie-Verlag, 1964.

Ridderbos, Herman. *Paul: An Outline of His Theology*. Translated by John Richard de Witt. Grand Rapids: William B. Eerdmans, 1975.

Russell, Walter B. "An Alternative Suggestion for the Purpose of Romans." *BSac* 145 (1988): 174–88.

Rutgers, Leonard Victor. "Roman Policy toward the Jews: Expulsions from the City of Rome during the First Century C.E.." In *Judaism and Christianity in First-Century Rome*, eds. Karl P. Donfried and Peter Richardson, 93–116. Grand Rapids: William B. Eerdmans, 1998.

Safrai, S. "Relations between the Diaspora and the Land of Israel." In *The Jewish People in the First Century*, vol. 1. CRINT, section 1, 184–215. Philadelphia: Fortress Press, 1974.

Safrai, S., and M. Stern, eds. *The Jewish People in the First Century*, vol. 1. CRINT, section 1. Philadelphia: Fortress Press, 1974.

Sampley, J. Paul. "Paul, His Opponents in 2 Corinthians 10–13, and the Rhetorical Handbooks." In *The Social World of Formative Christianity and Judaism: Essays in Tribute to Howard Clark Kee*, eds. Jacob Neusner, et. al., 162–177. Philadelphia: Fortress Press, 1988.

———. "Romans in a Different Light: A Response to Robert Jewett." In *Pauline Theology*. Vol. 3, *Romans*, eds. David M. Hay and E. Elizabeth Johnson, 109–29. Minneapolis: Fortress Press, 1995.

Sanday, W., and A. C. Headlam. *A Critical and Exegetical Commentary on the Epistle to the Romans*, 2d ed., ICC. New York: Charles Scribner's Sons, n. d..

Sanders, E. P. *Paul and Palestinian Judaism*. Philadelphia: Fortress Press, 1977.

———. *Paul, the Law, and the Jewish People*. Minneapolis: Fortress Press, 1983.

Sandnes, Karl Olav. *Paul—One of the Prophets?* WUNT, series 2, bd. 43. Tübingen: J. C. B. Mohr (Paul Siebeck), 1991.

Saß, Gerhard. "Röm 15,7–13 -als Summe des Römerbriefs gelesen." *EvT* 53 (1993): 510–27.

Schlatter, Adolf. *Romans. The Righteousness of God*. Translated by Siegfried S. Schatzmann. Peabody, Mass.: Hendrickson, 1995.

Schlier, Heinrich. *Der Römerbrief*. HTKNT, bd. 6. Freiburg: Herder, 1977.

Schmeller, Thomas. *Paulus und die 'Diatribe'*. Münster: Aschendorff, 1987.

Schmidt, Hans Wilhelm. *Der Brief des Paulus an die Römer*. THKNT, bd. 6. Berlin: Evangelische Verlagsanstalt, 1962.

Schmithals, Walter. *Paul & the Gnostics*. Translated by John E. Steely. Nashville: Abingdon Press, 1972.

————. *Der Römerbrief als historisches Problem*. Studien zum Neuen Testament, bd. 9. Gütersloh: Gerd Mohn, 1975.

Schreiner, Thomas R. *Interpreting the Pauline Epistles*. Guides to New Testament Exegesis. Grand Rapids: Baker Books, 1990.

————. *Romans*. Baker Exegetical Commentary on the New Testament. Grand Rapids: Baker Books, 1998.

Schrenk, D. Gottlob. "Der Römerbrief als Missionsdokument" In *Studien zu Paulus*, 81–106. Zürich: Zwingli-Verlag, 1954.

Schubert, Paul. *Form and Function of the Pauline Thanksgivings*. BZNW, beih. 20. Berlin: Alfred Töpelmann, 1939.

Segal, Alan F. *Paul the Convert: The Apostolate and Apostasy of Saul the Pharisee*. New Haven: Yale University Press, 1990.

Seutonius. *Seutonius*, vol. 2. *LCL*. Translated by J. C. Rolfe. Cambridge: Harvard University Press, 1979.

Slingerland, Dixon. "Suetonius *Claudius* 25.4, Acts 18, and Paulus Orosius' *Historiarum Adversum Paganos Libri VII*: Dating the Claudian Expulsion(s) of Roman Jews." *JQR* 83 (1992–93): 127–44.

————. "Suetonius' *Claudius* 25.4 and the Account in Cassius Dio." *JQR* 79 (1988–89): 305–22.

Smallwood, E. Mary. *The Jews under Roman Rule: From Pompey to Diocletian*, SJLA, vol. 20. Leiden: E. J. Brill, 1976.

Smiga, George. "Romans 12:1–2 and 15:30–32 and the Occasion of the Letter to the Romans." *CBQ* 53 (1991): 257–73.

Smith, D. Moody. "The Pauline Literature." In *It is Written: Scripture Citing Scripture. Essays in Honour of Barnabas Lindars*, eds. D. A. Carson and H. G. M. Williamson, 265–91. Cambridge: Cambridge University Press, 1988.

Snodgrass, Klyne. "The Gospel in Romans: A Theology of Revelation." In *Gospel in Paul: Studies on Corinthians, Galatians and Romans for Richard N. Longenecker*, eds. L. Ann Jervis and Peter Richardson, 288–314. JSNTSup, vol. 108. Sheffield: Sheffield Academic Press, 1994.

Soards, Marion L. *The Apostle Paul: An Introduction to His Writings and Teaching*. New York: Paulist Press, 1987.

Spicq, Ceslas. *L'Épître aux Hébreux*. Vol. 2, *Commentaire*. Paris: Librairie Lecoffre, 1953.

Stanley, Christopher D. "'Neither Jew nor Greek': Ethnic Conflict in Graeco-Roman Society," *JSNT* 64 (1996): 101–24.

Stirewalt, Martin Luther, Jr. "The Form and Function of the Greek Letter-Essay." In *The Romans Debate*, revised and expanded ed., ed. Karl P. Donfried, 147–71. Peabody, Mass.: Hendrickson, 1991.

Stowers, Stanley K. "The Diatribe." In *Greco-Roman Literature and the New Testament*, ed. David E. Aune, 71–83. SBLSBS, vol. 21. Atlanta: Scholars Press, 1988.

———. *The Diatribe and Paul's Letter to the Romans*. SBLDS, vol. 57. Chico, Calif.: Scholars Press, 1981.

———. "Paul's Dialogue with a Fellow Jew in Romans 3:1–9." *CBQ* 46 (1984): 707–22.

———. *A Rereading of Romans: Justice, Jews, & Gentiles*. New Haven: Yale University Press, 1994.

Stuhlmacher, Peter. *Paul's Letter to the Romans: A Commentary*. Translated by Scott J. Hafemann. Louisville: Westminster/John Knox Press, 1994.

————. "The Purpose of Romans." In *The Romans Debate*, revised and expanded ed., ed. Karl P. Donfried, 231–42. Peabody, Mass.: Hendrickson, 1991.

Suhl, Alfred. "Der konkrete Anlass des Römerbriefes." *Kairos* 13 (1971): 119–30.

————. *Paulus und seine Briefe: Ein Beitrag zur paulinischen Chronologie*. Studien zum Neuen Testament, bd. 11. Gütersloh: Gerd Mohn, 1975.

Tacitus. *Annals*, vol. 4. *LCL*. Translated by Clifford H. Moore. Cambridge: Harvard University Press, 1937.

Theissen, Gerd. *The Social Setting of Pauline Christianity: Essays on Corinth*. Translated and ed. by John H. Schütz. Philadelphia: Fortress Press, 1982.

Theobald, M. "Warum schrieb Paulus den Römerbrief?" *BLit* 56 (1983): 150–58.

Theological Dictionary of the New Testament. Edited by G. Kittel and G. Friedrich. Translated and edited by Geoffrey W. Bromiley. 10 vols. Grand Rapids: William B. Eerdmans, 1964–1976.
S.v. "ἀπαρχή," by Gerhard Delling. 1:484–86.
S.v. "βέβαιος, βεβαιόω, βεβαίωσις," by Heinrich Schlier. 1:600–03.
S.v. "δόξα," by Gerhard Kittel. 2:233–237, 242–51.
S.v. "כבוד," by Gerhard von Rad. 2:238–42.
S.v. "εὐαγγελιξομαι," by Gerhard Friedrich. 2:707–21.
S.v. "καρπός," by Friedrich Hauck. 3:614–16.
S.v. "μυστήριον," by Günther Bornkamm. 4:802–28.
S.v. "παρακούω, παρακοή," by Gerhard Kittel. 1:223–24.
S.v. "παρρησία," by Heinrich Schlier. 5:871–86.
S.v. "σκάνδαλον, σκανδαλίζω," by Gustav Stählin. 5:339–58.
S.v. "στηρίζω," by Günther Harder. 7:653–57.
S.v "σώφρων, σωφρονέω, σωφροσύνη," by Ulrich Luck. 7:1097–1104.
S.v. "τολμάω," by Gottfried Fitzer. 8:181–86.

Thielman, Frank. "The Story of Israel and the Theology of Romans 5–8." In *Pauline Theology*. Vol. 3, *Romans*, eds. David M. Hay and E. Elizabeth Johnson, 169–95. Minneapolis: Fortress Press, 1995.

Thompson, Michael. *Clothed with Christ: The Example and Teaching of Jesus in Romans 12.1–15.13*. JSNTSup, vol. 59. Sheffield: JSOT Press, 1991.

Thrall, Margaret E. "Super-Apostles, Servants of Christ, and Servants of Satan." *JSNT* 6 (1980): 42–57.

Turner, Nigel. *A Grammar of New Testament Greek.* Vol. 3, *Syntax.* Edinburgh: T & T Clark, 1963.

Vanhoye, A. ed. *L' Apôtre Paul: Personnalité, Style et Conception du Ministère.* Leuven: Leuven University Press, 1986.

Vielhauer, Philipp. *Geschichte der urchristlichen Literatur.* New York: Walter de Gruyter, 1975.

Wagner, J. Ross. "The Christ, Servant of Jew and Gentile: A Fresh Approach to Romans 15:8–9." *JBL* 116 (1997): 473–85.

Walters, James C. *Ethnic Issues in Paul's Letter to the Romans: Changing Self-Definitions in Earliest Roman Christianity.* Valley Forge, Pa.: Trinity Press International, 1993.

———. "Romans, Jews, and Christians: The Impact of the Romans on Jewish/Christian Relations in First-Century Rome." In *Judaism and Christianity in First-Century Rome*, eds. Karl P. Donfried and Peter Richardson, 175–95. Grand Rapids: William B. Eerdmans, 1998.

Watson, Francis. *Paul, Judaism and the Gentiles: A Sociological Approach.* SNTSMS, vol. 56. Cambridge: Cambridge University Press, 1986.

Wedderburn, A. J. M. "Purpose and Occasion of Romans Again." In *The Romans Debate*, revised and expanded ed., ed. Karl P. Donfried, 195–202. Peabody, Mass.: Hendrickson, 1991.

———. *The Reasons for Romans.* Minneapolis: Fortress Press, 1991.

Weima, Jeffrey A. D. *Neglected Endings: The Significance of the Pauline Letter Closings.* JSNTSup, vol. 101. Sheffield: JSOT Press, 1994.

———. "Preaching the Gospel in Rome: A Study of the Epistolary Framework of Romans." In *Gospel in Paul: Studies on Corinthians, Galatians and Romans for Richard N. Longenecker*, eds L. Ann Jervis and Peter Richardson, 337–66. JSNTSup, vol. 108. Sheffield: Sheffield Academic Press, 1994.

Weiß, Konrad. "Der doxologische Charakter der paulinischen Soteriologie." In *Theologische Versuche*, bd. 11, hrsg. Joachim Rogge und Gottfried Schille, 67–70. Berlin: Evangelische Verlagsanstalt, 1979.

Westcott, B. F. *The Epistle to the Hebrews*. Grand Rapids: William B. Eerdmans, 1984 [n. d. for original].

Westcott, B. F. and F. J. A. Hort. *Introduction to the New Testament in the Original Greek*. Peabody, Mass.: Hendrickson, 1988. Reprint, New York: Harper and Brothers, 1882.

White, John L. "Introductory Formulae in the Body of the Pauline Letter." *JBL* 90 (1971): 91–7.

———. *Light from Ancient Letters*. FFNT. Philadelphia: Fortress Press, 1986.

Wiefel, Wolfgang. "The Jewish Community in Ancient Rome and the Origins of Roman Christianity." In *The Romans Debate*, revised and expanded ed., ed. Karl P. Donfried, 85–101. Peabody, Mass.: Hendrickson, 1991.

Wikenhauser, Alfred. *New Testament Introduction*. New York: Herder & Herder, 1958.

Wilckens, Ulrich. *Der Brief an die Römer (Röm 1–5)*, 3d aufl., EKKNT, bd. 6.1. Neukirchen-Vluyn: Neukirchener Verlag, 1997.

———. *Der Brief an die Römer (Röm 6–11)*, 3d aufl., EKKNT, bd. 6.2. Neukirchen-Vluyn: Neukirchener Verlag, 1993.

———. *Der Brief an die Römer (Röm 12–16)*, 2d. aufl., EKKNT, bd. 6.3. Neukirchen-Vluyn: Neukirchener Verlag, 1989.

———. *Rechtfertigung als Freiheit: Paulusstudien*. Neukirchener-Vluyn: Neukirchener Verlag, 1974.

———. "Römer 13,1–7." In *Rechtfertigung als Freiheit: Paulusstudien*, 203–45. Neukirchener-Vluyn: Neukirchener Verlag, 1974.

———. "Über Abfassungszweck und Aufbau des Römerbriefes." In *Rechtfertigung als Freiheit: Paulusstudien*, 110–70. Neukirchener-Vluyn: Neukirchener Verlag, 1974.

Wiles, Gordon P. *Paul's Intercessory Prayers: The Significance of the Intercessory Prayer Passages in the Letters of St. Paul*. SNTSMS, vol. 24. Cambridge: Cambridge University Press, 1974.

Williams, Philip R. "Paul's Purpose in Writing Romans." *BSac* 128 (1971): 62–7.

Williams, Sam K. "The 'Righteousness of God' in Romans." *JBL* 99 (1980): 241–90.

Wilson, Walter T. *Love Without Pretense: Romans 12.9–21 and Hellenistic-Jewish Wisdom Literature*. WUNT, series 2, bd. 46. Tübingen: J. C. B. Mohr (Paul Siebeck), 1991.

Witherington III, Ben. *Conflict & Community in Corinth: A Socio-Rhetorical Commentary on 1 and 2 Corinthians*. Grand Rapids: William B. Eerdmans, 1995.

———. *Friendship and Finances in Philippi: The Letter of Paul to the Philippians*. The New Testament in Context. Valley Forge, Pa.: Trinity Press International, 1994.

———. *Grace in Galatia: A Commentary on Paul's Letter to the Galatians*. Grand Rapids: William B. Eerdmans, 1998.

Wright, N. Thomas. *The Climax of the Covenant: Christ and Law in Pauline Theology*. Minneapolis: Fortress Press, 1992.

———. "Jesus Christ is Lord: Philippians 2.5–11." In *The Climax of the Covenant: Christ and Law in Pauline Theology*, 56–98. Minneapolis: Fortress Press, 1992.

———. "Romans and the Theology of Paul." In *Pauline Theology*. Vol. 3, *Romans*, eds. David M. Hay and E. Elizabeth Johnson, 30–67. Minneapolis: Fortress Press, 1995.

Wuellner, Wilhelm. "Paul's Rhetoric of Argumentation in Romans: An Alternative to the Donfried-Karris Debate Over Romans." In *The Romans Debate*, revised and expanded ed., ed. Karl P. Donfried, 128–46. Peabody, Mass.: Hendrickson, 1991.

Yinger, Kent L. "Romans 12:14–21 and Nonretaliation in Second Temple Judaism: Addressing Persecution within the Community." *CBQ* 60 (1998): 74–96.

Zeller, Dieter. *Juden und Heiden in der Mission des Paulus: Studien zum Römerbrief*, 2d aufl., FB, bd. 8. Stuttgart: Verlag Katholisches Bibelwerk, 1976.

Zerbe, Gordon M. *Non-Retaliation in Early Jewish and New Testament Texts: Ethical Themes in Social Contexts*. JSPSup, vol. 13. Sheffield: JSOT Press, 1993.

Ziesler, John. *Paul's Letter to the Romans*. TPI New Testament Commentaries. Philadelphia: Trinity Press International, 1989.

Index of Modern Authors

Index of Texts Cited